# Acknowledgements

I dedicate this book to my son, Gary. Words cannot convey my undying love for you, son! You make me proud, and I am eternally grateful for having you in my life.

To my beautiful wife Ana, I also dedicate this book to you. You bring balance and tranquillity to my life. I love you and thank the universe that we met.

To mum and dad, you are fantastic parents, and I bet you never thought for one day I could write a book!

And finally, to you the reader. I sincerely hope that this book and our community platform makes a positive impact on your life.



ISBN: 978-1-9168793-0-0

# Prelude

I sincerely hope that you enjoy reading and participating in "Living your Life on Purpose" (LYLOP).

With the book and the LYLOP community at www.lylop.com, we aim to build the most comprehensive personal development platform on the planet.

A series of resources and support forums to help you in every area of life.

To kick off this book, can I respectfully request that at the start of every day, you do so with an attitude of gratitude.

Every morning think about the things you are grateful for and keep that gratitude close to your mind.

You have a wonderful life, and you live in a world of opportunity. With this book, and the community's interactions, we aim to build on your solid foundations and work with you to create the life you so desire.

People often question why I am always so positive, and my reply is always to do with gratitude.

Here is how I reply:

"I spent five years in the Army and went to Iraq, where I saw death, destruction and poverty first-hand. I then spent nine years in the Scottish Police Service. I had to deliver messages to children that their parents had died or committed suicide. Worse I had to tell parents their child had died. In the mix were the association of murderers, rapists, and downright horrible people."

"In one month, I went to 14 fatal road traffic accidents, one of which was my next-door neighbour who was on duty as a fellow Police Officer."

"I have an amazing son, lovely wife, fabulous parents, a loving sister, Charlotte and Matthew, my niece and nephew, and I live comfortably. Trust me, my life is amazing compared to the millions of others around the world."

Don't you see – you already have a brilliant life? Now is the time to take it to an entirely different level!

Let us crack on with this book, where you will benefit from over 20 years of my life's experiences.

**Life can be all jumbled up.**

Some areas of life can be working well, whilst others not so good. Wouldn't it be great to bring order to the chaos?

**Life out of balance**

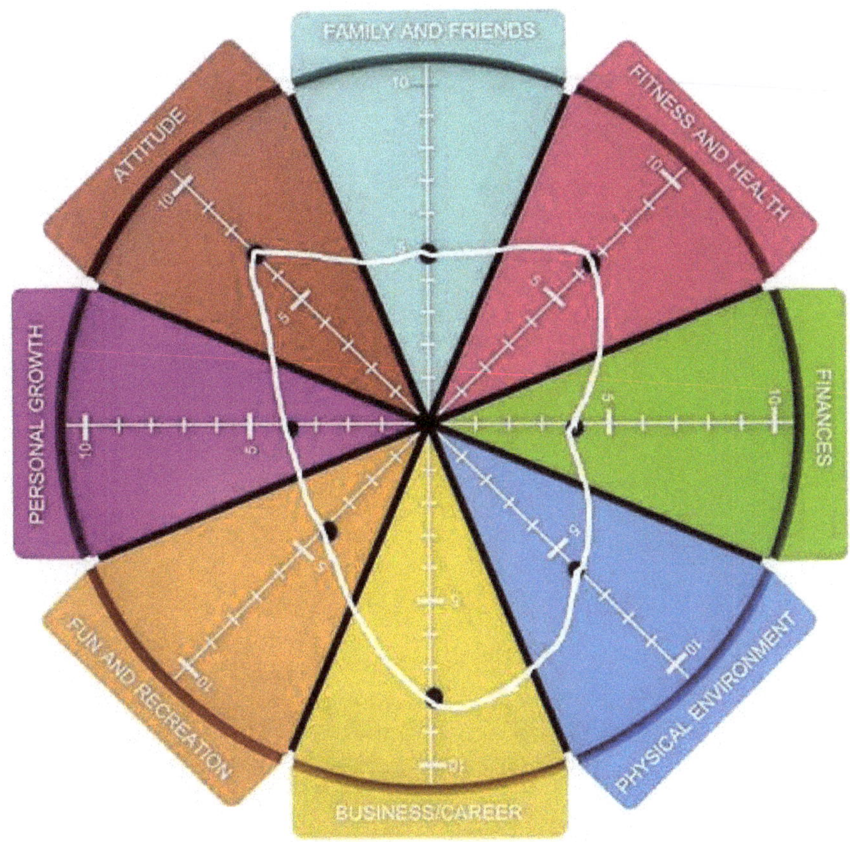


Living your Life on purpose will introduce you to concepts that will "Focus" on each segment in the "Wheels of Life".

**Life in balance**

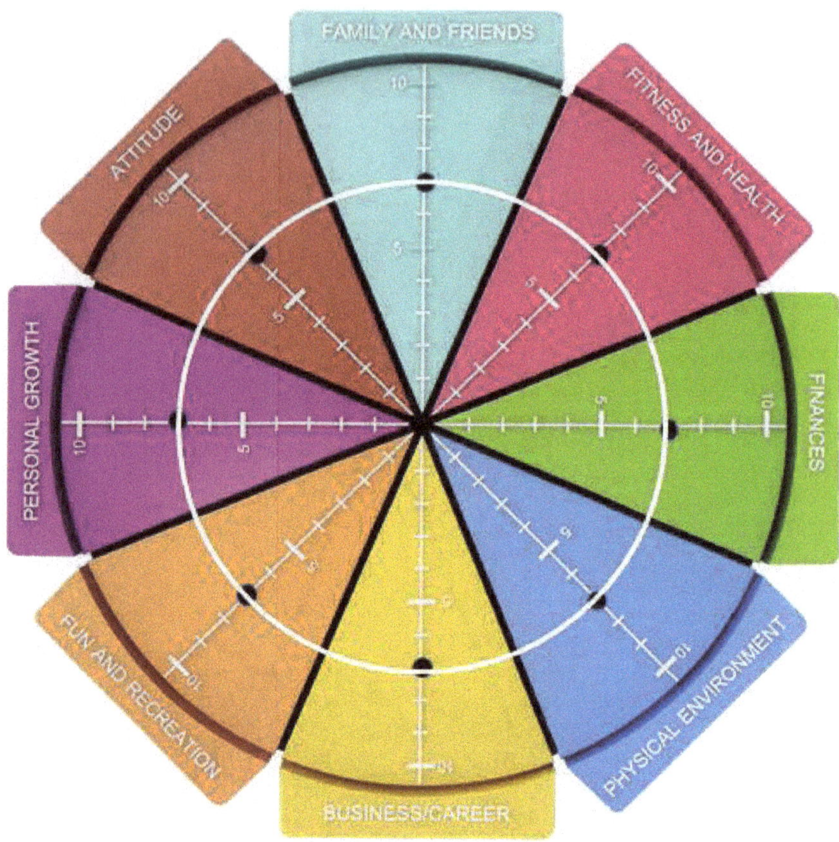


Once we have "Focus" we can work to bring balance to your "Wheels of life" making the ride of life more enjoyable and less rocky.

# Table of Contents

## Introduction

Do you ever look at other people and wonder why they seem to be floating through life with all the positive trappings, and you are beating your backside off and seemingly going nowhere?

Or maybe your career is on the up. You find work a great retreat because other parts of your life are not so good. Due to your out of balance work/life, your fitness is waning, you have put on some extra weight, family life is exhausting, and your relationship more a routine than enjoyable.

You look at your bank balance, and for the last five years, the same old story is clear. You have too much month at the end of the money.

As you check your current age and evaluate where you are in life, the hours you work, the holidays you take, and your accrued debts, are you happy?

Are you where you want to be?

And yet there are people that you know living an extraordinary life.

They have got balance. They have a lovely house, nice car, go on regular family holidays, and that family unit exudes love and unity. You also know that this lifestyle is not funded by increasing debt – somehow, they cracked the code, and it pisses you off.

It annoys you because you used to want that. When you played the fast forward button on your life, you felt awesome knowing that your mortgage was paid off by 55. The plan was your children were to be funded through university. You had a holiday home in the Spanish Costas that you and your loved one could escape to at any time it suited you.

You have a lovely home littered with photographs of family and friends having fun both at home and abroad – you made it!

You retired at 55, with enough money coming in to have no financial worries; the kids have kind of left home but still come to you for the occasional loan that you make a deal about to them. On the inside, you are so comforted you can help them. Well, you can't take it with you, can you?

When you fast-forwarded this future image of you, there was certainly no reference to the extra weight you put on, the lack of basic fitness, the poor diet, or the long work hours. There was no reference to the financial woes that bring about arguments or the fact your re-mortgaged home is still a burden, that the credit card interests each month could pay for the golf and gym memberships.

No, that was not your goal, and even as you read or listen to this book, you need to understand that it does not need to be either. Make the decision today, not tomorrow or next week – make the decision today to do something about it.

Make the decision to look at your habits. Think about which serve you well and serve you poorly; think about what you would like to have in the future and make the 100% decision from this moment to live your life on purpose.

Hey, stop for a minute. Seriously stop for a minute and put down the book or pause the audio.

That was a seismic thing you agreed to do. Your brain can't compute what you agreed to instantly.

You agreed to live your life on purpose, but what does that even mean?

Will there be no real change to your life, or will it mean a serious overhaul of your daily activity?

Of course, this is going to be a massive change. You are about to live your life on purpose, no more drifting on a Lilo on the beach after a burger and fries and a couple of beers.

You will be effectively kayaking up a Canadian grade 4 river where the torrents will be continuously trying to push you back to where you came from.

Wow-what a rush – paddling in a grade 4 Canadian river – upstream!

Ok, so it won't be that hard, but I can assure you living your life on purpose may sometimes feel that way.

If you want to improve your life, it will take some serious mental effort, and sometimes whilst you are aiming to paddle upstream, the force of the river or your bad habits will be pounding you, trying to get you back to where you came from.

But the actual reality of living your life on purpose is that it isn't even that hard, it isn't easy, but it isn't hard.

Instead of zigzagging in your world, you are going to straight-line it. Instead of searching for instant gratification, you will set your sail in the direction of your choice. Not the direction chosen by others, by your bank, by your limiting self-beliefs but chosen by you. Today, you make the decision that enough is enough.

Today you become the champion of your world. Today you set the rules for your race. You set the destination, set the dates you want to get there, and create your own rules.

Setting destinations and dates sound scarily like goals. Everyone does set goals; they do not appreciate them and do not document them.

Your flight leaves at 10 am to your dream holiday destination. You, your partner, and your children are going on your annual trip. You love these two weeks of your life.

It is a 2-hour drive to the airport. You need to check-in 3 hours before. You have booked to have your car valet parked for you when you arrive at the airport.

What time do you set off?

Well, the latest you tell yourself it should be 5 am, but to make sure you get there on time, you decide to leave at 4 am.

You chat with your partner, who agrees, there may be traffic on the road. Then you tell the kids. Wow, no resistance from them. They love this holiday too. It is, after all, one of the rare chances they get to spend two weeks with you.

So, your partner and your children have bought into this decision. They understand the goal of getting to the airport to ensure they can have this holiday. They do not want to get up at 4 am, but they know why.

What happened here is the whole family unit bought into the "win" of the holiday and understood the trade-off needed to ensure that holiday wasn't lost out on them. You, your partner, and your children engaged in a goal-orientated activity together. You did it on purpose.

You got to the airport way too early. There were no stresses at check-in as you were at the front of the queue. No tempers were lost. You got through into the departure lounge and had a cracking breakfast and at 8 am, you and your partner had a cheeky drink. You are on holiday, after all.

Everyone was relaxed as you boarded the plane, and you look to see another family rushing to the last call. The dad is screaming at his partner, who in turn is shouting back. One child is being dragged and drops her coat; the other child runs in fear of his life.

You've settled into your seats, stress-free and watch as the family are the last to board the plane. "I told you we should have left earlier", proclaims the partner. "oh, why don't you shut up", retorts the dad.

They managed to make it but only just. They are stressed and have fallen out, the kids cowering, scared to talk in fear of the wrath of both parents.

The 9-hour flight for you and your family passes quickly. You have excitedly discussed going on the Hulk at Universal Studios, Islands of Adventure, or the new Kong ride. Your kids prefer the idea of Blizzard beach and your partner, the shopping at the Orlando mall.

Giddy with excitement, you and your family have a most fabulous flight.

When glancing back at the family, you see they aren't talking to each other. They used the excuse of switching on the inflight entertainment, so they didn't need to speak. Thankfully, that isn't you.

You get a smug feeling that you set the goal, paid the price of organisation, followed through on our plan, and without any stresses, you achieved what you set out to achieve, and you are in such a great place right now.

But what if living your life on purpose in all facets of your life caused an improvement throughout it?

What if your partner and family bought into this process too?

As you pass through this book the first time, it will trigger ideas that you will start to employ. Your life will improve. Your finances will improve. The fog that stopped you from seeing a bright future for you and your family will lift.

You will see with clarity, and you will be heading straight towards the goals you set. No zigzagging you are heading straight there.

Slowly at first, but as you buy into all the suggestions within this book – Living your life on purpose and re-read it several times, you will cast off the weights that were holding you back.

You will gain momentum in all areas of your life, and the successes you earn will become like a life drug that makes you want more.

There is a great phrase, "Don't walk over the pennies to get to the pounds."

During this journey, you will start to experience small wins; these are the pennies; each penny you pick up will get you closer to the pounds.

But there is another brilliant phrase too, "A voyage of a thousand miles begins with a simple step.............. the first step must be in the right direction."

As you pass through this book and start to live your life on purpose, the excitement of an improving life will naturally cause you to set more glamourous destinations.

First, though, we need to take stock of where we are right now. You may have a burning desire to be on one of the first Galactic flights costing a cool quarter of a million. But the fact is you may need to settle for two weeks in a static caravan in a local seaside resort.

Having a two-week holiday in a static caravan isn't fine. It is superfine!

Some of the best family holidays and memories are forged in these family-friendly environments.

But how about paying for that holiday upfront, no use of credit cards and coming back home without a hole in your back pocket. No reflecting on how many ice creams you ended up buying, without the worry of the money running out.

Ok, you have the picture. Wherever you are right now has been created by the habits of what you did before. No point worrying about the past as this has already gone. If you are not happy where you are right now, it is due to your life habits.

When you look at your present, you may be fabulously wealthy, but your health and family life is appalling. When you look at your present, you may be frustrated about plenty of things. You might not see through that fog right now. You may not see any direction that could improve your life for the better.

**It is in the present that decisions are made.**

This is the best place to be in your life. Be in the present but not in the present time. Be present in your life.

Spend time reflecting on where you are right now. How is the relationship? How are your health and fitness? Is your home a dream home or a decaying box that needs repairs? When was the last time you had some fun? How is the bank balance and the plans for early and wealthy retirement? How well is your job or business growing, and on reflection, how have you grown as a person?

Now that you have reflected, even fleetingly, on your present circumstances, it is essential to understand that this does not need to be the future.

In fact, within one second, you can make the future better. One second. In a second, you can decide to change your whole life for the better.

You can decide to live your life on purpose. You can become a better you, a happier, fitter, healthier you. You can become more affluent, less stressed, and you can have the most fantastic family unit.

It takes one decision from one person, and that person is you!

If you are in a relationship, why not get them to read/listen to this book at the same time as you. If two people agree on living their lives on purpose together, the chances of success increase exponentially.

Why? Because you commit to improving your lives and following the tips in this book. You now have accountability.

The best thing about life is that there is no accountability. The worst thing about life is there is no accountability.

I can tell you the most successful people have accountability partners/success buddies. In Napoleon Hill's Think and Grow Rich, which incidentally is probably one of the best personal development books ever written, he speaks about the power of the mastermind.

We will cover Think and Grow Rich principles in this book later; suffice to say that if you have a partner to buddy up with and live your life on purpose, the results will be turbo charged in a positive way.

And if you do not have a partner that you live with, find someone you know that has a positive attitude and encourage them to live their life on purpose with you too. This will bring in accountability.

Living your life on purpose will have so many positive effects, both mentally and physically. For some people, it will be hard to comprehend how much improvement they will feel within their own lives and their relationships with others.

Far too many people are on autopilot daily and are drifting like the Lilo we mentioned at the seaside. This drifting mentality allows the brain to start to fill up time with stories.

Throughout living your life on purpose, we will share some top tips on how to eliminate those bad stories and how to replace them with positive ones.

Through the next 13 weeks, as a minimum, when you live your life on purpose and engage in a world of continuous and never-ending improvement, your mindset will start to take a turn for the better.

In our modern society, so many people have depression, or they don't seem to be as happy as they could be, and in the main, this is because they are carrying around with them so much baggage. Stories are percolating around their mind whenever there is downtime.

When I say downtime, it is the gap between doing something positively and actively. There are more gaps in their daily routine for lots of people, which allows for those bad stories to creep in. When you live your life on purpose, we will essentially bring organisation into an otherwise chaotic mind.

Testing your age right now, I want you to think back to the days with computers where we were asked to defragment the hard drive.

Before computers became as powerful as they are now, they would always slow down over time. One sure-fire way of speeding them up was to defragment the files.

But what is defragmentation?

When you started the defragmentation process, what you saw was a grid of broken up colours. Essentially, this was a broken up and disorganised filing system. If you wanted to open a file the computer had to go to multiple places to find the file, then reorganise it so you could see it.

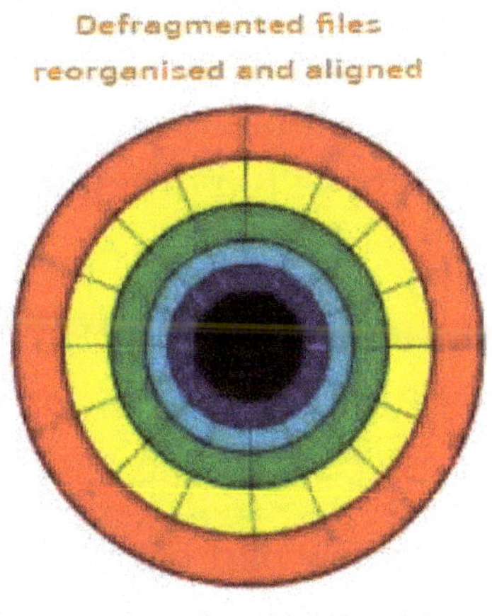


Once you had pressed for the computer to defragment itself, what you saw on the grid was that all the files were more compact, with no gaps between them. The broken-up files were filed in order and therefore more efficient operationally.

When we live our lives on purpose, what we are going to do is reduce the number of gaps, or downtime, where those stories can start to preoccupy our mind and instead, we will become more efficient and effective an organised in the things that we do.

What this means is that you will find that you will have more time to do the things that you want to do, rather than procrastinating or having a hit and hope Harry approach to your daily tasks.

Yes, you will become happier, yes, you will become healthier, you will become fitter, and you will become wealthier. You will be feeling brilliant with yourself, the way you transmit when interacting with other people is going to improve. So much so that everybody you associate with will notice!

One more thing, yes, we are going to do this all at the same time. We aren't going to focus on one segment in the wheel of life; we will focus on all the segments. There's no point focusing on one segment because variety is the spice of life. We will have fun during this process, and we will enjoy it.

During this book or audio, you will hear some fun ways in which we can change the jam in our doughnuts, eliminate that greedy mind monster and the way we can say no or goodbye to those people who, quite frankly, are grumpy gits.

You are now part of the living your life on purpose community, and this is not a book or audio; far from it, there is so much more at your disposal to help you have the most audacious and fantastic life. Living your life on purpose has an online presence via a website and an app. You will be able to take part in many community discussions in any of the wheel segments. If you are looking for hints, tips, and ideas, this is where you will find them.

Want to learn how to cook healthier food, it will be in the community. Want to engage in a couch to five-kilometre walk/run, it will be in the community section. Want tips on managing your finances better and to build more loving relationships with your family and friends? All of this will be here to support you in the community.

But with living your life on purpose, we need to go even further than having a community with top tips and recipes!

We've mentioned that one of the best things in life is that there is no real accountability and that the worst thing in life is that there is no real accountability. We have to go to work to generate the income to pay off our everyday expenses, and I guess that is accountability.

We have no choice but to do that. But to become happy in life and improve our chances of success, we will need to push ourselves a little bit further than we've done before.

There will be times when we are going to feel low, and there will be times when we fancy quitting.

Within the living your life on purpose community, you will find others to work with and support.

Like a dating website, without the romance, you will be able to put in your details, and we will automatically assign you a success buddy that is in harmony with you and your choice. Not a swiping right or left exercise!

To take this to a further level, Napoleon Hill in his book “Think and Grow Rich”, speaks about the importance of forming a mastermind group. We will certainly be covering this off later in the book; suffice to say that if you would like to join a mastermind group, we can also allocate you into one of these with eight to ten success orientated individuals.

As our community continues to grow, you will also have access to mentors on regular seminars keeping you in the loop in your own game.

With such an abundance of supporting information and resources, you can only fail if you do not commit to this programme. We are not asking you to break into a sweat from moment one, and indeed as you pass through living your life on purpose, you will notice that everything is done with a gradual improvement daily.

Feel energised that you have found this book and buy into the processes and the very fact that you can live your life on purpose and have a wonderful life.

Irrespective of who you are, where you live, your gender, religion, ethnicity, disability, or age living your life on purpose is for you.

We will draw down the wisdom and the teachings of many fabulous individuals worldwide. You will be absorbing some truly inspirational material, and you are going to find out so much about yourself and your mindset.

Many people desire to be successful in life, but a few weights hold them down from their rise to success. Imagine for a moment that you are a hot air balloon and each of the segments in the wheel of life represents a big weight. Over time, we will not cut the weight immediately; instead, through our daily operation of method, we will cause these weights to reduce ever so slightly regularly.

Eventually, the weights will be smaller and lighter, and the balloon will start to take off, but the balloon will still be weighed down. Whilst we are in the initial phases, we will not be rising as quickly as we think we should or want to.

Through the consistent application of theories and techniques, those weights will erode down to the size of a piece of sand.

Eventually, your balloon will soar up into the blue Sky of opportunity. The sky won't even be your limit you can pick wherever your destination will be.

So, without further ado, let us get organised with improving your life – let us live your life on purpose!

**Let's get organised for a purposeful for life.**

As we proceed with your personal development, we need to take stock of where you are right now in what we call the wheel of life. Don't pay too much attention to this exercise just now; however, this will form a great start point for us to reflect on during the forthcoming months and years.

Essentially, we aim to work with you to get a more fulfilled and happier life and want to get this fulfilment in all segments of your life, not just the odd one or two.

In your living your life on purpose Journal there are several of the wheels of life, and these are for you to complete monthly.

We will be working on a 13-week programme rotating every 13 weeks, and in reality, we will never stop engaging in these 13-week massive action plans.

The critical point about living your life on purpose is that we are not looking for seismic gains or instant gratification. We are seeking relatively small and yet seemingly insignificant enhancements in all segments of our life.

On a day to day basis, these enhancements and improvements may not be immediately noticeable. As we reflect every month by completing a new wheel of life exercise, we will start to see that balance is being restored in our life.

**Imagine that the wheel of life is a bicycle wheel and the purpose of life is to have an enjoyable ride!**

When we go through the first exercise of the wheel of life, grade yourself from zero to ten in each segment. Next join the dots together.

You may find that you have a bit of a wonky wheel. Do not worry; this is perfectly normal for most people who have never consciously analysed segments like this in their lives before.

You can see in the wheel there are different segments. There are lines along each piece from the centre to the outside of the wheel.

We will be working inside two different wheels.

The back wheel of a bike is the driving wheel. You can see from the graphic below that our driving wheel includes "Mindset", "Habits", and "Focus" elements.

The first 8 chapters of the book will cover these off. We need to get mentally fit for this!

The front-wheel will be showing ways to improve in all areas of our lives. Remember to be happy we all want balance.

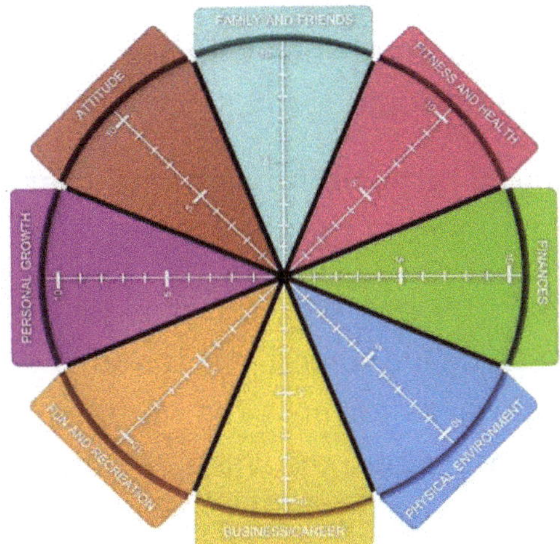


Incidentally, you can research using the wheel of life in various differing guises way back to early Buddhist writings. Interesting that chi plays an essential part in the balance of life.

You can see the circle has a centre point, and to complete the exercise, draw a dot from zero in the centre to 10, where you rate yourself in that segment.

Once you have applied your dots, now join the dots so you can move from family and friends through fitness and health, continue passing through finances and physical environment and around the wheel until you get back to family and friends.

This should be quite self-explanatory and easy to understand but spend some time with this because this will be the starting point of living your life on purpose. Of all the wheel segments, “Attitude” could the component that causes you deliberation.

Think about your attitude, not what you are externally demonstrating, but what you feel inside. Do you think you have a good attitude? Do you attract people into your life that are happy, smiley, and successful? Is your attitude playing a positive or a negative element in your career?

Once you have completed your wheel of life exercise, look at it. Is it imbalanced? Would it roll smoothly down a Hill?

Or are you likely to rattle your brain with every single bounce that each segment would cause?

We are doing this on purpose, but it is just a bit of fun and somewhere to start. Our objective is to move your grading's in each segment upwards towards the number 10 whilst always maintaining balance within the wheel. If you have a wheel that is balanced superbly at number 4 on each of the segments, well done! You are in balance now. Let us improve your lifestyle in all other areas of the wheel.

Within your Journal, we recommend you complete other starter exercises. These will include a check of some of your financial affairs, which by the way, you are certainly going to improve quite considerably as you pass through this book and audio.

We will also look at your health statistics, measuring your weight and certain parts of your anatomy because you cannot track what you do not measure.

You don't need to record any of these elements until you get to the book's relevant chapter.

The first part of this book is designed to show you how to get your mindset ready for the growth you will experience. During this growth phase, we will show you how you can improve every part of your life, but once we get you there, we believe it is vital that we at least keep you there.

Keeping you somewhere is not our intention; we want to show you how to improve right the way till you draw your very last breath on this beautiful world that we live in. We do not want to work with you momentarily to help you get somewhere and then drop back to where you started. That is not growing, and that is not living your life on purpose.

How many times do you hear of somebody winning the lottery in their country, only for them to lose it quite quickly! This is because their mindset could not cope with their new riches, and they squandered their income far too quickly.

Enjoy this book and the community and understand that we are all together in this growth, and we wish you every success in living your life on purpose.

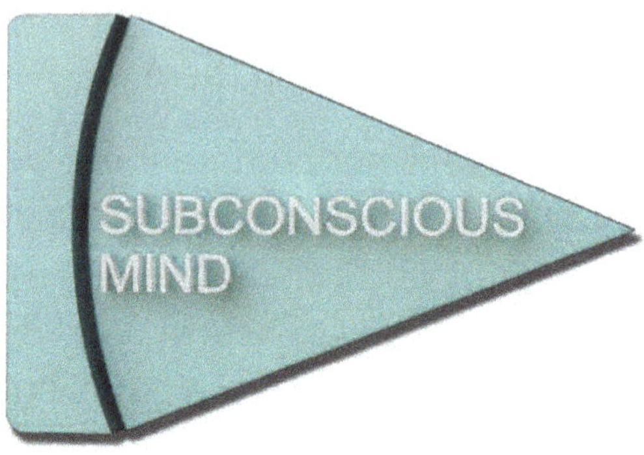


## Subconscious Mind

A human being's subconscious mind can be one of nature's most destructive forces.

It can work for you or against you.

Billions worldwide are beaten into a life of normality or poverty because of this incredible controlling system.

Most people have heard the word subconscious, but most don't understand what this is or what the subconscious mind does. That is the point, in a comical way. The subconscious mind doesn't want us to think about things. It works for us without thinking – this is subconscious.

Through your five senses of sight, smell, hearing, touch, taste, you have become the person you are right now.

If you are reading or listening to this book, it could be inferred that you are looking to improve the current "you". To do this, we must focus on the subconscious mind, for this is the natural controller of most of the things you do every minute of every day. Most people's current operating system has a bug in it, and we need to purge the bugs out and re-write the new piece of code.

The best analogy I've heard to explain this, is in an easy-to-understand way is Jammy (jelly) doughnuts, and I must thank Dr Tom Barratt for conjuring up this tasty image.

How do you put the jam (jelly) into a doughnut?

You inject it!

The doughnut is made, and then the jam is injected into it. I delivered a seminar once, and a gentleman in the audience was excitedly waving his hand when asked that question.

"I know how they put the jam into the doughnut", he proclaimed. Sensing his excitement and potential opportunity to deliver my point, I encouraged him to continue.

"How do you put the Jam in the doughnut?" I asked.

"My family owned a bakers", he enthusiastically replied, "and sometimes I was placed on jammy doughnut duty. Essentially, we had a device with two handles. The doughnuts were on a conveyor belt when they came under the device, you squirted in the jam."

Jokingly and with a big grin, he continued, "Sometimes I double squirted the jam into the doughnuts."

"How fantastic", I interjected. "Can you imagine being on the end of a double squirted jammy doughnut?"

So, we deduced that the jam is injected into the doughnut.

Now let us imagine your head is the doughnut and your subconscious mind is the jam. Who put the jam into your doughnut?

Let me help you out a bit.

When you were born, you had no real thoughts in your mind. Your parents, teachers, television, brothers and sisters, aunties and uncles and everybody around you inject their jam into your doughnut.

So, you see, you became the person you are due to the thoughts and beliefs of the people that surrounded you; they put the jam into your doughnut.

The big problem here is what if it is the wrong jam. Your parents had the jam in their doughnuts from their parents etc. If their jam is inaccurate, the wrong jam has been passed through generation after generation. What if you had received a double squirt of the wrong jam!

Your parents, teachers, brothers, and sisters did not intentionally put the wrong jam into your doughnut. They only know what they know, so they passed down to you to the best of their ability.

If your family is hypothetically earning, let's say 25,000 spondoolies a year they have a wonderful life, have some debts, and have a nice family holiday every year they may think that this is as good as it can get.

Maybe your family is used to watching television for four hours a day every day; perhaps they do a little exercise and maybe don't eat too healthily. This lifestyle would become the typical lifestyle for you because this is all you know.

They say, “You do not know, what you do not know”.

What you don't realise is that other families are coming home from work, they are eating together, they are talking with each other, and they are also participating in a variety of different hobbies.

A lot of families don't watch the income reducing box. Instead, they occupy their time doing things with each other and this, by default, creates a better family unity.

To improve as a human being, we have to identify some of the things in our life that we want to change, and then we need to go through a jam transfusion.

But what is the subconscious mind, and what is its purpose?

The subconscious mind saves your brain energy by automating many routine activities during your day. For example, you don't have to think about breathing; you naturally breathe in and out; your subconscious mind has automated this process, so you don't have to think about it.

Also, when you are learning to drive, you must think consciously about how you drive the automobile. With time, the subconscious mind makes this an automated process, so you don't have to think about it consciously, and therefore, the brain doesn't need to use much energy.

During your day, the subconscious mind is looking to automate as many of your daily activities as it can to free up space for other things that your brain needs to do. It wants to save energy.

Therefore, since you were a young child, your subconscious mind has been controlling you, and it has been controlling what you think is a regular daily activity. Your habits are your subconscious mind.

During your growing up phase, you see your dad returning from work. After work, he cracks open a bottle of beer, sits down and watches sport on television. You see this every single day of your life.

When you get to an age where you are employed, you have a house of your own; the chances are subconsciously, you come home from work you crack open a beer. You watch some on-demand television, and then you go about your evening much the same as your dad did when you were younger.

This is why we need to be conscious of our subconscious mind.

The thing that is important to understand, is that your subconscious mind cannot reject. So, whatever is going on in your world through those five senses, your subconscious mind accepts this into it. Remember, your subconscious mind cannot reject anything.

Your subconscious mind was accepting everything that your circle of influence, so your parents, friends, teachers etc, transmitted towards you and your five senses during your early years.

You had no maturity at this point to understand what was right and what was wrong, so therefore you did not have a barrier to stop all this information from going into your subconscious mind. This is perfectly normal and applies to everyone in the world.

If your subconscious mind cannot reject, you can consciously decide to overwrite or replace the jam in your doughnut with updated jam.

Imagine that you have jam in your doughnut, and this jam is not serving you the way you want it to; you need to engage in a jam transfusion! For example, I prefer custard doughnuts to jammy doughnuts!

For joviality, let us pretend that the custard is an improved thought process that I want to become part of my automated system. I would need to consciously be thinking about these custard doughnut thoughts all the time until eventually, it purged out the jammy element of my doughnut.

You cannot take something out of your subconscious mind that is already there. You can repeatedly overwrite that information so that the subconscious mind now accepts it as the new normal.

To put this into perspective, imagine you have a glass of water, and you start to put the sand into the glass. The glass can only contain so much content, and as you begin to pour the sand into the water, the sand is heavier than the water.

It will then push the water out of the glass until eventually if you put enough sand in, there will be little or no water remaining in the glass.

By employing a daily method of operation, we can change the jam in your doughnut so that we can put new jam into it and reprogram our subconscious mind to develop better as people.

We can delve deeper into the subconscious mind's science, but we don't need to do that right now. If we are armed with the knowledge, the subconscious mind is the master controlling system that effectively creates habits of everything we do, every single day of our lives what we can do is identify some of the things that we would like to overwrite so that we can improve them in our lives.

We started this chapter by stating that the subconscious mind is one of the most destructive forces to a human being. This is not being dramatic; the subconscious mind can stop a human being from achieving their full potential.

The subconscious has protective measures within it. The subconscious wants to protect you. It is always watching out for you. You don't know it because it's working in the background, but everything you do it is protecting your life. It is also preventing a better life.

It can only protect your life armed with the information that it knows, and this information is the jam in your doughnut that's being passed to you throughout your whole life.

When you look at some people who live a successful, carefree life, you may wonder why they are so happy. Why are they so successful? Why do they look so fit and healthy, and why do they have an outstanding attitude?

It will be entirely dependent upon two things: firstly, they got better jam in their doughnut from birth to their mature years and secondly, they also engaged in regular jam transfusions.

Treat the jam transfusions as though they were personal development. The people who embrace the philosophy of continuous and never-ending improvement are always learning, and they're still going through that jam transfusion process.

**It is untrue when somebody says that we are all born equal.**

When people are born into families of poverty or above poverty, it is ridiculous to believe that they have the same opportunities as wealthy people.

This is not discrimination. It is purely because the education system is not designed to help people grow their minds. Families who have wealth are generally better educated, not in chemistry, physics, and mathematics. They are generally better educated in life.

Because their parents have a better understanding of money, for example, as they grow up, they learn this better understanding about money. Remember the jam in the doughnut.

If their parents go to play golf and have a lovely life when it comes to recreation, their health, their eating habits are different from yours then, of course, you are going to be disadvantaged.

The fortunate thing is that this is not eternal. You can now decide to change the jam in your doughnut, to fill your doughnut with much better jam.

When a baby is born, the baby is essentially a blank canvas. Research found that whatever happens within the first eight years of their lives will be the primary way to think for the rest of their life. Unless they make an active and conscious intervention to change their subconscious mind.

Their current environment has pretty much programmed them by the age of eight years.

It does not have to remain this way, which is the excellent news. As we progress through living our lives on purpose, we will engage in some conscious activities repeated daily to positively alter your subconscious mind.

Being conscious in the moment, so thinking about things that you never thought about before is going to be the simple dynamic that changes your life forever.

For the record, whoever you are right now, whatever information you received in those first eight years of your life and beyond, your parents' social circle, from your teachers from the television, please understand that nothing was put into your subconscious mind wrong on purpose.

It is what they knew to be right at the time.

Think of your subconscious mind as you're some supercomputer; it is operating behind the scenes all the time; it is the operating system of your life. Since time began, these operating systems have all had bugs in them that are superseded by a new updated version of that operating system.

Throughout the next decades of your life, you may become consciously aware of how you want to live your life on purpose and how you'd like to improve your lives.

Suppose the subconscious mind is designed to protect us, to stop us from doing things that could harm us physically and mentally. In that case, we have to question consciously whether those safety parameters are, in fact, overzealous.

What I mean by this is, some parents are perpetual worriers in life. Because they are perpetual worriers in life, this then affects the jam in their children's doughnut. Throughout the child's life, they think it's perfectly normal to be a perpetual worrier, so by default; they become a perpetual worrier.

People worry about the simplest things that stop them from moving forward in their lives. They do not like to take risks. They want to be safe.

These perpetual Warriors won't even look at things that may enhance their lives if there is 1% of any risk. It is the way they are programmed.

On the other hand, some people actively take risks throughout their lives and see risk as the new safe. It is normal to take risks. These risks could be financial, these risks could be in the sporting world, and these risks could be perceived as necessary for continuous growth.

I have been very fortunate to go skiing in my lifetime, and I've been skiing since an early age. I remember, I became a cross country skiing instructor and took some troops to the Norwegian ski resorts of Lillehammer.

I was trying to teach older adults how to cross-country ski. They were so uncoordinated they were not used to this, and they had an inherent fear of falling.

My saviour was a kindergarten, yes, a kindergarten of children aged somewhere between three and six years. They skied past us in a line moving swiftly, entirely in harmony; they were skiing so naturally.

I asked the gents that I was skiing with to watch them and observe the natural skiing ability of these children; it was a sight to behold. Some of our gentlemen were from Manchester, some were from Wales, and some were from Scotland. They had never had skis on their feet before, so to them, this was alien.

Their subconscious mind stopped them from being fluid in their skiing ability because of the fear of falling. If you have skied before in your life, you don't mind falling as a young person because you know that falling doesn't hurt. And the more you fall, the more you master the art of falling. Who would know?

That is an art to falling. Yes, people in sports where there is a likely hood that they're going to hit the ground have mastered the art of falling.

When people are about to fall, they have fallen so often, you have guessed it, they aren't thinking consciously about how to fall; they fall naturally or subconsciously.

The central art of falling is to relax as you are falling, and when you relax when you're falling, there is less likelihood of things breaking. People scared of falling; if they sense they are about to fall, their whole body goes rigid.

Imagine an arm rigid when it lands on the ground. If it's rigid and therefore not flexible, there is a high likelihood that a fracture of that arm will occur. On the other hand, the natural faller relaxes, the arm is not rigid; they may fall on their forearm, they may fall on their upper arm or fall on their side and laugh about falling.

It is the subconscious mind that determined how to fall. You are not consciously thinking when you are going down "Oh, I must relax my body" through the repetition of repeatedly falling through the early stages of your development; you get used to falling.

As a child, I would always be climbing up trees. I'd be running around through the fields or on my bike. I would regularly fall, so now when I fall when I'm cycling, I fall in a relaxed way. I guess you could say that I fall softly. Some people fall like double the gravity rate, and they hit the ground hard and harm themselves—all controlled by the subconscious mind.

The subconscious mind can be so destructive because it can only accept and cannot reject. This means that so many negative forces have been implanted into our subconscious minds, restricting our personal growth.

A young boy lives in a happy world. However, his dad always says something negative to him, maybe about how he looks. The dad is not intentionally doing this because the dad was spoken to in the same way by his dad. The son, though, starts to take this quite personally. He doesn't like the negative way his dad is speaking to him. He starts to lose self-esteem and confidence.

The young boy starts to fall into a world where he would rather play computer games than socialise with other human beings. To a certain extent, he becomes introverted. There's absolutely nothing wrong with being introverted; however, this young boy started to withdraw from society.

When he daydreams, he daydreams about being a successful business owner creating computer games. He tells his father that he'd like to be a computer programmer. Instead of being supportive, the father demonstrates his lack of knowledge of computer games and his lack of ambition throughout his life by chastising the young boy.

Undeterred by this, the young boy finds a new interest and puts this recent interest and idea to the dad he loves and adores. Once again, the dad ridicules him for this silly idea and suggests that he should focus on getting a good education, followed by a good job.

Time after time, the young boy goes to his dad looking for some parental guidance hoping that one day his dad will support one of his good ideas, but time after time, dad said "Go and get a job" until eventually, the young boy decides that that must be the way the world operates. That young boys like him must go and get a job. Young boys like him cannot be like the other successful boys that he's read about in newspapers in magazines via social media. It can happen to the other boys, but it cannot happen to him.

The subconscious mind can now trap the young boy. He can submit to the father's will and never fulfil his dream of being a computer programmer or anything else. The young boy loses all ambition himself.

Remember, for most boys or girls, their mum and their dads are their heroes, so whatever they say is also accepted through the bond of love and trust.

He sees that his dad worked for the local council in planning. The chances are for young boy, his aspirations will be to work in the council in a job similar to planning.

Some of the most significant crimes in this world are the unconscious crimes committed by parents who chastise their children and stunt their growth so much that they never live up to what they could do.

On the other hand, a young girl living in a family that loved to take risks, that loved to grow and loved to develop, and whose parents loved to support whatever that she does has an entirely different opportunity in life.

Every time she went to her father with an idea throughout her early years, the dad would support that idea every time. The dad would speak to the young girl asking why she wanted to follow such a dream; they would talk about it; he would actively encourage her to talk about the vision of these dreams and her aspirations.

They would talk practically about the pros and cons of this idea. If it was a business idea, how viable was that business, what competition was there to that business, was it likely to be a profitable venture.

This conversation would continue; it would be an excellent way for father and daughter to bond and communicate. The young girl eventually starts this new idea, whatever it may be, and it fails. She is devastated by this failure; she cuddles her dad, and they talk about the disappointment. After the tears have passed by, dad teaches the young girl something quite spectacular.

Success is 99% failure; he teaches this young girl. You must never lose your dreams. You must understand that you might be lucky to have one go at something for it to be successful. The chances are that you will need to try a whole lot harder.

Still, he continues, the most successful people in this world that lived the most extraordinary lives in this world, have failed thousands upon thousands of times throughout their life.

Therefore, it is perfectly normal; he teaches the young daughter to try something and keep trying something perfectly normal and acceptable to fail. The biggest crime in life, he teaches her, is to stop trying.

Now we have two different children a boy, and a girl, born from the same blank canvas, the jam in the doughnut of their parents is highly likely to determine the jam in their doughnut and, therefore, move forward in their own lives. Life is a paradox. Many young people and adults lost their desire to achieve because they fear failure.

When and where did our support people change how they communicate with us?

As a young baby, when we were all moving from crawling to attempting to walk, our parents, our aunties and uncles, and everybody supported us and gave us lots of encouragement and funny noises in a high-pitched tone with massive cheesy grins.

None of us went from crawling to walking in one move. We kept failing and falling, and each time we fell, our supporters would encourage us to get up again. We would repeatedly fall until eventually; we would stand up with the assistance of a table or a nearby chair.

As babies, we did not see this as failing because we did not comprehend the word failure. All we knew is that we saw big people standing up on two legs, and we wanted to copy them. We also experienced the sensation of recognition from such an early age as people encouraged us to continue in our movement from horizontal to vertical.

At which point then did our supporters stop encouraging us to improve? It is absolute nonsense in our world today that we criticise someone who is attempting to better themselves when they fail for some reason.

For those of you who have failed and for those of you who have failed many times, well done to you!

I believe that all successful people in this world have failed so often. If they were standing around you right now, they would all be applauding you for every time you failed in your pursuit of personal improvement.

**Failing is acceptable, as long as we learn from each failure.**

We all must begin to associate with people that have a positive mindset. We will be talking about associations later in this book.

The subconscious mind has created your identity. The primary programming and conditioning would have occurred up to 8 years of age.

It would help if you looked in the mirror to identify who you are right now. Look at yourself and identify the strengths that you have, the good things in your life that you are more than satisfied with. The most challenging job of all is looking at your identity, who you are, and identifying what weaknesses you would like to turn into strengths.

Once you have consciously identified who you are, for example, your identity, then what we want to do is help you decide who you would like to become. Would you like to be a superb musician, a competent articulate speaker? Would you like to be a top-level golfer? Whatever you want to become, you need to be that person now.

There is a phrase that I don't particularly like in the wrong context, but when used correctly, it is absolutely fantastic and can help shape your identity by training your subconscious mind. The phrase is "Fake it until you make it".

Once you've consciously identified who you'd like to become, who you'd like your new identity to be. It would be best if you started thinking about that today and every day after that as though you are already that person.

For the record, many successful people regularly say affirmations. They don't say it when they feel like saying it; they say these affirmations all day, every day. They understand that this subconscious mind can only accept whatever they consciously put towards it, and therefore, they are positively reinforcing via affirmations.

This is not some mumbo jumbo; successful people talk to themselves to retrain their subconscious minds. It is not something you can do when you want to; you need to be doing this all day, every day, especially if you come across some negativity in your life. Each day, for training my subconscious mind, I say to myself a handful of questions. These form part of my purposeful morning routine.

Question 1: What are you grateful for today, Gary?

Question 2: What makes you so good?

Question 3: How organised are you today?

Question 4: what will stop you from doing your key pay off activities today?

Question 5: how will you become a better you today?

These questions form 5 out of 10 questions that I ask myself every day. I do this entirely to programme my subconscious mind. Remember, the subconscious mind can only accept it cannot reject.

Let us now go through these questions to show you how I answer them. You can see how I am consciously saying things, which I say aloud. My subconscious mind will then receive. You can create your own questions.

Question 1: What are you grateful for today, Gary?

I am grateful for my son, my wife Ana, my mum, dad, sister Gail, my nephew Matthew, my niece Charlotte for all my friends and family. I am grateful for the fantastic place that I live in. I'm grateful for my health and my well-being, and I am grateful for my businesses, all of which are growing at a fantastic rate.

Question 2: What makes you so good?

What makes me so good is that I'm a nice person. I live in a world of enlightened self-interest. I want to help as many people as possible to get whatever they want out of life. By default, I will get whatever I want out of life. I'm good looking;

I'm charismatic, I'm confident, I'm intelligent, I am a successful person in life. I'm well-liked by my family, friends, and anybody else who comes into contact with me. I am a people person. I am a money magnet. Because I know where I'm going, people and money are attracted to me, and that's what makes me so good.

You can see by going through the first two questions how I am answering them.

I'm answering it as though I am in the moment. If you wake up every morning with gratitude, you're going to have a wonderful day.

The big problem with creating a new identity, the big problem with changing the jam in your doughnut, is that this will not be an instant transfusion. Over years and years in your life, your identity, your subconscious thoughts have been formed through your current environment. Therefore, it is unlikely that in a week, you're going to transform your subconscious mind in the area you chose to do so.

Therefore, persistence in the following of this method is essential for you to create your new identity.

It could take you months to transform your new identity, so if we understand it will take months, and it's going to take persistence, we can manage expectations.

You are about to embark on something quite seismic in your life. It is worthwhile doing.

If you can live your life on purpose, you can improve it. You will need to create the habit of daily activity that will allow you to change your subconscious consciously.

**It's going to take a little while to do the jam transfusion.**

One of my favourite pop bands as a youngster was XTC, who wrote a song called "senses working overtime".

It highlights our five senses of touch, sight, smell, hearing, and taste.

I'd like you to imagine that human beings are natural transmitters and natural receivers.

You have probably heard the phrase good vibes or bad vibes. You may come across somebody you don't know through life, but you get a good vibe from them. This means they transmit something to you via their senses which have caused you to believe that they have given you a good vibe.

On the flip side, you've probably met somebody who you think I'm getting bad vibes from that person. So, they must be transmitting bad vibes to you.

If we are natural transmitters and we are natural receivers, we have to identify that the subconscious mind is playing a part in this receiving of this information. You will be receiving this information through the five senses.

For every single moment of every day, our five senses are working overtime, and they are working overtime to serve us.

You are blissfully unaware of how much activity is going on through your subconscious mind taking the slack so that you do not have to think about it and because you don't have to think about it, you don't have to spend energy doing it.

We have something called a reticular. The reticular is a filter that stops you from sensing everything around you. Otherwise, you would get overloaded with all the information that you're receiving. So, the reticular is the filter.

Every day you receive 10s of thousands, if not hundreds of thousands of pieces of information—all passing through your five senses, thankfully, your reticular filters out most of them.

You will have understood the power of the reticular throughout your life, but the chances are you did not know how it worked.

You go to a car showroom, and you decide to buy yourself a Volkswagen Passat. The moment you drive out with your new Volkswagen Passat, what do you see on the roads every time you drive your new Volkswagen Passat? That right, you see Volkswagen Passat's everywhere!

The Volkswagen Passat was always on the road, but your reticular was filtering it, so you didn't have to pick up on it.

Remember, your subconscious mind is an energy-saving device. If more energy were applied to every single occurrence of your five senses throughout your day, you would be absolutely shattered.

Understanding that the subconscious mind has created habits for most aspects of your life gives you full permission and knowledge to alter those thought process and the habits associated with them.

In developing your brand-new identity, what you will be doing is consciously activating the reticular.

You will be consciously thinking about how to improve yourself. You will be saying things daily to make sure that your subconscious mind accepts them. You will be reading or listening to personal development that goes into your subconscious so often that it becomes real. It starts to form the improving you.

The subconscious mind is the critical element that will help you become the person you want to be.

When we go through living your life on purpose, we will tame the subconscious mind and then unleash the power you have within it.

We will reduce any chances of fear of failure, and you will be motivated to do things you've never done before.

Because you are now achieving more success, your brain's hormone dopamine will be released. The body likes this release of dopamine. The mind loves this release of dopamine. It is the success hormone.

Some people called dopamine the happy hormone.

The more you feel the sensation of dopamine and the feeling of success, you will crave more success, and therefore, you will engage in the activities required to get that success.

Through-out this book, there will be a consistent reference to the subconscious's power. For the time, be consciously aware of everything you are feeding your mind.

## Habits

Habits define who you are.

"You are what you repeatedly do. Success is, therefore, merely a habit", Aristotle.

You wake up in the morning, and without thinking about it, you move straight into a daily routine. This is crazy, but you haven't even thought about some of these routines for so long, and why would you?

Some of our routines are perfectly fine, and they serve their purpose.

We already established briefly that our minds like to automate as much of our life as possible to save energy for more vital functions.

Think back to this morning if you put on socks, tights, or stockings, which foot went in first?

You've probably needed to think about it to get an answer, but there is a remarkably high probability that the same foot goes in every day. There is no need to change this habit. It serves its purpose. Have you ever jumped into a car and arrived at the destination but cannot remember most of the journey?

Do not worry. All your faculties were operating at the same intensity, but your supercomputer just automated much of the tedious journey.

Every day you have thousands of automated functions, and the vast majority do not even need changing. Some though may serve you poorly.

If you identify these bad habits and want to change them through a relatively short period, you can. This is the crux of the matter, though. You can only change your life and eradicate these bad habits if you want to.

Habit checking is a good exercise. During the next week or so, be consciously aware of everything you do. If this is a bad habit, write it down.

Use the Habit identifier document at www.lylop.com

A daily routine. Does any of this resemble yours, and what would you want to eliminate?

Jane's mobile phone is on her bedside table. At 630am, the alarm goes off; she rolls over, hits snooze and slips back into a comforting doze. Fifteen minutes later, the alarm reminds her it is time to get up. Her arm flops over and hits another snooze. "Just another 15 minutes," she thinks to herself.

After three alarms, she is ready to drag herself out of bed. First, though, she has a look at social media, and before she knows it, another 30 minutes has passed by. She pops to the loo and then goes downstairs and makes herself the first of two coffees before work.

She does not have breakfast; instead, settles onto her settee and watches the morning news for half an hour. After those two coffees, she goes for a shower, cleans her teeth before getting dressed and jumping into her car to commute an hour to work.

Traffic is not good today, much like any other day, so Jane's stress levels begin to rise in fear of being late for work. Fortunately, she gets to her desk with a minute to spare. She fires up the computer and gets to work.

A colleague asks if she would like a coffee. The answer was automatic "yes" The 3rd coffee of the day is consumed as Jane works away at her desk.

11 o'clock is break time. She makes another coffee and has a chocolate bar with some crisps (Chips for our International readers). Fifteen minutes later, she is back at her desk until lunch at 1 pm.

Jane walks to a fast-food restaurant and orders her usual cheeseburger and fries. She sits outside, enjoying her lunch and browses social media. At least her life is not as bad as her connections, she thinks.

She sees one of her friends is doing some weird and wacky diet, has lost a lot of weight and looks incredibly chuffed with herself. "Bitch", she thinks, looking down at her spare tyres visible in the ruffled jumper she is wearing. "Maybe I should lose some weight".

Lunch finished, Jane gets back to her desk and works until 3 pm and the mid-afternoon break. Another coffee and chocolate bar beckons.

At 5 pm, she hops into her car and sets off home. She pops into her local convenience store to buy some food for her evening meal. She gets lured by a microwave meal of Chicken Tikka Masala, rice, and a naan.

As she walks past the wine aisle, she automatically reaches for a bottle of sauvignon blanc. She sees her favourite biscuits and buys some too.

Arriving back at home, she throws her shoes off and settles on the settee, watching some quiz show whilst also tuning back into her social media. She posts herself. “Another same-same day in my boring job and about to have a curry and rice for dinner #allbymyself”.

Ping. Dinner cooked. Wine opened. On her lap, she devours the curry and slurps the wine. The plate gets thrown into the sink with yesterday’s crockery. Jane returns to the TV and her social media.

She opens her post to be reminded that her credit card payment is higher again this month. How depressing?

She is now watching a soap opera with one eye and still private messaging people or reading about the lives of her connections.

She spends more time reading about people’s heartaches than being inspired by people improving their lives. The wine is finished, and Jane automatically pops on the kettle to make herself a mug of hot chocolate to go with her chocolate chip cookies.

11 pm; she is getting tired, so she goes to bed. Just time for one last look at social media before popping the phone on her bedside table.

Each working day Jane does the same thing, and the weekend is only different because she tidies up her apartment and visits some family and has a total blow out on a Saturday with friends.

Sunday morning hungover, she does little other than feel sorry for herself. She is alone again.

The week starts, and the very same routine is followed.

Jane does not know it, but her lifestyle slowly dragged her down. It is not just a Jane that lives like this. John does too.

Millions of people with a boringly, repetitive lifestyle that does not serve them at all well.

Habits can be like a slow and unhappy demise, yet many people conquer them, and these little changes over time serve them well. Their lives become joyful, fun, and filled with positive interactions.

Jane decides to make some changes.

She places her mobile phone in another room before she goes to sleep. At 630am, the alarm goes off as she must get out of bed to switch it off. She stays up.

Rule number one.

To make or break habits, you want to make them easier (for ones you want to create) or more challenging (for ones you wish to break)

She still goes to the loo and then goes into her kitchen. The night before, she had placed her blender on the work unit. She picks up the blender cup and fills it with some fruit, a protein shake, and some oats. She has some honey on the work unit visible, so she puts a squirt of that in too.Once blended, she thoroughly enjoys her wake up drink and breakfast.

Jane walks through the corridor. She sees her training shoes already placed on the floor. A memory jogger that this morning is her walk morning.

She throws on some leggings, a top and gets her mobile phone. Jane has bought some professional development on Amazon Audible, so she grabs her earphones too. Training shoes on. Audible on. Jane enjoys a 30-minute brisk walk and returns home for a shower before getting dressed for work.

Jane enjoys a fresh orange juice and picks up her lunch that she had prepared the night before.

She kisses her partner and gets into the car, once again streaming some podcast. Traffic is lighter as she left nice and early for work.

Jane gets to work. It is her dream job. She gets to help others, visiting and meeting lots of different people. As she was always prompt and energetic, and full of life, Jane had been promoted. She had previously worked at a desk all day, every day. But that was not for Jane; she wanted more. At 11, she has a coffee. She decided months before to opt for Decaffeinated and dropped the two sugars she previously had.

At lunch, she enjoys sitting outside chatting with friends. She gets some lovely messages from her partner thanking her for preparing their lunch too. Jane loves it because they take turns in preparing each other's lunch pack.

She watches a couple walking, holding hands and laughing. "I'm so blessed," she thinks. "I have a wonderful partner too, with a great job, and I feel fantastic".

Work finished, she drives home via the gym. Tonight, it is her spin class. Her regular fit buddies are there, and one comments on how fabulous Jane looks.

She had shed a lot of weight, making simple changes. She got an increased level of energy and was transmitting happiness.

It was this transmission that attracted someone to look at her, and this then formed a relationship.

After spin class, she gets back home. As she had prepared lunch, it was her partners turn to prepare the evening meal. Lasagne, a side salad, some garlic bread – she loved it when he prepared for her.

It is a lovely night, so they decide to take a leisurely walk sharing their daytime experiences and daydreaming about holidays they planned to take.

Jane and her partner were so closely aligned. They liked to plan; they liked living their lives on purpose and were willing to make sacrifices to attain their goals.

Both had built up some credit card debt. They decided to save money, not buying lunch, or having excesses during the week.

As each month went by, they paid more than the minimum amount to their credit card and watched as the monthly interest payments began to drop. Finally, the debt was falling quickly. Soon they would be able to buy their own dream home.

Friday night was movie night. A glass of wine or two and some popcorn.

Saturday started with the park run, followed by visits to their friends and family and always something social. Saturdays were still great days.

Sunday was a lie-in, a lazy day other than going to the supermarket for their weekly shop. Jane loved her life, and it all started by making subtle changes. Jane introduced some very slight and positive changes in her life.

She moved the alarm out of her bedroom so that she needed to get out of bed to switch it off. This saved her a lot of time in the morning. She could start the day on her terms, not rushing to work because she had spent time doing irrelevant activities.

Jane had identified things that did not serve her well with her habits.

She had previously become immersed in social media and found that she was reaching for her phone first thing in the morning, after work, and last thing at night.

She disconnected from people that made negative comments and switched off the phone's notifications.

She did begin to read messages from positive people and liked the idea of starting her morning with a walk to clear her mind for the day. She did not watch the depressing morning news and instead was listening to professional development.

One such audio was Atomic Habits, written by James Clear.

Having listened to this, she identified those habits she wanted to get rid of and others that she wanted to build on or create.

She started to create triggers that made her more efficient and living a happier life. By making habits harder, she also naturally fell away from them.

In "Atomic Habits" James highlights the skill of habit stacking. You do one action that is followed by another and another and so on. The first habit was triggered by something you set up deliberately. Then as each day passes, the triggered stacks become part of your routine.

Jane had applied these rules in her personal and work life. She became healthier and fitter, her self-esteem rose, and she became to like herself. When applying good habits at work, such as arriving early, being more efficient in her tasks, her managers noticed. This led to a series of promotions and pay rises.

You may think this is just a story about Jane or John, but this is the wheel of life kicking into action.

By focusing on each element of the wheel and Living Your Life on Purpose day by day, week by week and month by month, small seeming unnoticeable improvements are made. At this point, your mind should be scanning your daily activity and monitoring to identify the things that you do daily, but which are not serving you well.

Time to live life on your terms, and the fact you are reading this book shows that you are looking to improve things in it.

Living your life on purpose is the right way to do that.

Some habits serve us well, and others serve us less well. If we overeat lousy food, drink too much alcohol, exercise infrequently, and sit around the house watching television every day, it could be said that these habits are not serving us well.

These bad habits over a day or a couple of days are not going to be catastrophic, but if these habits become the norm and we're doing these regularly each day, these could become a bad habit that causes significant health issues.

There is a common phrase known as the compound effect. The compound effect can work for you, and it can work against you, just like your good habits and bad habits.

The first time I heard of the compound effect was when it was revealed to me as the world's eighth wonder. The compounding of money was identified to me as this eighth wonder.

If you had 1 penny and that one penny doubled every day for 31 days, how much would that one penny have amassed to?

Isn't that crazy? When you look at the compounding effect of 1 penny on day one, you've got a penny on day two; you got 2 pennies on day three, you've now got 4 pennies, and on day four, you've now got 8 pennies, it does not seem like much is happening. But when you look further down the line, as the number starts to increase and the doubling effect accelerates, the compound effect is mind-blowing.

| Day | Penny |
|---|---|
| 1 | 1 |
| 2 | 2 |
| 3 | 4 |
| 4 | 8 |
| 5 | 16 |
| 6 | 32 |
| 7 | 64 |
| 8 | 128 |
| 9 | 256 |
| 10 | 512 |

| Day | Penny |
|---|---|
| 11 | 1024 |
| 12 | 2048 |
| 13 | 4096 |
| 14 | 8192 |
| 15 | 16384 |
| 16 | 32768 |
| 17 | 65536 |
| 18 | 131072 |
| 19 | 262144 |
| 20 | 524288 |
| 21 | 1048576 |

| Day | Penny |
|---|---|
| 22 | 2097152 |
| 23 | 4194304 |
| 24 | 8388608 |
| 25 | 16777216 |
| 26 | 33554432 |
| 27 | 67108864 |
| 28 | 134217728 |
| 29 | 268435456 |
| 30 | 536870912 |
| 31 | 1073741824 |

It really does double up to nearly 11 million spondoolies! 11million pounds, Dollars, Euro, Yen etc. The compound effect can be seen in all areas of our life.

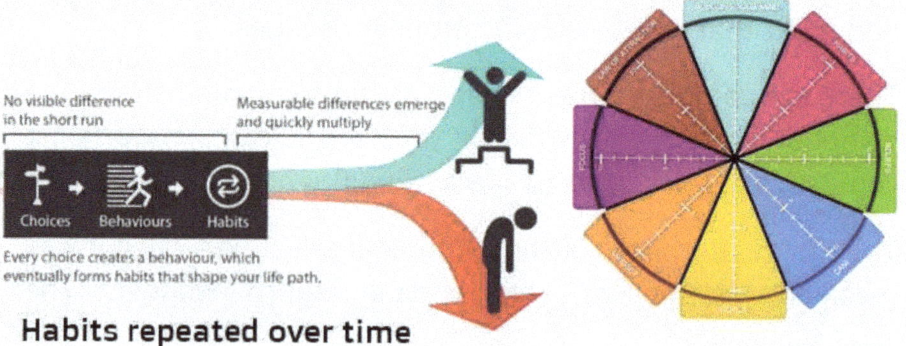

So, if we live our lives on purpose, we need to identify that if we have some terrible habits compounded over time, I guess they could kill us earlier than we'd hoped.

We then need to consciously create good habits that serve us well, understanding that by harnessing the compound effect's tremendous power, we will considerably improve our lives.

It will take a long time for these effects to take real hold in our life. But through the consistent application of the new habit, they will become the new norm. We shouldn't be fooled that changing patterns is easy.

The problem with habits going back to our old friend, the jammy doughnut, is that the habits have been with us for years and years. So, breaking a bad habit and changing it into a new pattern will not be easy.

Some critical steps can be employed to make old habits easy to break and new ones easy to make.

The first rule is you must understand it will take time to make a new habit. It will take time for your subconscious mind to automate this new habit.

Look at yourself consciously. Identify any of the bad habits that you may have that you would like to break totally and identifying some of the not so good habits you have that you're okay living with.

Now let's pay attention to the bad habits you would like to break entirely. You've identified the bad habit, and, in this example, I am going to use not drinking enough water.

You know that not drinking enough water is not good for you. You also understand that you could drink more water if you wanted to. You might also like to stop smoking or increase your exercising and maybe stop watching television. You may have a whole raft of habits that you would like to break.

It is not good practise to try and break multiple habits simultaneously. Therefore, we want to identify these bad habits and list them in the order that we would like to break them.

To create good habits, there are some things that we need to do, and one of those things is to make the new habit easier to do.

I don't like plain water. If I am running or doing sports, I love water, but I don't care for it around the house.

I did notice that whilst I wasn't a fan of plain water, I did like drinking carbonated water. So, I bought myself a soda stream. Another rule of creating a new habit is to make the habit easy to do and to make the habit enjoyable.

I just like the bubbles, the fizz, and the different flavour.

Before I went to bed, I would put one bottle of my newly carbonated water onto my desk in my office.

In the morning, when I went into my office to go through my daily method of operation (we will be covering a daily method of operation later), I would see my bottle of carbonated water.

The first thing I would do is have a drink of water because I had noticed the bottle was there, and it reminded me that it was an important task to start my day with. Indeed, during the first part of my purposeful morning, I would sip away a litre of water. This hydrated me quite significantly and made me more alert mentally. The skill in creating new habits is to use a trigger. The trigger in this instance was visually seeing the bottle of water ready to be consumed. The action was to drink the water.

If I had walked into my office and the bottle of water was not there, I would get involved with my daily method of operation; I would read my goals, I would say my afformations, I'd write down my things To-Do List without even thinking about wanting to have a drink of water.

But by walking into my office and seeing the bottle that that triggered my mind to say, "Oh yes, you want to drink more water, Gary." I then drink the water. I enjoy the water, and then I crave more water.

To make a new habit, we want to make the habit easier and break a bad habit; we want to make the habit harder.

One of my habits was that I drank a little too much alcohol during the week. I identify this as a habit that I would like to change. I like my wine, and I like my beer, and I do like a Jack Daniels from time to time.

I don't want to stop drinking alcohol, but I want to reduce my alcohol intake. Therefore, I need to employ a strategy that will make drinking alcohol during the week harder to do.

The easy thing for us to do was to ensure no alcohol in the house during the working week. If I wanted to have a glass of wine, I would need to get out of our comfortable home, travel to the nearest superstore, buy the wine come back, drink the wine and then, of course, when I did that, I'd feel bad because I'd broken my habit.

By making the habit harder, I am less likely to get the wine. I say to myself, "Oh, I would like a glass of wine".I go into the kitchen, but there is no wine in the kitchen. The trigger to my mind is that there is no wine in the kitchen. I question why is there no wine in the kitchen. I remind myself then that I have agreed that I will break the habit of drinking wine during the week.

What was also quite interesting is that I substituted wine with drinking carbonated water. I genuinely do like drinking wine, and I genuinely do like drinking carbonated water. I crave drinking carbonated water, which means that I've satisfied my number one goal of creating the habit of drinking more water.

As time passed and I became more habitual in my drinking of the water, I noticed that we were buying a lot less wine during the whole week, let alone just the weekdays.

What happened is a conscious thought pattern formed where I felt fantastic mentally. I would consciously say to myself I am enjoying waking up feeling fantastic without the effects of alcohol.

What then happened was during the weekends, if I wanted a drink, I would previously go for a glass of wine or a bottle of beer; I began to move towards the water first.

Drinking at home became less of a habit, both my wife and I started to feel better, we saved money and therefore, we're able to treat ourselves to other things.

Have you ever calculated how much money you spend on things like alcohol, cigarettes, and takeaway food? It certainly stacks up over a month or a year!

To create a new habit, we must employ a daily method of operation, and we must have triggers that remind us about the new habit we want to form and of course, we want to make things harder for habits we want to cease doing.

**Living your life on purpose is about creating those daily method of operations.**

When you have a purposeful morning, a purposeful afternoon, and a purposeful evening you will achieve more in your life than you could ever imagine possible.

From today, please start to employ a daily method of operation. Write down how you will begin your morning and the things that you are going to do to get your morning off to a purposeful start.

You could even call this your purposeful morning routine!

You choose your routine, implementing any triggers to ensure that you start creating good habits. Remember, your subconscious mind wants to automate everything. Repeating the same purposeful morning every morning for somewhere between 21 and 28 days, including the weekends, will create a natural start to your day.

No one has ever said that being successful in your life needs to be easy. It will not be easy; it will require discipline on your part!

Having a purposeful morning might mean that you have a drink of water, do some meditation, recite some affirmations, and write down a list of the things you want to do that day.

Successful people learn the skill of prioritising their tasks for the day. These do not need to be work tasks but everyday tasks in life. Many of us like the recognition of ticking off a task once we've completed it.

If your first task is to have a drink of water, write that down on the list and celebrate every time you tick that task. The second task might be walking your dog; this is a critical task to do, not just for you but because your dog may have crossed legs if you don't attend to them first.

Many people who own pets and go out and walk with them find this is a brilliant time to collect their thoughts, because there usually are not many other people out at that time to disturb them.

Write this in your daily method of operation and what you would do on your return from walking your dog.

Write down a full sequence of things you want to do first in the morning.

When you have written down all the things you want to do during the day, spend some time prioritising them. In Brian Tracy's book called "Eat that Frog", Brian alludes to the benefits of doing the task you like least first.

Therefore, he called the book "Eat that frog" if the worst thing you need to do daily is to eat a frog, get it out of the way as soon as possible.

The reality is that you have a horrible job that you need to do. Like administration for your local government agency or tax office, rather than putting off get it done, otherwise it would be in the back of your mind annoying you for days.

One facet of prioritising lists is that you need to focus on the most critical tasks first. We will have things that we write down onto our list, which are not that urgent. These tasks may be easy to do, and by consequence, we automatically go to do these first.

The fact of the matter is if these tasks were never done, the ramifications would be negligible. It is just that they were easy to do, so we decided to do those first.

When you live your life on purpose, you do not want to zig-zag; you want to straight line it to your goals.

**Prioritise the things that you need to do and do them first.**

So, in creating your new habit-forming, writing down a list of the things you need to do and then prioritising those activities will allow you to develop and push forward with this constant and never-ending improving attitude.

Discipline is of paramount importance in the new habit-forming process. It is so much easier to default back to type and default back to what was your previous norm, but this is not going to serve you well. Therefore, creating a purposeful morning and a daily method of operation is vital to your continued life progression.

If I could make alarm bells ring out of this book right now to demonstrate the importance of creating a daily method of operation where you write down a list of all your activities, this alarm bell would be ringing as loud as loud can be.

It is so dull writing down a list of things that you need to do and yet is probably one of the most useful things you can do to develop yourself personally and manage your use of the time available.

Try this just for 28 days and what you will find is that your dopamine, that success and feel-good hormone, will flood through your body each day because you're doing more of the tasks. Remember tick those tasks off and feel fantastic every time you tick one off.

Every time you complete a task, what is happening is you are moving forward. One little tick closer to the attainment of your goals, your dreams, and your aspirations. These may be seemingly insignificant activities, but it is more than just completing the activity that is happening here.

The fact that you complete your daily method of operation and the fact you are completing all these tasks means that you are creating a real habit, and a true habit that will serve you so well.

If you do not complete a task you roll it forward to the next day, and so on until eventually, you'll see that some of those low pay off activity tasks have been on your list for weeks. You can scrub these off because you now realise, they are relatively insignificant in the big scheme of things.

You set yourself a target of moving from couch to 5K, and you set yourself an ideal weight of 82 kilogrammes.

You write that you are going to do a one-kilometre walk or jog on your list. You make another entry that you're going to eat a good healthy breakfast and lunch, followed later by a good evening meal.

You complete your run, and you tick off the task. You have a nice healthy breakfast, lunch, and evening meal, and you tick off the task. You now have four accomplishment ticks, and you feel fantastic.

The next day because you felt fantastic, you write down the same four habits or tasks, and once again, you finish the day feeling fantastic with four more ticks.

You internally start feeling better with yourself, and you're congratulating yourself on the completion of your daily activities. Because you enjoy what you are doing, you want to do more of it.

Making a habit enjoyable is vital in the process too. To start with, you may not enjoy going out and completing your one kilometre, your two kilometres, your five-kilometre walk or jog. Most people who engage in some form of activity know it will serve them well to complete it and feel fantastic about themselves.

Of course, we are focusing on the couch to 5 kilometres just for something to focus on. It could be you want to go swimming, cycling, walking, dancing, or any other type of activity, the point is the more you do it, the more you enjoy it, and the more you want to do it.

So many people think that they don't like running. Their subconscious mind continually tells them they don't like running, but who put that jam into their doughnut. It would be best to go back to the early years of their life early to understand why they didn't like running.

A word circulates now about the younger generation, where they call these people snowflakes.

I like the snowflake generation because they are open-minded with their thoughts, and they share their values, and therefore we can work together in harmony, knowing how they think and how they feel.

Many generations ago, you were not allowed to display your thoughts or feelings because this was deemed a sign of weakness. I guess we could call these the hailstone generations—horrible frosty cold and hard.

Go back to your school days, your early school days, you were receptive to new jam being placed into your doughnut, and every week at school, they forced you to go on a cross country run.

For those who like being outside and running, this was the best day of the week.  It was a chance to get out and enjoy anything other than academia.

Those who loved academia, the arts or music; this could be their version of hell. They did not want to do any running; they did not see the purpose of running and would do everything they could not to do the running.

No one was ever taught why we would go running. It was seen to be just a punishment exercise, and the mind monster started to build in size. It grew and grew until the subconscious mind determined running was an evil and horrible pursuit.

If, however, we were taught more about the benefits of running at an early age, more people would understand its benefits and how it could improve performance in their preferred area of expertise.

As a young person, John loved academia, he loved the Sciences, and his teacher taught him the benefits of running. John and millions of other people worldwide realised that going out for a walk, jog or run is a brilliant way to free up the mind.

The teacher taught him that when he went running, forgetting the fact that there was a physical benefit of doing so mentally when you go running, you can use your creative side of your brain to think whilst you run, and many good thoughts come into the mind when you are free, and you are running.

At first, as a young boy, John did not buy into this concept. He believed the teacher was hoodwinking him. The teacher reminded John before each run to enjoy the exercise, but whilst he was running to think about the things that he wanted to understand more about in his pursuit of knowledge in the Sciences.

During those first few runs, John did start to think about the things that he enjoyed about his love of Sciences, and he found that whilst he was running, he forgot about the physical part of running; he began to embrace the fact that this was his excellent thinking time. John became an excellent student of Sciences, and in later life, John went on to run half marathons and marathons; he found that running was the best place for his mind to work.

This may or may not have worked with you. Still, the idea here is that if, as a young person, we were given a different angle as to why we would go running and one that we could understand ourselves would be beneficial to us, we would never have had that absolute hatred of running.

It is entirely about the jam in our doughnut; if our parents don't like sport or running, we are unlikely to enjoy sport or running. If our parents like music there's a high chance we will like music. If our parents like the Sciences, the chances are we will enjoy the Sciences and if our parents are doctors there's a good chance that we will follow them into that profession.

When looking to formulate new habits, consciously think about the habit and then identify what jam in your doughnut could restrict you from your successful acquisition of this new habit.

Once you can make sense in your conscious mind and educate your subconscious mind, you will accept this new habit far more quickly.

**Habit stacking**

When you live your life on purpose, you want to take out a lot of the time you are losing and become efficient in completing task after task.

This will then free up time for the more enjoyable things in life. It is good to employ a daily method of operation where you plan what task follows sequentially. Write down the list of tasks that you want to complete, and you then engage in this habit stacking daily.

Look at the diagram below to understand what we mean by habit stacking. These are contained within your Journal.

Ideally you should create a habit stack for different times of your day. Such as:

Purposeful morning habit stack
First thing in the morning at work habits stack
Mid to late morning at work habit it stack.
First thing after lunch at work habits stack.
Mid to late afternoon at work habits stack.
Early evening at home habit stack
Pre bed at home habit stack

This seems quite a lot of habit stacking, and I fully understand this. To make wholesale changes in our lives, we just need to be conscious of what we're doing throughout our day.

After your first month of habit stacking and doing it diligently, these will become art and part of your routine, and you will eventually forget that you even documented them. Once you have created your habits stacks an excellent next thing to do is work out triggers to activate you into the stacking mode.

Remember, the purpose of the trigger is to remind you to kick into the next phase of your activity, and you could even set a reminder on your smartphone.

This is what we would call stacking. You do something once, and then immediately after that, you stack other activities after it.

To become super-efficient in creating habits, create some form of stacking system so that you move from one task to another task to another and so on. You make this part of your daily method of operation, and you write down the order in which you are going to complete the habit.

You write down what you want to do, follow it by other sequences of other things that you want to do, and then tick them off each time you do them.

**To summarise:**

1: You need to identify the habit you want to make or break.
2: You need to make the habit easier to do if you wish to form a habit or harder to do if you want to break a habit.
3: Create a trigger to remind yourself to make your habit.
4: Create habit stacks.
5: Satisfy a craving. If you satisfy a craving by substituting something new that stops you from doing something old, that will make it easier to create or break a habit.

During later stages of living your life on purpose, we will introduce ways in which you can create habit triggers to start new habits in each facet of the wheel of life. These will serve as memory joggers to help you create a better life for yourself, your family, and everybody around you.

# Beliefs

In this chapter, we want to focus on the mindset that will encourage you to improve in every facet of your life. Remember that you will benefit from small, seemingly insignificant improvements, by living your life on purpose.

Day by day, you will be growing in your self-confidence, self-esteem, and belief.

As your life starts to shape how you design it, minuscule and unnoticeable enhancements to your internal belief system start forming a better, more balanced, and confident you.

As time passes, certain things you believed you couldn't do become easy to do. Your mind begins to want to stretch and try even more challenging tasks. Limits in your mind begin to fade, and confidence begins to grow.

So much is made of limiting self-beliefs, yet the reality is that these are simply the constant injection of the same jam into the doughnut. You just need different jam 😊

You can achieve anything you want, just not in one day. When you look to the future, do so without the goggles of yesterday, as you aren't the same person. A different person with a different mindset will get an alternative result.

But what is a belief?

For this book's purpose, we will split belief into two main categories.

**The belief that you can do something and the belief that you know something.**

As you live your life on purpose and engage in continuous, never-ending improvement, you will start developing new skills and new mindsets. With this greater awareness and confidence, your ability to do more in your life will increase.

This is a critical chapter in the book. It is a crucial factor in the book because this is the chapter where you decide to improve your life.

A flawed belief system will get you nowhere. A belief system that is always improving and upgrading will get you everywhere.

It does not matter where you are in life now; it is where you are heading that is important.

No more zigzagging or going around in circles; you will straight line to your destination.

We cover goal setting within another chapter of this book, but did you know that so many people in our world do not write down their goals in fear of failure!

Step by step and heading in a forward direction, literally everything you want to achieve can be achieved with belief. Add daily activity into your goal-setting process, and you are onto a dead cert winner. If only life was that easy!

The first thing we would recommend that you do is to immunise yourself. Set the target and go for the goal. If you have an absolute belief that this is the direction you want to head in your life, do not let anybody put you off.

Those dream stealers out there do not want you to be successful. The laws of association determine how successful you will be in your life. If you associate with happy, success orientated people, they will improve your personal beliefs.

At this stage in your life, you may be uncertain about where you want to head, and that is perfectly fine. Give yourself 100% permission to start to think of a better life.

Each of us reading this book is at different life stages, so when we speak about something, we may be either behind or ahead of the eight ball with the topic we are discussing.

When we run through some life scenarios, change the scenario to fit your anticipated direction if you are further ahead in your life.

The whole premise of living your life on purpose is helping people grow in every aspect of their lives.

You may have heard the phrase limiting self-beliefs; these are protective barriers within your subconscious mind that prevents you from doing something. Even if you have a burning desire to do this, your limiting beliefs will stop you from even attempting to do so.

But where did these limiting self-beliefs originate from?

They indeed were not in your mind when you were born, so you must have received them from another source. Our good old friend, jammy doughnut, comes back into the game. Every single person has their very own unique belief system. Some beliefs are just little beliefs lying just beneath the surface.

Other beliefs are entrenched firmly down the bottom of a coal mine shaft.

There is no way that positive thinking alone will allow many of your beliefs to be altered from their current state to the state you want them to be.

Imagine that during the year 2020 and 2021, your life has been drastically affected by the pandemic. You have lost some loved ones to the disease, your business has failed, and your finances are in a negative balance that you've never experienced before.

Somehow, your loving partner has stayed with you, even you wonder why.

But don't worry, you can fix all of it with positive thinking! Stop having a pity party and start to think positively, and everything will be okay. Get a grip on yourself and change from being negative to being positive.

Get real!

That does not happen; having a positive mental attitude is a good thing to have, but it should not be a mask. It won't remedy problems. It is a good start that is all. Being practical is far better than having a positive attitude that masks more significant problems. When you live your life on purpose, you have effectively decided to change your life for the better. You have chosen to make a change, a positive change, in all segments of the wheel of life.

You are accepting that the same winds blow upon all of us.

> **Jim Rohn Quote: "The same wind blows on us all; the winds of disaster, opportunity and change. Therefore, it is not the blowing of the wind, but the setting of the sails that will determine our direction in life."**

How we respond to those winds are the key determining factors on future successes within our lives.

When you are practical, you understand that there will be no quick win. That by focusing on your daily method of operation and moving your life, and the lives of your family more purposefully, that day by day and week by week, you will start to see the shoots coming through the ground of a better life.

You cannot have pity parties.

Did you know that when people hear you moaning and groaning, most of them will give a nod of sympathy and maybe cuddle you, but the reality is, if you keep talking that way, they will start to distance themselves from you?

Instead, give yourself a major shake and start writing down where you want to get to.

For clarification, we are not assuming that you, as the reader, are in the depths of despair or are having a pity party. This is mainly a demonstration that positive thinking is not going to help you alone.

Have you ever tried to do a Rubik's cube?

For some, this is a seemingly simple task, yet it seems practically impossible for others, including myself.

As a youngster, I genuinely never correctly completed the Rubik's Cube. I did get all the colours on all the sides back to where they needed to be. But I did it my way!

When I tell people about my way of doing the Rubik's Cube, you would be surprised by how many people confess and say that they just took the stickers off the squares, that's how they completed the cube.

I just took the whole thing to pieces and rebuilt it back to where it should have been. I never read the rules of the Rubik's Cube. Therefore, I did complete the task. Granted, I did not use my brainpower by moving the cube around and by some wizardry get it back to all colours on all sides.

The other people I spoke with also completed the Rubik's cube puzzle, although I suspect that we may have gone into a slightly grey area! But we still completed the Rubik's Cube. We did not complete it the way it should have been done, but we still got there.

Life is like a Rubik's Cube or like a box of chocolates. But as this is my book, we aren't going to talk about somebody who likes running or shrimps!

Through the goalsetting phase, you set yourself your very own targets. Maybe it is the couch to five kilometres or running your very own marathon or making 100,000 spondoolies in a year.

It is your life. They are your rules. You get there, however, you feel appropriate.

You are not in competition with anybody; you are only challenging yourself.

While these are your rules, and it is your game, and you can play it however you want to play it, understanding some basics rule need to be followed.

**Basic rule number one:** Is that if you think it will happen overnight, you are going to beat yourself up because, frankly, it won't.

**Basic rule number two:** Is that if you think it is easy, you are going to beat yourself up because it won't. Prepare for a challenge.

**Basic rule number three:** Irrespective of what it is that you are looking to improve in your life, you must harness the compound effect of daily and repeated activity.

**Basic rule number four:** Accept that when you start, you may not be good at it!

**Basic rule number five:** Equally you should understand that the more you do something, the better you will become at it!

**Basic rule number six:** Invest in a lot of jam for your jam transfusions. Engage in regular professional development by reading books and audios. For help, refer to the list of books and audios found within living your life on purpose.

**Basic rule number seven:** Understand that for things to change, you need to change, that your current mindset and beliefs may need updating.

We have so many beliefs that are so far down that coal mine shaft, that genuinely we do not know where they originate from, or indeed if they are 100% true!

This does sound deep and profound, and really if you can take some time out and start to think about some of your critical drivers in your brain. Question where they came from and are the sources bona fide and correct?

When you go deep into your thought processes and analyse the source of some of the nonsense in your mind, it starts to confuse you even more.

So, don't go down there too long because you might just get lost and never come back out.

I was sent to borstal as a child. Well, it wasn't borstal, it was a boarding school, but both my granddad and I agreed it was like borstal!

We called the school Alcatraz.

I know it wasn't really like borstal, and of course, it was nothing like Alcatraz. But it might as well have been!

My dad was successful in the armed forces, and at the time, they began to part-fund private education. Instead of going to a military school in Germany, I was packed off to a boarding school in Yorkshire, England.

At the age of nine and being so far away from home was just the tip of the cold iceberg. My family were not well off by any stretch of the imagination. My mum and dad were probably the wealthiest of our entire family unit.

With around 20 aunties and uncles, that is some going!

Most of our family, though, are poor.

My grandad was the best in the world to me. To his sons and daughters, he was nothing but a big bully! A proper hailstone to them. He meant well but he brought all those kids up by himself and his oldest daughter, my mum!

At school, I had to develop a thick protective layer. Whilst most of the other children at the school would have designer label clothes, or when it came to cycling, they would have well-branded cycles. I had none of that; I had just the basics.

At the weekends, bearing in mind my parents were in Germany, my grandad would drop me off at the school. Most people will never have heard of his car, and those that do will fully understand where I'm coming from.

Granddad would drop me off at school and park next to the Rolls Royce's or the mg sports cars in his dirty Brown Vauxhall Viva. Worse still, the aerial for the radio had been broken off long ago and was now replaced with a wire coat hanger. I would go from having a loving weekend with my aunties and uncles and their children, my cousins, to dormitory boys' instant hostility. For the next six years, I learned to defend myself, and I learned to cope with this hostile environment. When I left that school, my belief structure had been written.

For the next 15 years, I had surrounded myself with a shield. Through my days in the army, I found that it was easier to respond with aggression than open up with trust.

I am not a fighter; I have never been and undoubtedly never will be. Even though you do not fight, you can demonstrate hostile intentions just by the way you talk, the way you look at people and by the way you verbally and physically push people away.

In hindsight, I wasn't a bad person, I wasn't a nice person, but there was never any malice. It was just total protection, and I didn't want to get hurt.

On leaving the army, I joined the police service, and during the next nine years, the same personality traits remained.

I had weird beliefs; I believed no one was there to help me. My perception was it was them against me. I thought I had to beat everybody. Not in the physical sense, and not even in the competitive sense. Which makes it so weird!

I just had to beat them by knowing stuff. I always needed to be right, and I would put my opinion in so firmly that eventually, people would agree with me.

In hindsight, most people agreed with me just to appease me.

I soon left the police service, thanks to a unique business opportunity. Over the next years that passed, I was opened to the world of personal development. What is this new phenomenon? It was unknown; it had been there all my life, and nobody had ever spoken to me about personal development. This stuff should be taught at school!

There is such an abundance of brilliant personal development material out there; millions of children like me would have turned out to be different young adults had we been taught it.

By implementing personal development during the early years of our children's lives, continuing through their teenage years and then into their early 20s and 30s, we would have more harmony and cooperation in the world.

With a series of regular jam transfusions, and yes, there have been many jam transfusions through my subconscious mind!

As a direct result of these jam transfusions, I was able to eventually look back into my mind that was. I was able to look back at the person I had become. I built such a protective barrier it took over a decade to break it down.

At boarding school, I was alone. When I joined the army because I spoke without an accent and because people knew I had come from the boarding school, I was alone. I joined the Scottish police service, and with an English accent, I was alone.

The crazy thing is I am so Scottish, but they heard an English accent and assumed what they wanted.

On joining this unique business opportunity, that transformed my life and my mindset forever; I was thrust into the limelight like never. Turned out I was very good at this new business and caused a buzz. I loved it; in fact, I yearned for it!

I loved to be the person that others were raving about. That boosted my ego, and I think it probably reached either Saturn or Uranus. It was definitely Uranus because I was so far up my own backside!

The spotlight was regularly on me, and I was the beacon of hope. The fact of the matter is I enjoyed the limelight so much that I lost my focus on the task at hand and stopped building my business.

Whilst I was the racing snake, and the person on the pedestal, more and more people that were the tortoise would slowly pass me by. They never wanted the limelight or never seemed to.

They were quite glad that I was strutting my stuff, delivering seminar after seminar exalting how fabulous the company was and how brilliant the opportunity was.

They were building their businesses, and they were growing wealthier than I was. They had harnessed momentum, and in my own business, it started to slow down.

I needed the feeling of euphoria and success, and I needed the feeling of being loved. More importantly, though, I needed to understand that my old belief system, this protective system, would not serve me in my life. Or it was not going to help me well in any case.

And through this personal development, I soon discovered different terms for different people. I heard that some were extraverts, and some were introvert, and either vert was perfectly fine.

Retrospective thinking has led me to believe that I am a public extrovert and a private introvert. Put me in front of a stage of 10 people, 200 people or 2000 people and I will come to life and deliver educating, empowering and entertaining sessions. Not for just one hour but literally for hours on end.

My wife used to joke and asked me if I had prepared for my talks. She knew full well that I could just stand up on a stage and wax lyrical about all the things that I had learned in this world of personal development.

I am though a private introvert. There are lots of us just like that. I thoroughly enjoy going to our local pub and having some drinks with the men and women of the village. I thoroughly enjoy going out for nights with some of our friends and some of our family members.

After maybe 2 hours, though, I start to yearn to get back home. There is no badness or ill will intended, but I'd just like the quietness of our humble abode.

Allow me to spend a year travelling around the world with my son, and I would snap your hand off right now.

To be fair, though, if he was in Australia and I was in the UK, if he asked me over for a game of golf and a couple of cheeky schooners, I'll be on the next plane like a flash.

My wife and I, along with Cookie, our chocolate Labrador dog, spent seven weeks travelling around Europe in our motorhome.

Just the three of us living an adventure not quite like Tom Sawyer and Huckleberry Finn, but we were navigating down our very own Mississippi. We had no idea where we were heading, and we frankly did not care. Those six to seven weeks were the holiday of a lifetime.

I've been on plenty of holidays that are labelled the holiday of a lifetime; they just weren't! They were lovely luxurious holidays, but I have had the better Holidays of a lifetime with people I want to be with.

My dad and my son and I went to Majorca in Spain. Three generations playing golf over three or four days and playing golf, drinking beer, and eating food. That's a holiday of a lifetime.

My wife, mum, and husband Dennis and I went to New Zealand for a month. Getting to spend that quality time with people you love is a holiday of a lifetime.

Climbing up Kilimanjaro with my friend Neil was the holiday of a lifetime as was touring around Australia following the British Lions with Mark and John.

When my Iron Man buddy Steve and I go away for our events, these would be classed as Holidays in my lifetime.

So as an introvert, I do like my own time. The difference, though, is that unlike at school, in the army or at the police, where I felt as though I had to be alone, now I do it by choice.

But if you want to go out for a beer, please pick up the phone, and I'm out with you, if you're going to go for a golfing holiday pick up the phone, I'm with you, if you want to do anything exciting, pick up the phone and I am there. But if I go for a little walk or a swim and you see myself by myself, it isn't because I don't want to be with you. Sometimes, I like my own company.

That was a quick insight into my jam transfusion. As you can imagine, throughout our lives, we learn so much about others, and we know so much about ourselves.

One of the biggest things to understand in life is that you should never worry about what other people think about you.

The moment you start to worry about what other people think, you put a limiting block on your potential.

**Belief in yourself starts with you.**

You are where you are right now as a direct consequence of everything you've ever thought, said, or done. That is the truth of life.

Unless you have developed some form of time machine, what happened in your history has already happened and can never be undone. What you do today can shape your future. What you do tomorrow and the following days after can create the most remarkable life.

No matter where you are in your life right now, make that decision to start living your life on purpose.

Plot your course of where you want to go. Then work out what you need to do to get you there. You do not need to believe that you have the skills or the ability even to get there right now!

Through the continuous and never-ending improvement and resilience, you can get there. Of that there is no doubt.

Like a muscle strengthens by correct use, so can you and your beliefs.

There are plenty of people who have a damaged belief system so entrenched in the depths of their minds. Like a the bottom of a dark mineshaft. If you are such a person, or you know people, remember the jammy doughnut analogy.

From an early age you didn't have the maturity to understand that things that were said or done could have been avoided. As an adult you should now know that you and only you can allow negativity into your mind.

Through power associations and regular jam transfusions you will be able to quickly identify what you wish to pass into your subconscious. Look back throughout your life and forgive those who put the wrong jam in your doughnut. Then make a pledge to yourself that day by day you will participate in personal development.

There are so many people before us pursuing inspiring things only to be ridiculed by the masses. Times have never changed; there are still negative people who tried to stop others from doing something they could never do themselves.

Can you just imagine the Wright brothers saying to the world they were going to fly an aeroplane?

I wonder how many people of that generation fell about laughing at such an absurd idea. Do you think it was some, none, or lots?

That was back in the days when it was hard to communicate your message with the rest of the world. If the Wright brothers came up with the idea of flying an aeroplane and could have shared that with the rest of the world, do you think they would have given up on their dream to fly an aircraft?

In a perverted twist of technology, let us pretend that they posted on Facebook and tweeted that they would try and fly an aeroplane. What type of response globally would the Wright brothers have received?

Even though millions upon millions of people would have mocked them and laughed at their absurd suggestion via an archaic social media system, they would still have pursued their dreams.

Fast forward a century or so as humans, we don't just fly aeroplanes around our world; we send people into space and probes and vehicles to land on Mars. The Wright brothers are not revered as some wacky scientists; they are pioneers, The pioneers of flight. Sadly, though, you will need to understand that some people will prefer you to stay exactly the way you are right now. Banish these people from your associations and have nothing to do with them.

In this scenario, you have set yourself a target of increasing your income to 100,000 spondoolies a year. You are currently earning 35,000 spondoolies a year. You, therefore, need to increase your annual spondoolies by 65,000.

You speak to one of your friends and tell them you will be earning 100,000 spondoolies by this time next year. They laugh at you, they mock you, and they ask you to stop being stupid. How do you feel? Could this have stunted your belief in your ability to hit that knew designated wage?

Imagine a round table with three legs. These three legs are your belief, legs. You go to see your friend, and your friend mocks you, effectively chopping off one of those legs. You now have a two-legged table! The two-legged table is likely to fall over.

The problem with a three-legged table is stability. What you need is a table with 1000 legs. You set yourself the target of earning 100,000 spondoolies a year. Understanding the laws of Association, you go to the most successful person you know.

You ask this person for advice, and this person gives you some sound advice, the best of which is that "If you believe you can, you can".

Having spoken to this one person, your table grows another belief leg.

That successful person encouraged you to read some books and develop yourself personally. You read a book called "living your life on purpose", and you start to understand that you really can earn 100,000 spondoolies a year. Another leg grows beneath your table.

Your table now has five belief legs, and as you start to understand the way the world rotates and the way the world operates, your table starts to grow belief leg after belief leg. With 100 belief legs underneath your table, if any of your negative associations begin to mock you for where you are heading, even when a leg is chopped off your table, there are still plenty more keeping it stable.

The power of a mastermind group should never be undervalued. Within the living your life on purpose community, you will have access to joining a mastermind group. A group of like-minded individuals will support you in your quest to earn your 100,000 spondoolies a year.

The mastermind group will help you earn the living you so desire, but they will help you in every segment in the wheel of life. You will have a balance in your life, and life will be fantastic.

**A good belief set is intrinsic to your success.**

Whatever you desire in your life, whether it was the perfect partner, a lovely physical environment, the business you so crave, or your health and fitness, if you live your life on purpose, you can achieve it!

But belief does not arrive in bucketloads overnight. If you are entering into new worlds and are doing new things, you will feel uncomfortable starting with, which is perfectly normal.

Growth in all areas of our life will require determination and persistence. It is going to require focus. You will need to understand that sometimes you will feel despondent, and sometimes you will think about quitting.

Every successful person you have read about or hear about success is more than likely to have wanted to quit in their pursuit of goals. If it is good enough for them, it is good enough for you.

Immunise yourself from the negative forces around you and absorb all positive energies. Ying and Yang are out there, and they are always out there. They are not exclusive to you; every other person on the planet falls to them at some point.

**Tough love.**

Tough love is where somebody who cares about you, tells you something because they want to help you, not stunt your growth. It is called tough love because sometimes we need to hear the things we don't want to listen to act as a catalyst, to help us to get to where we want to.

Here is a dose of tough love. Please take this in the loving way it is intended for you.

You've got to wherever you are in life right now by coasting along and doing just enough.

That may have offended some people. The first response could be, how dare you? I've worked hard to get to where I have got to; how very dare you?

I wasn't even talking about work or career; I was talking about all the segments in the wheel of life.

Granted, you could have some Starship Wing Commander title in your job description, and you could be earning lots of spondoolies every year. But what about your health and fitness? What about your relationship with a loving partner?

What about the relationship with friends and family? There is a high chance you've just been coasting along and thinking that everything is okay, but seriously do you have balance within your life? Are you happy with every single aspect of your life?

I am not talking about the way you look, by the way. The first thing you need to do is to become happy within your skin. This is a genuine reason why everybody should engage in personal development.

It does not matter if you are tall or short, thin, or fatter, white coloured or black, hairy, bald, male, or female!

It is who you are. It is about you being happy and being in pursuit of happiness, not just selfishly, but in the pursuit of helping others to be happy too.

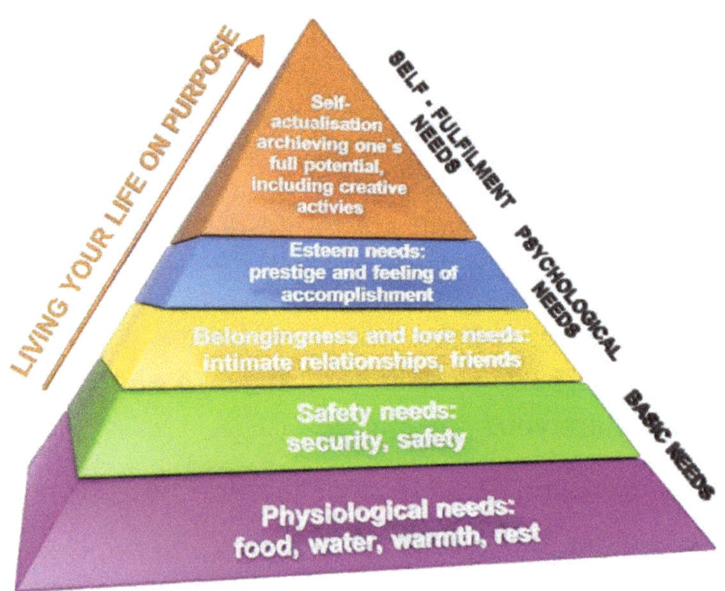


When we go through Maslow's hierarchal of needs, work a route to self-actualisation. Becoming the better you is far more valuable than owning things.

When you are happy within your skin and feel internally satisfied, then you will have conquered your beliefs. You will have evicted that horrible mind monster and said goodbye to those limiting self-beliefs; you have arrived at your chosen destination.

It is not up to anybody else to dictate where you are going or how you get there; that responsibility lies entirely at the foot of your path.

Once you realise that there is an abundance of people out there that want to help you to grow and achieve whatever it is in your life, your mindset will alter forever.

Within our LYLOP community, you will find so many people that will work as part of your back-office support structure. You will approach life differently with an open mindset.

One way you can instantly change is to try to look at things from another perspective or point of view.

If you come across a scenario that you know to be true, but others are questioning that validity of truth, take a moment to view it from their perspective and paradigm.

Why do you think that this fact is right, and where did you initially get the information in your mind? Was the source of your data correct!

This is quite a profound way to operate. Instead of automatically thinking you are right, pause and validate. When you start to question your information source and respond positively to the findings that your initial thought process was wrong, you can begin to grow significantly.

The belief that you can do something. Think about something you have never done before and then think could you do it?

For this example, I will use myself in a scenario. I have never played the guitar before.

That technically is not true, I have picked up a guitar before and run my fingers through the cables attached to some wood, and it made a noise.

I have demonstrated my lack of understanding of a guitar using the word cables. I have also purposely used the term noise because it was not a tune.

I have never played the guitar before, but could I learn to play the guitar? Do I even want to learn to play the guitar?

Yes, come to think about it. I want to learn to play the guitar! How will I learn to play the guitar? Guitar lessons!

Think about anything that you want to do in your life, and even if you haven't done it before, you must question whether you even want to do it in the first place.

If you do not want to do it and are forced to do it for some reason, you will enter that activity half-hearted at best.

After one guitar lesson, will I be able to pick up a guitar and strum it like Brian May from one of the best bands in the world called Queen?

We all know the answer to that question. I don't even know the right way to hold a guitar or whether it is upside down or not!

Through continuous and never-ending improvement and many guitar lessons, I am confident I could learn to play that instrument. I also know that because it is not a passion of mine, it won't become an all-absorbing hobby, whilst I may play the guitar. Therefore, it is fair to understand whilst I may be able to learn to play this instrument, there is no point when

I will master that instrument. When we go and live our life on purpose, there will be very few occasions when we need to be a master of the disciplines.

You may aspire to be a successful business owner, and you may have an outstanding product or service to sell. You do not need to be a specialist in marketing or sales. You are encouraged, though, to find a master in those departments to help you sell your outstanding product.

You may aspire to run a 26.2-mile marathon. You don't need to run as fast as Mohammed Farrah, and you could run that marathon in six hours. You will still have completed your goal of running the marathon!

If you want to run the marathon in three hours and have never done this before, you will need to enlist the help and support of a running and a nutritional coach.

Whatever facet of life you want to improve on, the simple philosophy is to surround yourself with better people than you at that discipline and learn from them.

Time always wins out.

Your belief in yourself and your ability to do something will increase over time and the repeated application of the disciplines needed in that activity.

**You cannot apply yourself once and become a master at anything.**

Goal setting and having a big WHY will be the motivating factors for you succeeding in life.

For example, if there was a 12-foot plank on the floor, and I said, "can you walk along the 12-foot plank"? There is a high chance that you would walk along the 12-foot plank without even thinking about it.

Nice and easy, no danger there, and was no skin off your nose to do it. You didn't even miss a heartbeat.

We then put that same plank on 2 A-frames, and those A-frames now mean the plank is one metre above the floor. I ask you now to walk across the plank.

Your brain will now calculate whether this is a risk worth taking, and most people would think it's only a metre I'm going to fall; I'll give it a go. You climb up the steps onto the plank, you wobble a little, and then you tentatively walked to the end of the plank and jumped off.

What is quite bizarre is that it's the very same plank only elevated one metre, but your beliefs and your fears start to impact your ability to walk 12 feet along a plank that you had already walked along when it was on the ground with no danger.

You did it, all the same, so congratulations to you. We now move that same plank, and we placed that plank between two skyscrapers.

I then ask you to walk across the plank. Some crazy individuals will say okay, and they will walk across the plank without any worries whatsoever. After all, how hard can it be they walked along the plank on the ground?

They walked along the plank at one metre, so 500 metres in the sky should not matter one little bit.

Though most sane people would not want to walk along the plank, there is just no reason to justify such a dangerous activity. But if you had a reason to walk across that plank and that reason was so compelling, you would indeed walk across the plank.

In this hypothetical scenario, you are on one side of the skyscraper. The plank leans over to the other building, which is on fire. Your two children are on that side of the plank; most parents would not even hesitate to walk across the plank, pick up one child or back across the plank, deposit that child and then return and rescue the other child saving them from that burning skyscraper.

There was certainly no difference to the plank. It's still the 12-foot plank, but the reward for going across the plank justified the danger.

So, in summary, to increase belief in yourself, you must repeatedly engage in an activity so that through this activity, a repeated application becomes competent through the number of times you engage in the activity.

That alone isn't sufficient for most people.

There must be a reason why you want to do something that is going to take you out of your comfort zone.

**The bigger the why, the more significant the power. Why power!**

John and Jane have decided to take part in living your life on purpose. They have two teenage children, of course, a boy and a girl. They live in a mortgaged house, a 3-bedroom semidetached. They each have a car that is on credit, and they have 10,000 spondoolies outstanding on combined credit cards.

They haven't been on a foreign holiday for several years, claiming that they prefer staycations. Both John and Jane have good jobs, each commanding a salary of 30,000 spondoolies a year. The household income exceeds the average household income, and yet they always have too much month at the end of the money.

Jane came home one day having heard about living your life on purpose and shared her findings with John. At first, John wasn't listening to Jane and was instead concentrating on the game that he was watching on the income reducing box.

This time though, Jane was not giving up and switched off the income reducing box. "Things need to change", John she professes emotionally.

Sensing the love of his life needed some talk time John, started to pay attention.

"We have no real income to spend on enjoying our lives", Jane continues, "we want to give our children the best lives possible, but the fact of the matter, John, is that we are struggling to make ends meet".

"It's not that bad", replied John "everybody is in the same boat", he continues.

“Exactly” retorts Jane, "everybody is in the same boat, and we are sailing with them. John, don't you see we aren't getting steadily richer we are getting steadily older and poorer".

"It fills me with dread that we may not be able to afford to send our children to University, let alone take them on that Floridian holiday we've been promising since they were young children".

Jane explains that she has found a programme called living your life on purpose where, according to the finance section, we could reduce and eliminate their 10,000 spondoolies worth of debt within less than three years. They could create a happier, more balanced life in no time at all. They just needed to make some subtle and yet consistent changes.

She continued that rather than having a life of debt and liabilities, she wanted to have a life of abundance and assets.

John began to buy into Jane's idea and loved it as they started to plan out eliminating their debt, living mortgage-free, and in two years, taking their children to stay at their Hard Rock Hotel Universal Studios, Florida.

The synergy between John and Jane created the 2 + 2 = 5 effect.

They pledged that they would engage in personal development, and they were going to grow together. John and Jane wrote down their goals, and they decided that it is was essential to the family unit.

They got so giddy with excitement that they were already there; the happy hormones were flying around so much momentarily they forgot the current world they lived in.

The next day though, Jane started to have some doubts. John began to reassure her that over time and by working consistently step by step towards their dreams, goals, and aspirations, they could do this together.

Jane's wobble was over for that day, but it would not be Jane's last wobble in the journey, and John wouldn't be immune to it either. One day John would feel that the task was impossible, and the next day Jane took over, but their reason "why" was so powerful that they worked it out between them.

John and Jane participated in the LYLOP community. They began to build relationships with other success-oriented people, and they began to enjoy the experience thoroughly.

They became fitter and healthier, they became happier and more satisfied, their children began to spend more time with them, and they hadn't required them to do so!

They were making overpayments on their outstanding credit, and they could see that the interest on each of the cards was reducing at quite a rate.

Inwardly they began to feel as though they were gaining momentum. “It is working”, they began to proclaim to one another.

It's working.

It can work for you too, and it can work in every aspect of your life; for it to happen, you have to make it happen.

**If it is to be, it is up to me.**

You set the sail of your ship, and the winds will blow you one way or another. Sometimes the wind will drop, and it appears that you are not moving at all, sometimes those winds will blow against you, and they will keep blowing, and they will test your resolve.

But if it can work for others, it can work for you.

Imagine right now a year from now. Imagine that you now know that it is working.

Put yourself into your own life and think about where you are right now and all your current life circumstances. Now project yourself forward one year.

Write a movie of your life that contains you as the lead actor or actress. Where are you going to be within the next year? This film is not about a family who does the same things every day, without any change, where the debts are growing? Quite the opposite.

Is it going to be about a family much like John and Jane above?

Put yourself in your own movie where you want to be in a year!

Seriously, stop reading the book right now!!

Put the book down or stop the audio and start to think where you want to be in a year. Write a movie of what your life is going to be like in a year and put yourself in that picture as the lead role.

Yes, I have deliberately repeated what I'm asking you to do because repetition is the number one rule of all learning.

I'm not even going to ask you to think about where you want to be in one year just now. I'm going to respectfully suggest that you think about where you want to be in one year every single day from today and for the next 365 days as a minimum.

It is working.

It is working!

You now see it is working for you, and it is working for your family. The hard graft and the hard grind to get it going are bearing positive fruit. It is working.

It was not some overnight instant gratification result; you deserve to give yourself an incredible amount of credit for getting it working.

It is a year from today. You have achieved some wonderful things, and now I want you to think that you are a year ahead, but now I want you to look back to today.

How much have you grown as a person? You are successful, you've reduced your expenses, and you've increased your income, you're feeling better, healthier, and fitter, you are happy, and things are working out simply fine.

Thinking back a year, how much have you improved mentally, and how are your beliefs now?

If only we had that dastardly time machine. If only we could project you forward by one year, three years or five years. Wouldn't that be fantastic to propel you forward in time so that you can see a much better and happier life?

If we could move you forward in time just for a fleeting moment and then brought you right back, how much effort do you think you would put in if you knew, without doubt, you could succeed?

The great thing is, we don't even need The Time Machine. Your subconscious mind is so powerful, and it cannot reject; we can feed the subconscious mind that it is already a year from now!

It is called the power of autosuggestion. Every morning you get up, you read your affirmations and goals, and you recite these daily statements in the morning at lunchtime and in the evening if you can.

The more you read your affirmations to yourself an answer them, the more your subconscious mind will accept them as real. That will take some practice, and that is going to take belief.

In this circumstance, the belief that you want to buy into is the belief that this process can work.

The old jam in your doughnut may think that this is some form of hocus pocus wizardry, but your new mindset needs to be “I will do this”.

Of course, you are right either way you think. Personally, that is sufficient evidence for me to understand that these processes do work.

If Napoleon Hill interviewed over 500 successful people in the United States of America, and each of them attributed belief and autosuggestion as one of the factors that help them to become successful, who are we to argue?

Move to the modern era and listen to the way some of the most successful people in business, sport, and life, in general, talk about having belief and talking about autosuggestion. Some call it visualisation.

Some of the greatest golfers in the world talk about visualising the shot they're about to hit before they've even hit it.

Successful people leave clues. We need to listen to these people and to find out what attributes help them to become successful and embrace them into our mindsets without hesitation.

Throughout your journey through living your life on purpose, your beliefs will alter.

Beliefs in what you can do will improve because of regular activity engagement. Your beliefs in what you know will also change because you start to question what you previously understood to be true.

We will realise that what we knew to be true for most of our lives was just untrue for many of us.

There won't be any drama about finding out this new information; it will just be part of your natural growth.

## Constant And Never-ending Improvement

You cannot manage time.

Contrary to belief, no one in this world can manage time. The best people manage their use of the time available.

We all have 168 hours a week. Most people spend a lot of their time working on their job or business, watching the television, and sleeping.

In 2015, people in the United States watched television for an average of 274 minutes a day!! That is 32 hours a week.

The ramifications of this bad habit alone are significant.

A person living their life on purpose does not sit and watch the TV for that long. Naturally, they enjoy their movies, sport, nature etc.; these come as a reward, not as a routine.

The most successful people form habits that serve them well. Reducing time watching the TV could improve your relationship with a loved one, your family, health, and fitness and much more. Do something with your family and/or a loved one. Form hobbies together that may improve your relationship whilst enhancing your health.

Start a part-time business together. With 10 hours a week (saved by not watching the TV), you could create an extra income stream that could help pay off your debt/mortgage in a fraction of the time.

We have already covered that to live your life on purpose, you may need to alter your mindset and beliefs, to create better habits and that it is essential to focus on all the elements in the wheel of life.

We will continuously revisit these elements as they are vital to your continued improvement. We can call this C-A-N-I : Constant and Never-ending Improvement.

C-A-N-I is where you, as a person, always strive to become better. It will not happen overnight. But over time, when applying simple and yet seemingly insignificant C-A-N-I principles, your life improvement can be seismic.

Having a constant and never-ending improvement mindset means that even if you improve 1% on any given discipline in your life and focus every day on improving yourself, eventually, over time, you will enhance yourself immeasurably.

When you live your life on purpose, moving forward in every area of your life is the focus. Standing still in this world is not standing still because if you are standing still and not improving due to this world's fast-moving pace, you are falling behind.

Becoming a master of time management will be one of the biggest C-A-N-I successes. Want to become healthier – you need to engage in C-A-N-I.

Have a desire to be more successful – C-A-N-I is your route.

Want to be financially free? C-A-N-I will be your process.

Love to have more fun in your life? Your C-A-N-I is your release.

Having a daily improvement is easy. Most people do not improve daily because they don't focus on the process of improvement.

In life, in everything we do, there are four stages of competency:

Unconsciously incompetent
Consciously incompetent
Consciously competent
Unconsciously competent

**Stage 1 – Unconsciously incompetent**

This is the most dangerous of all stages and where many people are.

You do not know what you do not know – right?

In stage one, some people think they are good at something. Yet, they have never actually questioned that fact, and they have never sought advice to help them improve.

Because they do not have an active pursuit of C-A-N-I, they stagnate.

Some people accept that they are in a good place. This the jam in their doughnut. They could do so much better – it is just because they do not know.

John is 35. He is earning 29,000 spondoolies a year living in rented accommodation; his car is on credit, he has credit card debt and some small loans. He has too much month at the end of the money.

Yet, John comes from a family that never earned this income level, let alone have a nice car. On the preface, he thinks he is excelling in life. It is easy for his subconscious mind to blank out the debt element because he assumes that is normal anyway.

John's belief that he is excelling in life is fuelled further by the glowing comments he receives from his less fortunate friends and family members. John has made it.

John may have just hit the ceiling of his belief system. But by living his life on purpose and with C-A-N-I, John could continue to improve his life and even learn that debt is a trap and not good.

Every day at 6 am, Jane walks out of her rented apartment in London. She walks 10 minutes in the morning rain to jump on the London Underground. An hour later, having suffered the "sardine effect" in the tube train, she settles at her desk.

Jane works Monday to Friday from 8 am until 6 pm and has a habit of starting early and working later. She arrives home at 730pm shattered.

She has been doing this same old routine for double-digit years. It pays well and, on the weekend, at least she gets to hang out with friends and family. But Jane lives in London. The cost of living is extortionately high. She does not own her property and rents, but everybody does that, so it is normal.

Once again, there is nothing wrong with this. The fact is a heck of a lot of people spend over 10 hours of their working week commuting to a job they do not like but suffer just because it pays the bills.

Over 70% of people engage in a job they do not like. Someone once told me the definition of a JOB. JOB = Just Over Broke.

When the employee does just enough, they don't get fired, and the employer pays them just enough; they don't leave.

Naturally, this isn't every job, but how sad is that?

Through time, the subconscious mind settles into the habit of doing that same old job. It becomes so automatic that people do not even think about it. If you are pursuing C-A-N-I and love the idea of living your life on purpose, this is a state of mind you cannot occupy.

People need to be aware of being unconsciously incompetent and focus on continuous and never-ending improvement.

If you are in any stage of your life and have stopped trying to improve your chances, you will likely regress.

In 2020 Lewis Hamilton became the most successful Formula One driver of all time. Asked what will motivate him for the 2021 season – Constant and never-ending improvement was his summarised reply. Ask any sportsperson in the world; they will always give you a variation of C-A-N-I's theme.

Speak to any successful person in your society; the same theme will apply.

Ask any CEO of significant businesses that collapse why they failed – they will give the reverse of C-A-N-I. We were unable to adapt to a changing world. We failed to improve.

High Street and well-known names are going or have gone bust in countries worldwide because they failed to C-A-N-I.

As ordinary people, we look at these major companies and could be stunned at some of the reasons they failed. They have high-level Directors leading the company. They will have think tanks to improve and all the financial data on hand yet, they still fail.

The most noticeable failure I have heard repeated company after company was that they did not have an excellent online presence.

It is like the internet was a surprise.

Established companies that spend large amounts of their money having shops are being beaten up by the slimline companies online. They have fewer overheads and can offer a similar product cheaper without the inconvenience of leaving home.

The world is changing. Things are happening quicker, and there are more opportunities to improve life than ever before. So why aren't more people jumping on board?

They are unconsciously incompetent. They think life is excellent, and they do not engage in C-A-N-I.

By declaring an intention to start living a life on purpose, you immediately move from unconsciously incompetent to being consciously incompetent in the game of life.

Of course, this sounds severe, but it is not meant to. It is a reality check statement.

I love to participate in Ironman triathlons, and I have currently completed 14 of them. This triathlon consists of a 2.4-mile swim, a 112-mile bike ride, and a 26.2-mile marathon.

As a whole event, let us hypothetically state that I am a world-class cyclist and a super-fast marathon runner, but I cannot swim 100 yards, let alone 2.4 miles.

Would I be a competent or incompetent competitor of the Ironman?

It would be the latter, as I will not complete the event.

We could be super good at our business in the wheel of life, generating lots of money but with no fun or recreation, a low work/life balance and no connection with our family.

So, by living our lives on purpose, we can improve our finances whilst also dedicating more time and energy to all the wheel elements.

As time passes by, you will naturally move through the stages of competency due to the new habits you have formed and a daily method of operation.

One way to live your life with constant and never-ending improvement is to introduce a routine to your life. Successful people call this a daily method of operation.

## Daily Method of Operation

Mastering the mundane is a sure-fire way to getting more fun and satisfaction in life.

Have you heard the phrase night owl or early bird?

This is a phrase that effectively determines whether you get up nice and early and get to the task or stay up late and get to the job.... or no functions for incompetent people.

"I'm a night owl", states one person, whilst another proclaims, "Not me, I'm an early bird all the way."

It is like they say these statements as though their DNA has genetically programmed them to work morning or night more effectively.

It has nothing to do with DNA but back to our old favourites, the Jammy in the Doughnut and Habits.

What we do from an early age habitually dictates our clock.

I have always loved the sport. From the moment I wake up to the moment I sleep, I could play sport. For as long as I can remember, that was always the case.

As an 8-year-old in the height of summer, I remember Dominic and David Harker knocking on my window at the agreed time of 5 am to play soccer. All-day, we would play outside. Sports or kids' games such as tag, British bulldog (a favourite of mine) were the activities of literally every day. By night-time, I was shattered and in need of sleep.

I, therefore, became more of an early bird.

One of my friends, Chris, has always liked computers. From the ZX spectrum to all-singing super-fast computers in this modern era, Chris played with them all. For some reason, unbeknownst to me.

At over 50, Chris is still a self-proclaimed geek, still loves technology and still classes himself as a night owl.

But it does not need to be this way. I could introduce habits that could allow my body clock to alter to night owl status, and Chris could likewise be an early bird.

The problem is I would need a massive reason to commit to such life-changing body clock activities, and the same would be said of Chris.

I could do it, but it would need to be worth it. And so, could you.

If we wish to master our use of time, we need to identify what time of day will be the most significant period for us specifically.

If I were awarded a crazy 3-year contract that would pay me lots of extra money for less time and doing something I love doing, but that contract was working from the UK remotely with the Australian market, trust me, I would change my working hours.

I would need to form the absurd habit of sleeping during the UK daytime to wake up around 8 pm UK time and 8 am Australian. Going to bed around noon at the peak of daylight hours in the UK would be bizarre.

It takes different people differing times to become used to their new body clock. There is no ideal time.

NASA did a study with Astronauts and made them wear a headset every moment of every day. The headset turned everything upside down. For days, these astronauts became nauseous, and then eventually, something remarkable happened.

The brain did not like things upside down and corrected. Your brain is so clever it can help you adapt to your environment.

For some astronauts, it took 17 days and others longer for this correction to occur. It became the new norm. When the headsets were removed, this correction took time to return to the previous normal.

It is essential to understand that it will take weeks for this new normal to alter your body clock. It needs to be a continuous activity too.

If we live and work in our own country, it would be advantageous to work out which times we could be most effective in our pursuit of happiness. It is your call but remember to consider ALL factors in your wheel of life.

When is your partner at their peak – could you alter your peak to match theirs?

When are the children back from school – could you free up some time for them?

When is the peak contact time for customers for your job or business?

When are you most likely to do a spot of fitness in terms of health?

Analyse each element of the wheel according to your location. Then make a conscious decision to create a daily method of operation to suit your new pursuit of living your life on purpose.

Far too many people drift along in life, and that is why they do not achieve true happiness.

Have you ever gone on a beach holiday, jumped on a Lilo in the sea and maybe dozed into a light sleep?

Those of us who have it is quite amazing how far you can drift away from your original point. You then need to paddle back to where you started, and of course, you must paddle against the current, so it is harder to get back to your start point.

**When you live your life on purposes, you do not drift.**

The most common daily method of operation starts at 6 am. Although I must confess due to my work's flexible nature in the winter hours, I start my daily method of operation slightly later and in the summertime somewhat earlier.

For some, that has just been a shock and awe gut-wrenching statement. For others, that was great. I already get up at 6 am moment.

Either way, 6 am is known to be a good starting point.

There is no point allowing the alarm to go off at 6 am, though without a pre-determined daily method of operation and a powerful reason why. We referred to setting goals earlier in the book.

The bigger and more exciting the goal, the more drive and enthusiasm to achieve it.

If your intention to improve your life is significant and exciting, when that alarm goes off at 6 am, you jump out of bed and set to your formulated daily method of operation.

Remember the top tip of the alarm setting in the habits section. Place your alarm out of reach from your bed. To switch it off, you must get out of bed. When out of bed, you may as well stay up, making your habit easier.

If it takes weeks to become the new norm, we must discipline ourselves. We must be committed to this C-A-N-I, and we must understand that this pursuit of improvement in our life means sacrifice and uncomfortable situations. Hitting that snooze button isn't damaging you, but it could be delaying your opportunity to progress further in your life. So, don't ever press the snooze.

6 am, one such uncomfortable habit that will soon be your biggest ally.

When you get up at 6 am, you do so because you know this is when people will not bother you. You can get so much more done.

If you have children, they may still be in bed. If not, agree with your partner, who will take the early morning shift. Remember participating in this C-A-N-I and living your life on purpose works better with your partner doing it with you too.

When we go back to our good old friend, the jammy doughnut, it is also essential to understand that 6:00 am an average time to rise for lots of people. For those who think that 6:00 am early and it's far too early to get out of bed, it's only the jam in the doughnut.

Probably their parents got up slightly later, so they got up slightly later during their early years, and that is something that is now ingrained in the way they operate. But trust me, lots of people get up far earlier than six am. You don't know what you don't know, right?

Write out your daily method of operation and tweak it over time, but here is my morning routine an example:

6 am. Alarm rings. Up and have a pee. Then go into my office. There is already a bottle of carbonated water on my desk. This means I now drink significantly more water. Having the water on my desk makes my habit of drinking water easier.

I have a drink of water.

6.05 am. I then read through my afformations. You have probably heard of affirmations before. Muhammed Ali would always say, “I am the greatest”, and many other successful people have these positive statements.

Understanding that the subconscious mind can only accept, I created a series of afformations.

Questions that I ask myself daily and then reply to. I do speak these out loud in my office.

> What are you grateful for today?
> What makes you so good (insert name)?
> How organised are you today?
> What will stop you from doing your Key Pay-off Activities?
> How will you become a better you today?
> What is your weight and fitness level on (13th-week date)?
> How much extra income will you generate by (13th-week date)?
> How does that make you feel?

You can create your own. I always start the day with gratitude.

On more than one occasion, people have asked me why I am so optimistic in life. My reply usually is along the lines of

“I spent five years in the Army and went to Iraq in 1990; then I spent nine years in the Police service. I have seen death and destruction, real poverty; I have delivered death messages to children that their parents have died, and worse to parents that their children have died. I’ve been in the company of murderers and rapists that have wreaked a lifetime of misery on innocent families. In one month, I went to 14 fatal road traffic accidents, one of which was my next-door neighbour serving on duty as a fellow Police Officer. Trust me; I have a lot to be grateful for".

And so, do you. Having a pity party about how your life is right now will not serve you well. Afterall with the rules of blame and responsibility, you are where you are right now as a direct consequence of everything you ever said and did.

Starting my day with gratitude reminds me of how fortunate I am. I start my day in the right place—every day, and this form the platform for C-A-N-I.

You already have a wonderful life. Of course, you may be up to your neck in debt, doing a job or business you don't like, living in a home you don't like and worse, still dislike the location.

You drive a car that is financed and therefore a liability blah blah blah.........but you have a wonderful family, friendships, you have your health, and you have opportunity.

You can live your life on purpose, embracing C-A-N-I in the wheel of life.

Create a series of your afformations. Those that are meaningful to you and recite them every day. The positivity and direction they create will be high pay off activity.

6.10 am. I read my goals that are placed on my desk. I love the idea of having a home in Spain, travelling around the world, buying material things that would enhance our lifestyle.

Reading my goals excites me. These will encourage me to live my life on purpose and focus on goal-directed activity.

After my purposeful morning routine, I go downstairs to the kitchen, make myself a nice cup of chamomile tea, have breakfast and pop back up to the office to continue with my daily method of operation.

6.25 am. I open Spotify and play my morning music. A series of uplifting favourites. At the same time, I start to write down my tasks for the day.

Buy yourself a “things to do” book. These typically have a series of lines to write down your tasks with tick (check) boxes.

I love writing down tasks for the day. I love ticking (checking) them off as I do them. Hey, I often write down a job that I had to do that was not on the list and tick (check) it off!

This is a massive time-saving activity. By writing down your daily tasks, you live your life on purpose. They do not need to be solely income/business related; they should include each segment of the wheel.

One daily task which seems insignificant but when formed as a habit repeated daily but offers a massive impact in your life is making a cup of tea/coffee for your partner just before they are due to get out of bed. It is a tick off your list that will be so appreciated by them.

Another daily task, written down and checked off, could be walking the dog.

The more things you tick off your list, the better you feel and just before you go to bed, have a look at your list and see how many ticks you have entered into your daily Journal.

It is quite bizarre, but if you go to bed satisfied with your day, there is a high chance that you will sleep better because your brain is content with the day's activities.

On the topic of sleep, one of the biggest reasons people don't sleep well is that when they go to bed their minds wake up, and all of the world's worries run through the mind causing poor or broken up sleep.

Once you have committed to living your life on purpose and engaging in a daily constant and never-ending improvement, your brain will start to be more content with the future that your life shall hold.

Because you have gone through your daily afformations and read your goals, your brain starts to understand that life is getting better and heading in the right direction. You then start to relax during the evening resulting in a better sleep pattern.

With improved sleep, you feel better when you awake, and getting up earlier becomes the new normal.

In the spirit of continuous and never-ending improvement, we want to look through our daily routines to maximise our use of time. Creating a daily method of operation that spans throughout the whole of the day, will allow you to do more in that day than you thought previously possible.

Another way to participate in continuous and never-ending improvement is to understand the difference between the two words of blame and responsibility.

The successful people in life take full responsibility for everything they ever do and everything they ever did. The less successful people tend to blame others for why their life is mediocre.

Blame and responsibility are either key drivers or a brake holding back people in this world in literally every aspect of life.

If you have a blame mindset, you will blame everybody for everything. Firstly, the chances are you will associate with other people who have a blame mindset, so you are always right, and you are probably not living the best life you can.

Having a responsibility mindset works so much more favourable in the long run. If you have a responsibility mindset, your life's conflicts reduce significantly, which is unbelievable.

One way to understand the rules of blame and responsibility is to accept responsibility for absolutely everything in your life right now.

Now, this may seem hard, and there are certain exceptions, where people have been subject to something criminal or illegal that was out of their control due to coercion or bullying or through some form of other manipulation.

But take responsibility, whoever you are, wherever you are in your life right now.

Take responsibility for how you talk, how you act, the way that you conduct yourself with others, the place that you live, the car that you drive, and the debt or the credit you have in your bank account.

Take responsibility if:

> you are not happy with your life,
> if nothing exciting is happening in your life,
> if you don't have a partner to live with to love and to cherish,
> you are slightly or obesely overweight,

Take responsibility. That is what you need to do to progress in this world.

In the pursuit of constant and never-ending improvement, I'd like to introduce you to the two circles.

**The circle of influence and the circle of concern.**

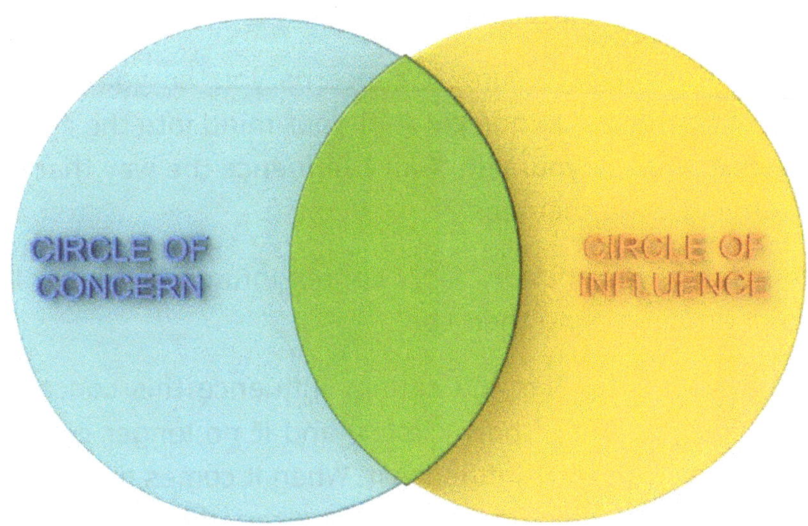


If you live your life within the two circles of influence and concern, you can reduce stress levels and take responsibility for your actions instantly.

I would like to imagine that you are going through your everyday life, and then something happens that concerns you.

For this example, let us pretend you are driving along on the motorway or the highway if you are in America and you see a driver speed past you. Then they pull into your lane, what appears to be just metres from the front of your car and then continues to drive on away from you.

For too many people, the immediate thing is to get into a bad mood, into a high temper and then keep that bad mood and high spirit with you for the rest of your journey.

In fact, you are so incensed by this when you get to your destination, you then tell everybody about this dangerous driver that threatened your life.

You keep it for the rest of the day until you forget about it.

Now, this type of mindset is not going to serve you well. How about operating within two circles?

The same incident occurs; it concerns you, so you're in the circle of concern. You quickly shift your mind into the circle of influence and ask yourself, “Can I influence the way that idiot person is driving their car”?

Immediately you answer, “No, I cannot influence the way that stupid idiot is driving their car”.

Once you deduce that you cannot influence this concern of yours, you pop out of both circles, and it no longer concerns you because you can't influence it. When it comes to blame, so many people are holding onto so many negative things in their life from their past that it just bogs them down.

The subconscious mind is just chewing it up, all the time. This negative thought pattern is stopping them from moving forward. It is time to release the things that you blame in your life.

Spend some time with a pen on a piece of paper and go through all the things that you are not happy with within your life. Then start to analyse each of these individual negative parts of your life and work out ways to eradicate them.

Can you influence them? If not, ditch from your mindset!!

In this exercise, you have to understand that most of these thoughts you write down will be negative in your mind.

The first reaction might be blaming other people or other circumstances because they are hurting you.

It would be easy for me to say, though once you've written down this list of negative anchors for you to say, "Yes, I take the blame for this".

But you still want to blame somebody that's entirely within your remit within your brain.

Why not go through the list and write down those that you accept blame and those you take responsibility for?

Go back through the list again, see if you can discharge more from the blame list – so take more responsibility.

You cannot blame your parents for everything negative in your life. If you are at the stage of life that you have decided to buy this book or audio and decided to live your life on purpose, you made a conscious decision in pursuit of improvement.

There are thousands of phenomenal personal development books or audios around the world, and you could have chosen any one of those professional books or audios at **any time** in your life.

You could have gone to the most successful people you know and just ask them a simple question "How did you become successful"?

Successful people leave clues, and one of the most important clues that they will give you is to engage in regular personal development.

Maybe your parents didn't have access to the same amount of information that you have. Still, you could now go onto YouTube, Tik Tok, and a whole raft of other social media platforms, including the search engines of Google, Yahoo Bing, etc.

At any point in your life, you could have watched or listen to something that would help you improve yourself. You either didn't because you didn't know it existed, or you just couldn't be bothered!

At this point in the book, accepting and taking responsibility for everything in your life is one of the most challenging yet most liberating things you can do. It is one of the most awkward, uncomfortable, and horrible things to do.

But it is liberating at the same time. It is fair to say that some of these negative things you have blamed somebody else for throughout your whole life have held you back. The moment you take responsibility and decide that they are in the past, jump into the circle of influence and concern.

For each of them, and then you put them to rest, your subconscious mind will put them to rest once you accept responsibility.

In this process of living your life on purpose and in the pursuit of constant and never-ending improvement, the very fact that you're engaging in this process means that you have made the conscious decision to improve your life. Enhancing your life gives you a buzz; the dopamine goes through your body, and you're excited about your future.

With this constant and never-ending improvement philosophy in mind, it is also essential to focus on the actions and not on the results of what you are doing. People who focus on results expect an immediate effect.

Those who focus on the activities understand that the results will follow time.

By simply going through the action of writing down the negative things in your life and then accepting responsibility for some or, if not hopefully, all those things, this straightforward action in itself will allow you to move forward in the pursuit of increased happiness.

But you will need to keep going through this exercise. Periodically, you will still need to go to your mind's depths and keep questioning what is negative in your life.

If in the space of two or three paragraphs I could say to you yes, go into your mind, write down everything in your life that is unhappy and then accept responsibility, and everything is magically restored to perfection, I would be the most famous mind guru in the world.

If you regularly go through the exercise, identifying the negative things in your life and if you keep accepting responsibility for those things, what will happen is that as your life starts to improve in so many different areas. These negative things that you write down will slowly reduce in size, and some of the lesser ones will indeed vanish, but some of the deep-rooted ones will probably with you for the rest of your life.

As you continue to improve and develop as a human being, as your physical environment and your relationships with other people start to improve, the consequences of any deep-rooted or negative thoughts start to reduce over time.

In pursuit of constant and never-ending improvement, when we understand that we are focusing on the actions and not on the results and that results won't come immediately, we are managing our expectations.

We will take the analogy of becoming physically fit. If I go for a one-kilometre walk or jog on my couch to 5K on day one, would I be physically fitter? The clear and obvious answer is no.

At the end of 90 days, when I can now run a 5K without walking, would it be fair to say that I am physically fitter than I was when I first started the couch to 5K? The answer is a resounding yes.

If I wanted to engage in a hobby with my partner, I had a limited skill level with salsa; if I went to my first salsa lesson, would I instantly become a salsa dancer? The answer is an obvious no. If I keep going through the pain and the discomfort of feeling so uncoordinated, but I go to salsa lessons each week for six months, would it be fair to say that I would have improved as a salsa dancer? The answer is a resounding yes. Would that improve my relationship....well, that depends on how many toes I stood on!

I weigh 89 kilogrammes, but my ideal weight is 82 kilogrammes; if I have a protein shake for breakfast, a salad for my lunch, and then a light protein-enriched meal for my evening meal, would I instantly be 82 kilogrammes? Of course, I would not be 82 kilogrammes!

If I were to maintain a good healthy diet for 90 days whilst also engaging in my couch to 5K, is there a higher or a lower chance that I would reach my 82KG target weight? Of course, there's a higher chance I'll reach my 82 kg target weight.

For each of these examples to occur and for me to become a master in each of these areas, I need to understand that time will win out; through the constant and never-ending application of small but seemingly insignificant tasks daily, I will improve. And so can you!!

So now we need to accept that in this world of instant gratification. In a world of short YouTube or short tik-tok videos.

The microwave meal is cooked quickly, that for us to attain a higher level of success within all segments of the wheel of life, the results are not going to be instant but instead accumulate over time.

One sure thing about you entering the world of continuous and never-ending improvement, is that you will rattle the cages of some people you associate with the most.

There are laws of association. One of the laws of association is that **you will become equal to the average of the five people you associate with the most**.

Ponder that for one moment. Who it is that you are spending most of your time with? Then realise that you are the average of these five people.

In the pursuit of constant and never-ending improvement and in the quest of living your life on purpose, and in the goal of you growing as a person and having a better life, you may have to make some difficult choices.

One choice is to share that you are going on this journey with all the people you know, like, and trust, and you ask them if they'd like to join you on the journey. Maybe working together as a mastermind group, you could work with each other to grow as human beings.

If you share this with some of the people you associate with, do not be surprised when they cannot be bothered to change their lifestyle. When you do come across these people, please don't blame them.

Take responsibility for what's going on in your life because if you dive into the circle of concern, ask yourself can I influence the fact that they want to stay where they are and the fact they don't want to improve their life? Well, you could maybe suggest more often to them that they could change their lives, but the chances are they are happy where they are right now. It is just the most comfortable option to live a life of normality.

Over time your friends and family will start to see that you are slowly but surely becoming a more rounded and happier person. They will know that you are achieving the goals you set yourself though seemingly far out targets.

If some of your friends and family have a small inkling to improve their lives but didn't want to say it in fear of failure, they will follow your beacon of light and join you in their ongoing, never-ending improvement programme.

Remember, successful people leave clues. In this scenario, you are a successful person. You are leaving clues, and people will want to follow you. How fantastic is that?

But now is a good time for a personal development warning. Right now, I would like you to have alarms ringing around your head, loud sirens going on around your head, because this is a personal development warning.

You have decided to improve in your life and understand the laws of association. If you are hanging around with people who are not focused or forward thinking. If you have dreams, goals, or aspirations of improving your life. You must understand that some people won't want you to improve.

They will go out of their way to tell you and to show you why developing yourself is not worth the time or the effort, and because they have no goals, dreams, or aspirations of their own, they want to keep you exactly where you are right now.

Do not listen to these people because as you continue to develop, as you continue to grow, as you continue to feel the successes of your small but seemingly insignificant wins compounded over time, you will start to associate with more successful people. Rather than restrict your growth, these people will encourage your growth. They will give you support and suggestions to help you do just that.

**Beware of the GUPTR or the IBE or the POOR person.**

The GUPTR, you probably know lots of these people right now. GUPTR stands for "Generally Unsuccessful Person Talking Rubbish". Do you know any of these?

IBE stands for "Instant Bleeding Experts". Do you know any of these?

POOR people stands for people who "Pass Over Opportunities Regularly". Do you know any of these?

We all know people just like this, but would you take advice from the generally unsuccessful person talking rubbish, or would you take advice from a more successful person? Hopefully, you've decided on the latter!

As you engage in constant and never-ending improvement, people that are threatened by your growth and by your goal-setting mindset are likely to try to pull you back to where they are.

This is where your self-discipline comes to the fore. Do not let anybody put you off from engaging in your daily method of operation.

In this pursuit of living your life on purpose for you and you alone must know that where you are right now is a direct result of the people you associate with currently, or the beliefs that are presently in your mind.

You have the time, and you have the power, and you have the ability and the wonderful world to become more. Now that you have decided to live your life on purpose, and have decided to adopt this blame or responsibility attitude, do you understand that you can make a significant difference in your life?

Our world is not perfect, the crime, the unnatural disasters, the war zones, and the crazy politicians that come into power from time to time are around the world, and they have been since time began. But our world is full of opportunity, our world is full of abundance, and you can get whatever you want from it through your pursuit of development.

The rules that apply to an Olympian apply to you in the pursuit of improving your life.

The rules that apply to a successful businessperson apply to you in the pursuit of improving your life.

I cannot do anything but sit and watch in awe of Olympic athletes. I watch the ones coming last and admire them for getting onto the world stage of their chosen discipline. You cannot even imagine the number of hours they have spent training and practising their profession.

I can tell you, though, it is not just 100 hours a week; it is much more. I can also tell you that they failed, that they cried, that they became so enraged with their failure that at times they even considered quitting. But it was the pursuit of success in their discipline to be an Olympic athlete to be on the top stage in their chosen sport with the chance of winning a gold, silver or bronze that drove them through the hard times.

These Olympic superstars, winners, all of them had set themselves a goal and a target, and they put in systems in place to use and to train with every day.

Elon Musk is one of the most successful people in business this world has ever had. He is one of the world's wealthiest people, and it is only a matter of time before he becomes the richest person in the world.

Interestingly, Elon Musk is not motivated by money. The doomsayers have ridiculed him for all his wild and wacky and superb ideas. But he is a driven individual, and during the build-up to launching and developing his electric cars, he would regularly work for 120 hours a week. This is a superhuman being someone that, when you peel the onion and get to the core, is someone that wants to help humanity.

A lot of what he is engaged in right now is in pursuit of helping humanity and helping its survival of it?

This man is living his life on purpose, and he engages in continuous, never-ending improvement. But he is not motivated by money.

Pursue your passions is one of his key motivators.

Don't be afraid to think big is another.

Be ready to take risks and ignore the critics and enjoy yourself. Just part of the mantra that Elon Musk and braces daily.

Now you may not want to amass a fortune of 185 billion dollars, and that's not what this programme is about but understand the fundamental principles that Elon Musk lives by. The key and overriding principles of living your life in a world of constant and never-ending improvement are that you are going to pass through different stages.

To start with, things will feel uncomfortable. You will test your comfort levels daily, regularly during the day, and each time you conquer those fears and move further forward in your life, those comfort zones will improve; they will increase.

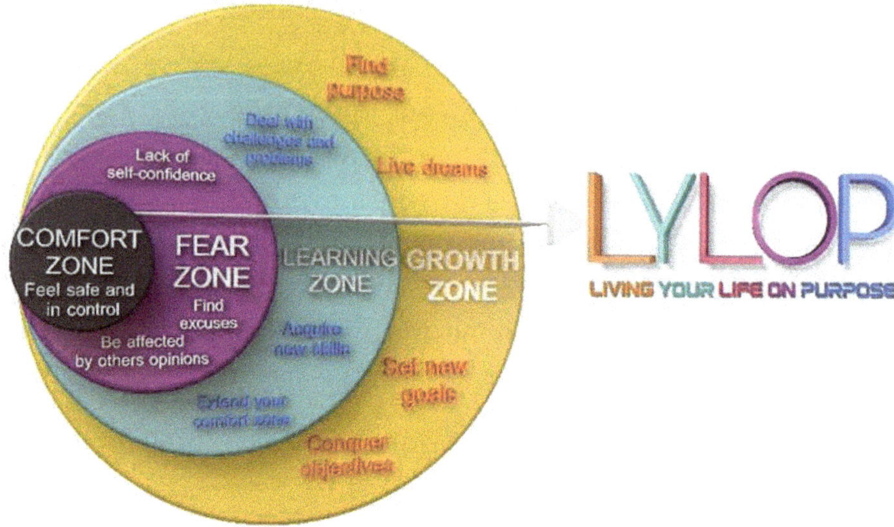


For change to happen, you will need to change; the amount of time you spend on yourself will increase. This is worth it! It is worth it! The feeling of adulation as you pass by some of the targets you set, and you continue to make bigger, more exciting goals and plans.

Nobody will see the number of times that you have felt frustrated. Nobody will see any of the occasions when you wanted to quit. Your success will be attained in the darkest, loneliest moments. You and you alone are going to be responsible for your success.

In pursuit of continuous and never-ending improvement, the pain, heartache, and lows will be all worth it in the end.

# Goals

I don't want to start with a negative in this chapter of the book, but most people who set goals don't achieve them.

Not because the goal-setting process does not work, goalsetting can and will work if systems are in place to help you in the direction and the attainment of those goals.

Many people write down a goal, yet this goal is just a daydream.

Because they don't engage in a goal-directed activity using a specifically formulated system to attain that goal, they are likely to fail.

A friend of mine was a salesperson. He often tells the tale of the day he went into somebody's house to sell his wares.

"I'm walking into the house in the hallway was a large dog. As I walked through the hallway, I heard the large dog moaning and groaning.  Throughout my presentation, I could hear this dog moaning and groaning; it was continuous and never stopped.

After the deal was won, I turned round to the home occupants and said “I'm sorry to say this, but I think there's something wrong with your dog. It hasn't stopped moaning or groaning since we've been in here".

The dog owner smiled and said, "Don't worry, that's just old Duke. Duke is lying on a rusty nail. It is bothering him but just not enough to move".

The moral of this story is that most people are sitting on a rusty nail themselves, and whilst they moan and groan about it so often, it isn't bothering them enough to move to a better place. Instead of being an old Duke, get off your rusty nail, stop being complacent and start to work towards the life of your dreams.

So, boom, we started with the negative but also, we've explained a little of why goal-setters generally fail. And because they have been not taught the correct implementation of a system for the successful attainment of those goals, people lose the desire to write down goals.

People don't achieve their goals because sometimes they set big, massive goals. Setting big, and I mean huge goals, is fantastic so please understand when I say what I'm going to say next, it is not in contradiction to the process of setting big, big goals.

I challenge you to set big goals; I challenge you to set massive goals! Just don't expect those big and fabulous goals to be attained quickly.

When we mention time, it is also essential to understand that the goal setting process's time element is sometimes damaging.

Let us go back to our couch to the 5K habit we spoke about previously. I have a goal to run 5 kilometres within 90 days without stopping walking but just pure jogging or running.

This is a brilliant goal. It has a date, and it has an objective, and both the date and the purpose are entirely possible.

I am 89 kilogrammes in weight, and I have a target weight of 82 kilogrammes. Would it be healthy or possible to maintain a healthy diet and a simple fitness programme to lose 7 kilogrammes within two weeks?

Unlikely and unhealthy. So, the goal-setting process in the last scenario was to reach the target weight of 82 kilogrammes that is an entirely reasonable goal. The problem was the time frame.

I currently earn 30,000 spondoolies a year, and I want to make 100,000 spondoolies a year, and I want to be making this 100,000 spondoolies within four weeks. While this is not an entirely impossible task, it is highly improbable. There is nothing wrong with setting the goal of 100,000 spondoolies a year income because we know that when you live your life on purpose and live in a world of constant and never-ending improvement that through the goal setting and the goal achieving process, this is undoubtedly achievable.

I currently live-in rented accommodation. I want to buy a house that is detached with four bedrooms in a lovely village, and the cost of that house is 450,000 spondoolies. I want to do that within six months. I need to have a deposit of 65,000 spondoolies, of which I have zero deposit now. This is, once again, an entirely attainable goal. The problem with the plan is the time frame.

We can set those big goals, but we have to be clear that the time we achieve those big goals is realistic.

If I set a goal and the time frame is unrealistic, and my mindset is that I have failed to achieve the goal, I will stop setting goals because I believe that I am failing in any of my goals. There are many books and audios in circulation about the goal-setting process. All of them will encourage you to set your goals actively, and all of them are likely to demonstrate that the time needs to fit the potential attainment of your dreams.

**A friend once told me never to walk over the pennies to get to the pounds.**

He was referring to setting a big goal and visualising that big goal be the pounds. On the way to collecting the big goal, put lots of little plans in the direction needed to get to the big destination.

Set lots of little goals in the direction of the big goal. Gain satisfaction in achieving the small goals along the way and what will happen is that you will be inspired to do more. With a burning desire to pick every penny along the way, you will move towards your primary target.

Another big problem in the goal-setting process is that some people set some goals that are so big, and the time for attainment is so far in the future that you cannot focus on the activity needed to get to that goal. Because the goal is so big, the little activity you engage in regularly through a long-time defined plan doesn't seem to hit the mark in achieving anywhere near the goal.

For example, the goal is massive. We are doing lots of work to get to the destination, and yet the work we're putting in doesn't seem to be getting us anywhere closer. Now the reality is that the activity we are putting in brings us closer, but the goal was so big-, and the-time frame was so far away that it just doesn't seem that we are making headway.

We are making headway, but it just isn't noticeable. Because it is not evident, we start to lose focus. As we lose focus, our goal-directed activity slows down, and then the goal becomes more unrealistic as each day, week, month, and a year pass by.

Therefore, in the goal-setting process, rather than have a five-year goal or a one-year goal, a good strategy is to employ a 13-week massive action plan.

You set the big goal and leave it as a target, and you don't need to put a time frame on attaining the big goal.

Once we have set the big goal, we then chunk down little goals to attain the big goal and the small goal we would fit into a 13-week massive action plan.

We are doing a 13-week massive action plan because there are four 13 weeks in a year. It is also easier to focus on what you want to achieve within 13 weeks than within a year or a five-year plan.

Let's face it if somebody implements a one-year plan to achieve a goal, the high chance of starting that one-year plan will be somewhere in the region of three to four months before the end of the project.

Even a year's plan is an extended plan, and it is hard to generate enthusiasm and motivation to engage in the daily activity required to attain the goal.

A 13-week massive action plan, on the other hand, is easy to focus upon, but we breakdown that 13-week massive action plan even further. We work out what we want to achieve by the end of the 13 weeks. That is our penny goal. And then, we split that 13 weeks into 13 weeks of activity.

In goal setting, 13 weeks or around 90 days is the regular length of time for setting goals.

Remember, we can focus on a 13-week plan. It's hard to focus on a one year or a five-year plan.

Let us go back to our couch to 5K. We don't run now, but we would like to complete a 5K run within 90 days. We could break that down into this 13-week massive action plan. By the end of week one, we could set the target that we have completed the one-kilometre section of the five kilometres, and we want to have run a little but walked most of it.

If we have gone out for seven days and have walked most of the one kilometre, but we have jogged some of the one kilometre, we live our life on purpose, and by the end of the first week completed that task.

We set ourselves the target by the end of week four to be running at least 50% of the one km. Notice the goal is achievable. We don't want to go from sitting on the couch to running one kilometre in one go within four weeks.

Whilst our brain says, "yes, we can do this", we need to understand that the physiology of the body does not want to be overly stressed in the early stages of any new activity.

At the end of the first week, we celebrate because we have completed the goal of walking mostly but running some of that one kilometre.

We are celebrating the continued improvement during weeks two and three and the fact that we are now jogging or running more throughout that first kilometre.

At the end of week four, we celebrate that we have run or jogged over 50% of the time.

This is a seemingly insignificant improvement on its face, but this is a massive achievement, and the celebration is well-founded. Our target for the end of month two is to have extended the distance to 2.5 kilometres and for us to walk or jog at least 50% of that 2.5 kilometres.

The target for the end of the third month or 90 days is to run that 5 kilometres in its entirety.

As we pass through weeks one to month one to the end of months two and then to the end of month three, our minds and bodies are congruent, and we believe that we can successfully do the 5K run.

During these 13 weeks, we will have set one of our goals, and we will have successfully achieved that goal. We will feel fantastic, and we will believe in the goal-setting process.

Over the next 13 weeks, we may set a target to do our first ever 10-kilometre run. This is entirely possible because your body is now used to the running process. You may need to run and walk some of that 10K, but the objective is to complete the 10 kilometres distance.

If you were keen and had set yourself an ambition to run a marathon, there is no reason why you cannot run a half marathon in the third of the 13-week massive action plan goal setting process. Then in the last 13 weeks at the end of it, which is a full year, there is no reason why you cannot run or run and walk a full marathon of 42.2 kilometres.

This goal-setting process is guaranteed to work if you commit to implementing the system needed to get you some success along the way.

Within later chapters within this book, we will run through lots of different systems that you could use to achieve the goals that you set within each segment of the wheel of life.

Do you remember the daily method of operation we spoke about earlier in the book? Yes, the one that recommended you get out of bed earlier, and set your day off to a great start with your daily method of operation?

Suppose you set meaningful goals that you can achieve regularly. In that case, you will find that implementing your daily method of operation will become more enjoyable because you will be feeling and attaining the results you set in your goals.

One such goal could be that for the next 13 weeks, you will create a habit of working on your daily method of operation.

You will set yourself the goal of getting up at 6 am or any other time that you wish to start your daily method of operation.

This may seem crazy, but your alarm goes off at 6:00 am on day one. You jump out of bed and switch the alarm off; you then move into the area to do your purposeful morning wake up routine. Once you have got up out of bed and maybe like me, you have had that first drink of water; you are ready to rock and roll. You are prepared to go.

Just before you get ready to go, congratulate and celebrate the fact that you got out of bed at 6:00 am, and you drank your first drink of water for the day.

This celebration is all part of the system of goal setting. The very fact that you jumped out of bed at 6:00 am motivated by the improvement in your life and the goals that you are going to achieve. The mere fact that you did this is the successful attainment of one of your goals, and you should therefore celebrate it every morning because this will help in solidifying the habit of you getting up in the morning.

This self-celebration every day throughout everything you do is so good at solidifying the habit.

For example, I am a fair-weather sports person, and I sometimes like to follow the least resistance path. Where I live, I regularly do a run, which is approximately 12 kilometres. Along the route, I can go and do a 5-kilometre run. I can divert and do an 8-kilometre run because of the road's intersections, or I can continue round and ignore both of those intersections to do my 12-kilometre route.

I have set a target of going for a run, and on the day of the run, it's been lightly raining. I look out of the window and think, "Oh no, I don't like the rain. I think I will give it a miss".

Then the other side of my brain shouts at me and says, "Gary, you said you were going to do the run so go and do it because you know that once you complete it, you will be delighted that you did".

I put on my running gear, and then the moment I walk out of the house and feel the rain on my face and start to run at this moment inside, I begin to congratulate myself. I start to celebrate that I've gone and done the run.

This may sound crazy, but I am saying to myself "Well done, Gary", inside my mind.  The run continues, and I get the first intersection to deviate and do the shorter route. There is a point in my mind when I think, "Shall I do the 5 Kilometre instead of the 12-kilometre run"?

I start to approach the intersection, and as I run past the corner once again, I celebrate. I do actually say, "Well done, Gary ".

I continue my run, and then I come across the next junction, the 8-kilometre route.  The same negative path of least resistance thoughts go through my mind, and yet once again, I pass. Once again, I celebrate that I did not quit, that I did not take the path of least resistance. I did not take the easy option. And you've guessed it on completion of my 12-kilometre run, I feel delighted with myself, and I celebrate my success.

Embrace the same celebration process in every single area of your goal-setting process within living your life on purpose.

**In any area of life, one of the things we need to do is to learn the skill of discipline.**

Daily disciplines repeated over time that is focused, which will work for us, and will generate significant compounded results.

Many people don't achieve their goals through lack of discipline and the fact they made the goals too big with an unfeasible time frame to achieve them.

During your enjoyment of living your life on purpose, and I don't mean the book, I mean by actually living your life on purpose, when you feel success in your life, this affects your mental state.

It affects your abilities to go out of your comfort zone, which creates further fuel for you to do and become more.

When you learn the art of setting and achieving your goals, they become like a positive drug; you want to achieve and take time after time. You become addicted to the attainment of success; you become addicted because you are improving your life.

The word addiction is not negative; by the way, it is perfectly OK to wake up in the morning to be fuelled by a burning desire to achieve something to help yourself, to help your family and for your personal growth.

When we go through the book's stages and particularly in the finance section on the wheel of life, we will show people how they can reduce and then eliminate their debt. Where they can build assets rather than liabilities and where they can enjoy the fruits of life rather than be worried about when the next pay-check or income is going to enter their lives.

If you have embraced any goal setting, you will have heard the goals need to be smart.

S = specific

M = measurable

A = attainable

R = relevant

T = timely

**Being specific.**

Can you imagine walking into your favourite restaurant sitting down at the table, and the waiter comes to serve you and asks you what you would like to eat. You reply, “Bring me food”.

That is not specific, and there's a chance you might get something that you don't enjoy. However, if you had looked at the menu and saw the starters, the mains, and desserts, wouldn't it be true to form that you will pick something that you would like to eat at that moment in time.

So, when you set the goals, you want to be specific.

**Measurable.**

If you have a target to be a certain weight and are above or below that weight now, the only way, you can measure when you achieve your goal is to set a target.

In this scenario, I am currently 89 kilogrammes. My target weight is 82 kilogrammes. Throughout the goal getting journey, I can track my weight difference. So maybe at the end of week one, I am 88 kilogrammes; at the end of week two, I am 87 kilogrammes.

Each week I weigh myself, and I can see that I'm getting closer to my target weight of 82 kilogrammes. The closer I get to my target weight, the more enthusiastic I become about this because I now understand that I'm getting closer to my goal and my target weight of 82 kg.

Within my system, in this weight goal, I have decided that I will weigh myself each week at the same time on the same day. I am engaging in my couch to 5K activity, and I am eating a healthy balanced diet.

This is undoubtedly a measurable way to watch how I'm progressing towards my goal. On a side note, your mind works better if it has a target to aim for.

Notice that I did not state that I wish to lose 7 kilogrammes. Instead, I set a target of 82 kilogrammes. Your mind can focus so much easier this way.

**Attainable.**

You must believe mentally that you can achieve the goal. If you set a goal that is not achievable within the time frame, your subconscious mind won't allow you to go for the goal. Remember, when we spoke about your subconscious mind earlier, it has a job to protect you.

If the goal is just wildly out of reach because of the time constraints you've put on it, your subconscious mind will stop you from doing the activity that's required to get you moving towards the target. So, the goal needs to be attainable. We chunk down the big plans. Remember, don't walk over the pennies to get to the pounds.

Maybe your goal is to run a marathon within one year. Our mindset is to go from couch to 5K within the first 13 weeks of our massive action plan. We have chunked the goal down, so we know that it is attainable to go from a non-runner to completing a 5K run within 90 days. It would be foolhardy to say that you can go from the couch to running a marathon in 90 days.

So, we set the goals of their attainable. It could be that during your goal-setting process, you make your goals easily achievable on purpose. And this is perfectly good because if you make your goals easily attainable and start to tick them off, you begin to congratulate yourself, and that dopamine runs through your veins. That is good news because you will be more engaged in the future goal setting and goal getting processes.

**Relevant.**

This step is about ensuring that your goal matters to you and aligns with other relevant goals. It must also be congruent with your environment, values, and resources.

Your subconscious mind and your whole entirety of your body would not allow you to do something if it compromised your values.

The relevant section of the goal would also include this worthwhile to you. If you are not going to buy into the relevance of your objectives, there is no chance that you will even move towards the achievement of that goal or set of plans.

**Timely.**

“It is the 30th of May 2021, and I am delighted to have reached my target weight of 82 kilogrammes”.

You can see that this is how a goal could be written down. It is pleasant and straightforward; it has a date which is the timely section. It has a target of 82 kilogrammes, so that is specific.

When you set goals and write them down, a top trick is to write them down in the present tense as though you had already achieved them.

So, it could be day one of the 13-week massive action plan, and you have 13 weeks to achieve your goal of 82 kilogrammes. But on day one and every single day leading up to the accomplishment of your goal, you say, "it is the 30th of May 2021, and I am delighted to have reached my target weight of 82 kilogrammes."

Remember, your subconscious mind only can accept it cannot reject it. So, when you make this present case statement, your subconscious mind believes it to be true. You repeat this statement daily the jam in your doughnut is being transfused. You are engaging in the system's activities to get to your target weight of eight 2 kilogrammes, and your goal will be achieved.

At the time, JFK said a similar thing, not about weight, but he did say that I will put a man on the moon by the end of the decade. In 1969, that goal was achieved.

Therefore, it is vital to put a date when the goal will be accomplished.

You can set goals in literally every area of your life. You must apply the “smart” principles, and when you set those goals, make sure you achieve them. Develop and implement systems to achieve them. **Systems are essential in the fulfilment and attainment of goals.**

Within the wheel of life are different life focuses. Each area that you are looking to improve will require a system. The system may vary according to the other segments of your life.

During each of the later chapters in this book, we will give some examples of systems that you can use to help you get started with goal getting and goal achieving phases of your life.

We have already established the importance of having a big goal or a big target and reducing that big target into smaller chunks.

People who failed to reduce a large goal into smaller, more achievable targets generally float aimlessly through an abyss. Just imagine a void of time, a massive void of time.

At one end of the time is where you are now and the other end of the time in the very far distance is where you want to be. It is easy to get lost in that void of time, be distracted, and lose hope that you will ever achieve that goal.

When you set smaller and yet meaningful goals on route to the primary destination, you become more motivated each time you achieve the plan you've now set. You become more motivated because you know you are getting closer to the end goal.

Those who do set big goals should still be complimented for setting any plans at all. The reality is, though, they will be drifting in this big void or alternatively, they may be zigzagging so much and wasting energy.

They will lose their straight-line ability to hit some goals. If you have small plans, you are more likely to straight line to that goal. You achieve that goal. You straight line to the next destination and then another and keep repeating this winning formula. This is a top strategy for setting goals and getting those goals.

So instead of Zig zagging, you are straight lining. Each time you achieve one of those smaller goals, your confidence increases, your belief in what you're looking to achieve grows, and you become fuelled and motivated by the next target and so on.

If you want to live your life on purpose, not only should you engage in constant and never-ending improvement, you should also employ and enjoy the goal-setting process.

I want to introduce the concept of why you want to set a goal.

The very word why is such a small word, but, in the big scheme of things, the word why can be massive, and it can be a word that sets the dream alive.

Let us say that you set a goal, and you like the idea of that goal, but you're not that bothered whether you attain the goal. It could be fair to assume that the reason for setting the plan was not big enough. The why was not big enough.

Suppose you have a little why you will have little power. So, with a little why you have little power, you don't move towards achieving that goal because the reality is it does not excite you sufficiently.

If, on the other hand, you have a big why you will engage in big power, we could call this why power.

When you set goals, these goals need to be goals that activate your mind's excitement and within your body. This then causes you to jump out of bed in the morning to engage in that daily method of operation and for you to do the things that need to be done to move you closer to that goal.

With a significant why power, you will achieve anything you want to achieve. Failure is not an option. You will not be distracted. People cannot switch your mind off the goal, and even through times of hardship, apparent defeat, and worse still ridicule from your friends and family, you will not fail in achieving your dream because the Why Power is massive, and you are resolute.

The biggest catastrophe of life is the catastrophe where people die with their dreams still inside of them.

I once heard a heart-breaking story of a lady in Midwest America. This lady loved the opera. She had never been to an opera, and later in life, she contracted Alzheimer's. She was put into a care home, and every single day she would sit by the window looking outside humming an Aria.

Her daughter would visit from time to time, but when the daughter left the care home, the lady would forget who she was. Yet she could still hum an Aria every single day staring out of the window.

This lady loved the opera, and yet even occasionally, a visiting opera had been only three to four hours away; she had never been to one. Sadly, she died, and when the daughter came to collect her belongings, she broke down and cried.

The older lady had newspaper clippings of operas that travelled around the American states. Some were so close by she could have walked to them, yet she died with her dream inside of her.

Whatever you dream, whatever you want to get in your life, do not die with the dream inside of you.

They say that a goal shared is a goal declared. Engaging in this goal-setting process should be fun. It should be exciting and is better practised with a loved one or possibly a support buddy.

Doing this alone can be difficult, and in Napoleon Hill's "Think and Grow Rich", he talks about a mastermind group's power.

Working with a family member, your partner, or somebody who could be a support buddy will increase your likelihood of success.

Let us go back to our couch to 5 Kilometre run. You can do this by yourself. Of course, you can. If you have big enough why power, you will do the couch to 5K, there is no doubt about that.

If you have a success buddy, on the other hand, you are more likely to go and do the daily task at hand because your support buddy or your success buddy will be doing the same thing as you.

It is raining; you know that you need to go and do your one kilometre, but you don't feel motivated because of the rain. Your success buddy Contacts you, and between you, you decide to go and do the 1K. You celebrate going out of the door. You celebrate while walking or jogging and celebrating when you finish.

A little bit of rain will not stop you from pursuing your goal because you have a significant why power.

You had a why; you had a reason for engaging in this couch to 5 kilometres. That reason could be that you wanted to reduce your weight from 89 kilogrammes to 82 kilogrammes.

Part of the system you are employing to achieve your target weight of 82 kilogrammes is this couch to 5 kilometres in conjunction with eating a healthy and balanced diet. You are creating brand new habits to make sure that nothing will distract you or take you off course.

Remember that we want to make bad habits harder to do. So, during your 13-week massive action plan to complete your couch to five kilometres, you have made sure that there are no terrible treats in the cupboards. This means you cannot be distracted by them.

Considering our process of reducing the goals into smaller, more achievable targets, you have charted the days you run and chart your weight.

Each day you run; you tick it off in the journal. Ensure that you have the journal in front of you each day. Have a look through your ticks. This will help you become fuelled to make sure you get more during your day!

**Make the journal fun and a pleasure to do.**

With your balanced diet, make sure that you keep ticking in the Journal. It could be that you have a coloured tick for physical activity and another colour tick for healthy food activity.

Part of the weight target is to measure your weight by standing on some scales. When you first start, you may want to stand on the scales each morning at the same time. This is motivational because even if you alter your weight ever so slightly and it is heading towards your anticipated goal of 82 kg, you feel inspired by that progress.

In this dialogue, have you notice the target is 82 kilogrammes. It could be that I weigh 78 kilogrammes, and I feel as though I want to put on weight. It could be that I'm 89 kilogrammes, and I want to reduce my weight. Either way, the target is 82 kilogrammes, which is why I'm purposely using grammar this way.

I want to imagine that you are 89 kilogrammes, and you have set yourself a target of 82 kilogrammes. You have given yourself a 13-week massive action plan time frame. Within this 13-week massive action plan, you have decided you will go from couch to 5 kilometres and eat a healthy and balanced diet.

On day one, you measure your current weight. You may also want to get a tape measure and measure specific parts of your anatomy.

On day two, you may weigh yourself again. The chances are you are still 89 kilogrammes on day two. On day three, you may still be 89 kilogrammes. On day 4, however, your weight is now 88.8 kilogrammes.

It is such a small difference in weight for those first four days of hard work, yet you are now moving towards your anticipated target of 82 kilogrammes.

On day five, six and seven, you continue to weigh yourself, you continue with your physical exercise, and you continue to eat a balanced and healthy diet. Each day ever so slightly, you are moving closer to your target. But it is the small wins that continue to motivate you to put those running shoes on and choose a nice healthy meal rather than that gorgeous Five Guys burger.

Please understand it is perfectly normal to have days off, maybe one day off a week; treat yourself to that delicious Five Guys burger with fries and those monkey nuts. Have a break from running. It is suitable for your body to recover anyway. As time passes by, this daily method of operation starts to become a habit, a habit that you are enjoying doing and a habit that is generating results, moving you to your big target.

It is why chunking down your big goal into small goals is vital. It works in every single facet of the goal getting process.

You want to be out of debt. You work out a system to get out of it; you can measure your debt reduction often because you are engaging in regular activity to decrease it. We will cover this off in the finance section of the wheel of life.

If you are a business owner and want to increase sales, the same rules apply.

As a sales coach, I spoke with one of my clients. He had a printing business and had owned this for over 16 years. It was quite a small concern, and he had an annual business sales turnover of 335,000 spondoolies.

While speaking with him, I worked out a plan to help him and his business move to a 500,000 spondoolies business turnover within 18 months. Aghast, he proclaimed this was not possible. It had taken him 16 years to achieve 335,000 spondoolies in business sales. How on earth could he increase it by such a large amount in such a short period?

On a scrappy piece of paper, I showed him just how easy this could be. He worked the business alongside his son. So, there were two of them within the company.

500,000 spondoolies minus 335,000 spondoolies equals 165,000 spondoolies of new sales required.

The average client value was £1000 a year. Therefore, we required an additional 165 clients over the 18 months. When you divide the 165 clients into 18 months, you then require an additional nine new clients a month. That works out to be just over two a week.

Both my client and his son were only required to focus on bringing in one new client each a week every week for 18 months.

We have a big target of increasing sales by 165,000 spondoolies, but that is merely the aim. The actual target is introducing one new customer each as both he and his son would be involved in that process.

All we needed to do was introduce the system that both he and his son would implement daily, to ensure that enough people were looking at his business, so that through the pipeline, a minimum of 1 new customer a week would be introduced.

Both he and his son were motivated to complete the weekly activity required to move forward, and I'm delighted to say that not only did they smash that target they superseded it.

**A ship without a rudder is undoubtedly to end up on the rocks.**

In any area of our life, for example, in the wheel of life, if we set goals, whether they are small or large, the consequence is that we will be moving forward.

Focusing on each segment of the wheel and embracing constant and never-ending improvement will improve our lives.

A voyage of 1000 miles begins with a single step. That step must be in the right direction.

In summary, we have identified that the goals are significant for future development and improvement and enrichment of our lives. We have covered the fact that having a big goal or target is good and is essential. We have identified that if we have a big goal that covers a considerable period of time, it makes common sense to break that big goal into smaller, more achievable goals so that we don't get lost in the ether.

We don't zig-zag. Instead, we are straight-line goal getting people.

We have employed a smart process for achieving these goals. If possible, we will move forward with our dreams, goals, and aspirations with a loved one, a family member, a friend, or a success buddy of any description.

Remember, in the wheel of life, we're going to cover off some tips, tricks and techniques in each of the wheel of life segments to help you in the pursuit of your happiness.

The best thing about life – there is no accountability. The worst thing in life, there is no accountability!!

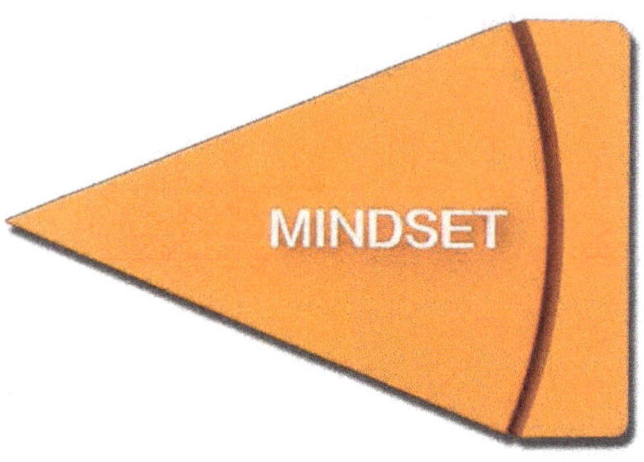


## Mindset

The right mindset with suitable systems can allow anyone to achieve anything and become anyone they wish to become.

We hear about mindset in the sporting arenas or associated with successful people in the business world.

Yet, many people do not realise that having the right mindset in all-wheel segments accelerates lifestyle improvement.

With the right mindset, you become a more pleasant person; you achieve and do more with your life with the right attitude.

But what is the mindset?

First, we must revisit our good old friend, the jammy doughnut. In a perfect world, wouldn't it be fantastic to have a total operating system rewrite?

The jam in our doughnut is likely to be partially the right jam, and somewhat the wrong jam. If we could do a total transfusion of all the jam in our doughnuts in one simple process, it would be so much easier. The problem is we can't do that because we don't know what we don't know, and we don't know what the right jam or, in the big scheme of things, the wrong jam is.

Therefore, through the rest of our lives, we can consciously seek out information and knowledge and consciously decide what goes through to our subconscious mind. The more we repeat that message to our subconscious mind, the quicker the subconscious mind will accept it to be true.

When it comes to the mindset, you may have heard two definitions of mindset. **One is a fixed mindset, whilst the other is a growth mindset.**

We mentioned in previous chapters how the subconscious mind forms over time. By the age of eight, much of our personality has already been created by the jam in the doughnut. There is a massive problem with society and the education system that serves it.

Our school's teachers want to help the children passing through from year to year to year. Unfortunately, schools have a habit of creating young people with a fixed mindset.

Even from the earliest of ages, children are subject to tests. A government agency creates these tests and depending on the success ratio of those tests; it determines how the school is graded throughout the country.

Therefore, a school's purpose becomes more about providing data to the government agency than the purpose they were first created. Teachers show a curriculum to the students and teach them how to pass the curriculum. The students become conditioned into a process where they learn information tested. They are highly congratulated, lauded, and placed on a pedestal for the ability to pass a test.

The fixed mindset is where a human being only does enough to get to the grade they expect. During these early years, the students get into learning something and then repeating something without lateral thinking.

When a person with a fixed mindset comes across something that challenges them or questions their intelligence, it is normal for the person with a fixed mindset to recoil and move away from that scenario rather than tackling and overcoming the scenario.

This is not the teaching profession's fault; instead, the environment that teachers find themselves. They must justify their existence by making sure more pupils get higher grades.

Higher exam pass marks mean that the school gets awarded to a higher level, making it more appealing for parents to send their children.

This is quite bizarre because the schools with the higher grades could be the schools that encourage students to have a fixed mindset and a mindset to learn nothing more than the curriculum to get an "A "grade in their exams.

A fixed mindset still wants to succeed, but they crave validation for that success. The problem with the education system and the creation of people with a fixed mindset is that they feel judged throughout their lives. They believe every part of life is a test and must pass the test to get the validation they crave.

If a person with a fixed mindset does something that ends up in what they deem to be a failure and do not get the grade they are expecting, they feel devastated internally.

The fixed person thrives in a life that comes easy to them; they do not like to be challenged.

So, understand that the fixed mindset needs to be #1 in their world, they must be special, and they must be recognised for anything that they do. People within the fixed mindset category blame everything for going wrong in their life on other things than themselves. Their successes measure their lives, and they avoid failure or any chance of failure.

**The fixed mindset believes that life is about successes and failures. There is no grey area.**

Fixed mindset people believe that failure is an imperfection, and they hide these imperfections. Some fixed mindset individuals are even known to cheat to get the recognition that they so crave.

Fixed mindset individuals believe that it is their talent that causes them to succeed in life. They believe that their intelligence and their skills have been pre-determined at birth.

Because they think that these skills and intelligence were pre-determined at birth, they see failure as a limit to their abilities. Therefore, they believe that they are good at it or are not good at it.

It is as black and white as “I can do it” or “I can’t do it”.

Fixed mindset individuals are unlikely to take feedback or criticism as constructive moreover; they would take it personally. They don’t like to be challenged, and they stay within their comfort zone for as long as they can.

Teachers attempt to educate their students that a growth mindset is a right way to develop. While this is a sound message being passed to the pupils, the priority is still on the school getting a student to regurgitate the curriculum.

The pressure on students is all about getting results, so the idea of a growth mindset is lost in the ether. In a school lesson or even later in life in the work environment, someone with a fixed mindset will not put their hand up or ask questions in fear of being ridiculed or wrong.

Many people with fixed mindsets failed to reach their optimum level because they believe that their intelligence or talent will carry them to the top of the game. They do not practise sufficiently, and they failed to engage in continuous and never-ending improvement.

40% of people have a fixed mindset.

With such an innate fear of failure or rejection, or humiliation, it is hard for someone with a fixed mindset to change that mindset. This stops them from achieving their full potential.

However, if you are prepared to embrace the jammy doughnut philosophy as a fixed mindset person, just being conscious that you have a fixed mindset is a fantastic starting point. Each time a conscious fixed mindset person engages in anything, if it becomes uncomfortable, they can question "What I would do if I had a growth mindset"?

A growth mindset is all about developing talent and ability, understanding that doing isn't about failing more about learning. Believing their skills can be cultivated through the learning and the activity process and that failing in this process is part of the process.

Growth mindset individuals thrive on stretching themselves to a new limit. The growth mindset person attempts something and wants to learn from their experience of improving and continuously improving.

**The growth mindset will have persistence and resilience as core skills and traits.**

A growth mindset individual will always question. They will not mind asking question after question. A growth mindset person would accept any constructive criticism even if it hurt them, and they would dwell on that criticism and then find a way to work back to improve themselves. They believe that effort leads to progression and improvement, and if they respect the person that has given them the criticism, they will learn from it.

People in this mindset can change every part of their perspective. Thus, people in this mindset group by default their life improves through the time they put in high effort, if they have low skills and get results that probably outperform expectations.

They see failure as being perfectly okay. Fixed mindset people think failure is the end, whereas growth mindset people see failure as part of the beginning.

A fixed mindset limits growth and achievements; growth mindset encourages growth and achievement.

So, failure is nothing more than another chance to grow for the growth mindset and that they can learn to do anything they want. If there is a challenge, they will learn new skills to overcome that challenge and try new things.

The growth mindset individual accepts responsibility and knows that they can maximise their performance in any chosen discipline by taking this responsibility.

People with a fixed mindset may appear to be well ahead of their growth mindset associates during the early years of life. In the long run, people with a growth mindset are more likely to accelerate past a fixed growth mindset individual later in life.

A typical example of someone with a growth mindset would be Sir Richard Branson. If you look at Sir Richard Branson's legacy and how he performed so well in his business, it was because he surrounded himself with so many fantastic people.

He took advice readily and enjoyed the growth in his mind of building his businesses.

A person with a fixed mindset certainly could be highlighted as the Ex-President of the United States, Donald Trump. In such denial that he failed to be re-elected, he embarrassed the American nation. He still believes that his correct and failed to win the election.

A fixed mindset person always wants recognition for whatever they do within the relationship and never accepts any blame for anything that goes wrong in the relationship all the household.

If you live your life on purpose and you're engaging in a process of continuous and never-ending improvement, you must remove the fixed mindset's shackles in a slow yet purposeful manner.

Even making the decision knowing that you are a fixed mindset individual that you are prepared to go through a seismic change will be challenging by itself.

The transition from having a wholly fixed mindset to a partial growth mindset will be challenging but will be extremely rewarding through conscious awareness of the change.

When looking for a success buddy to go through the wheel of life or any wheel of life segments, a good first conversation would be to highlight if you have a fixed or a growth mindset.

By declaring that you have a fixed mindset to yourself and any success buddy you are doing is opening yourself up to say this is my weakness, but I wish to turn this into a strength.

Please be patient with me if I'm not forthcoming or if I seem a little bit awkward in the situation.

When transitioning from a fixed to a growth mindset, the jam in the doughnut could take decades to be entirely transfused. Therefore, it is a smarter objective first to identify if you are a fixed mindset and then accept that you will employ a growth mindset in a certain number of areas of your life.

Let's now get onto something a little bit lighter, a little bit more fun and something we can all sink our teeth into and thoroughly enjoy.

You are listening to or reading this book called living your life on purpose, and the whole idea is that by using the wheel of life, we're going to bring balance to all areas of your life.

In this mindset chapter, we've done enough talking about growth and fixed mindsets. How about we switch to the "I can" mindset.

"I can" improve myself in all the segments in the wheel of life. I can enhance my life full stop; I will do whatever it takes to make sure I live a well-balanced and rewarding life.

I love my life, and I'm incredibly grateful for all the things associated with it. Over the next 13 weeks, I will engage in a 13-week massive action plan. I will track what I am doing to see the results I'm achieving.

And this is the very essence of the mindset, just being optimistic, just giving this a go, can bring about so many extraordinary improvements to your life.

Imagine living without any debt; imagine having more money coming into your bank balance than you've ever had before, spending more time with your friends and your family doing the things you've always wanted to do.You are going on those lovely holidays without it hitting a credit card or buying the car of your dreams and living somewhere that you've always wanted to live.

Imagine all the beautiful things you could do by engaging in this process of continuous a never-ending improvement. By focusing on the wheel of life segments, understanding that there is no instant win, and through the compound effect of doing a little bit of activity in each of those segments of the wheel, your life will improve.

The critical overriding reason people engage in living their lives on purpose to gain balance within their lives is to become happier. A happier person with less stress will transmit precisely that.

Remember, we are human beings' natural transmitters, and we are natural receivers. We can transmit good vibes or bad vibes, happy vibes, or unhappy vibes, stressed out or not stressed at all.

When you are free of stress, everything you do seems to go tickety-boo. Through the transmission of your internal feelings, people are detecting no worries in your life.

As you go through living your life on purpose and improving in different areas of your life, what will begin to happen is you will worry less, you will become more enthusiastic, you will be a more pleasant person to associate with.

Don't be surprised a year down the line when somebody you know well, love, and trust compliment you on your new persona. You may even question yourself about how good you have become.

If you can improve yourself 0.3% a day every day based over a year, you will have improved yourself by 100%.

But we need to apply the right mindset at the start. We need to use an "I can" attitude from the start.

We must understand that we will be challenged along the way and that being challenged is perfectly normal in life's growth phase. Also, conscious that sometimes the results are not going to go the way we want them to as quickly as we want them to. Remember, most people live in this instant gratification society. They want things done right now.

But it probably took you years and years to get overweight and unfit, or in debt, or working yourself to a job you don't even enjoy.

Therefore, it would be ludicrous if we had the mindset that within a month, our world will be transformed. It just does not work this way.

But what can happen in a relatively short period is this contagion. When I say contagion, what I mean is your application into the activities you're doing daily in this world of continuous and never-ending improvement can become contagious. It can become quite addictive. Not in the wrong way.

You start to engage in the couch to 5K. On day one, your mindset is, "I'm going to do this, I'm going to do this, I'm going to do this".

On day five, you start to lose a little bit of your ambition. You are losing a little bit of your motivation. Fortunately, you did engage this process with a success buddy or your partner, so each of you gives the other some accountability, and you breeze through day five.

At the end of week one, you've enjoyed getting out and about, you've enjoyed the fresh air you enjoyed doing the jogging and walking. On completion, you've enjoyed congratulating yourself on your excellent work. You've also maintained that good healthy balanced diet, and you are feeling much better with yourself apart from the odd ache here and there in the leg region. On day seven, you weigh yourself.

You are delighted that you can see an improvement, and you are getting closer to your target weight. When you mentally acknowledge that you are moving in the direction of your goal, this will fuel you further to keep moving towards the goal.

Your mindset improves quite considerably around days 21 to 28.

What has happened is that your daily method of operation, has now become more of a natural habit. Your subconscious mind is not having to overthink it and instinctively go about your tasks.

In the early stages, where it is more challenging, your mental status is challenged more; as you pass through days 21 to 28, the mental challenge is less within your comfort zone, and you enjoy your development.

At the end of the first month, engaging in this continuous and never-ending improvement and following a well-set series of systems will see a noticeable difference. It is at this point you buy yourself into the process. For the first 28 days, you are forcing yourself into the process and the systems that you have created.

You are now straight-lining to your goals. You are no longer zigzagging. You are now living your life on purpose, and it's now just a matter of discipline. Irrespective of what mindset you are regarding fixed or growth, let us just put this aside for one more moment.

Are you living in your dream house, driving your dream car, going to your dream job or business, living your dream family fun and recreation life?

If the answer is no, it didn't matter what mindset you were in because it isn't working as well as you wanted it to work.

When you live your life on purpose, and you focus on those daily activities that you have identified, and you grow each day in those areas. Eventually, everything around you will improve.

With your new "I can" attitude used in every facet of your life; you must also understand that some people need validation. Some people need some form of external reward from people close to them.

**What motivates you determines your engagement in this process.**

Your goals create the "why power". The reality is for you to succeed in living your life on purpose; it is absolutely nothing to do with anybody else.

The only person that can determine your success in your life is you, and you must take full responsibility for your daily actions. You do not require any form of external reward. You are doing this for yourself, and you are doing this for your family.

If you are serious about improving your life, reduce the amount of time you spend on social media sites such as Facebook. Also, try to limit your exposure to bad news on the television or via newspapers. Make a conscious effort not to associate or respond to people with a negative mindset.

Remember, you will become equal to the average of the five people you associate with the most. Find people who have an "I can" attitude.

Searching through and reading posts on Facebook about how dull people's lives are, about their food intake, and how they are so stressed out with the world will not serve you well. It will only cause a thing called emotional contagion.

Emotional contagion is where two or more people agree on something. You hear somebody talking about how bad their life is and when you feel the same way about your life. You comment on the Facebook post, and then you think unified you have found somebody that has life as bad as you. You will not be surprised to find thousands of people just like you, so now the emotion contagion suits your immediate wants and needs.

Spend time listening to or reading other personal development material and listening to the many "TED talks" available online via YouTube. Immerse yourself into the mindset of the movers and shakers of the world.

Find somebody that you can relate to, somebody that shares the same desires, vision, and values that you want to attain. There are so many people who have supplied so much fantastic material to help the mindset. Buy it!

To develop, we must strip back to basics; if you want to grow within your mind, you must understand that our sound old friend jammy doughnut principles come into play. Remember, what we think we know may not be accurate, or it may be just partially right, and what we know may be holding us back from achieving our true potential.

A significant problem in humans' growth is that they don't want to be seen going backwards in life. They have an ego, and their ego gets in the way of professional development.

Add a man into this mix; you then have ego and testosterone. High levels of testosterone in a man are equivalent to kryptonite and Superman. Combine testosterone with your ego and a refusal to identify this as a weakness, and the chances are you are unlikely to grow personally at all.

I challenge you to open your mind and engage in this philosophy of continuous and never-ending improvement. I challenge you to as much as possible adopt a growth mindset. Understand that you may move through your comfort zone into an area you do not like.

The more times you enter a new area of discomfort, the more times your brain starts to accept it. Keep visiting the danger zone. If you watch Top Gun with Tom Cruise, think about the highway to the danger zone. For those of you of a certain age, you are now humming that song in your mind.

If you did start humming highway to the danger zone and have not thought about that song for many years, this highlights just how powerful your brain is.

We all have a perfect memory, don't we? At this point, you may be thinking that you do not have a perfect memory. Many people think they have got a poor memory. This could not be further from the truth. You do have a perfect memory. What you lack is a perfect recall.

We all have some profound things hidden within our brain, something that the subconscious mind may be deliberately trying to suppress to protect us.

When you move out of your comfort zone, the subconscious mind starts to raise the alarm. You begin to feel nervous, maybe get sweaty palms, maybe if the trauma has been so significant, feel nauseous, and want to recede to your comfort zone.

But what if this fear that was in your subconscious mind was not a real fear at all. It could have been your parents' thoughts or as you were growing up people close to you. Therefore, without its ability to reject, your subconscious mind has automatically accepted fear of someone else that you know.

Some fears are real. You cannot jump out of an aeroplane without a parachute and expect to survive. You cannot defy gravity laws, and with your fragile body doing such a stupid task would be fatal.

That isn't true. But you probably agreed with me straight away without even thinking about it. If the plane were flying, let us say 10 metres above the ocean at the slowest possible speed, and you jumped out of the aircraft correctly, and most safely, there's a high chance that this act would not be fatal.

That sounds like fun. I can hear lots of people shouting.

You see, we put things into our minds each day, and some things have been put into our minds long before we were consciously aware of what they were. These are the things that create our comfort zone. These are the things that can limit our growth, yet these are unfounded fears.

What is crazy is that we could engage in some simple tasks right now, where I could read out a set of words, and then I could ask you to write down all those words. You would write down words that I did not say purely because of the subliminal message that can be hidden within the stories I talk about

There is fantastic personal development audio called "I know what to do, so why don't I do it" by Nick Hall PhD.

The book is lightly delivered, but it does delve quite deep in Nick's fantastic way. Indeed, one to consider buying.

As human beings, we interpret things how we want to see them. With an "I can" mindset, we can evaluate what we are about to do, recognise the fear level and determine that the fear level is insufficient to stop us from doing the task.

You have set a goal of completing the couch to five kilometres. On this morning, you wake, and you see outside the clouds are heavy; it looks like it will rain.

You set a goal of completing the 5K, also reaching your target weight of 82 kilogrammes. You may have set the 82 kilogrammes as a target because you have an event to go to and you want to wear your favourite suit or dress, or you have a sporting event.

Within this goal, there are many other reasons you are doing it. Such as living longer, feeling, and looking better with yourself etc.

Because you have an accountability partner, a success buddy, you look out the window and consider whether you want to engage in your couch to 5K activity. For a second or two, you think missing just one day won't matter. But then you think about why you are doing this goal, get on the phone, or text your accountability partner, who, as it turns out, has the same back-out thoughts.

You both agree that the rain will only make you wet if it does fall. You will not experience any significant trauma, and therefore you both agree to go and do your run. During the run, you're congratulating yourself; after the run, you congratulate yourself, and together you congratulate each other.

You feel fantastic that you have completed yet another run in your desire to reach 5 kilometres. Every time you pass through that comfort zone, your willingness to achieve your goal becomes more realistic, and therefore you become more motivated to do those daily activities.

You will experience some discomfort, which is all part of the stretching process. But when you stretch in your mindset and grow this comfort zone, these will become art and part of a typical day's activity.

**Procrastination, ego, and testosterone are three-bed partners that should never meet.**

Procrastination is the killer of all dream's goals and aspirations. Putting things off for another day that will never arrive is futile, and the problem with putting things off is that it is so easy to do.

If you wake up every morning, engage in your daily operation method, and you have a big enough why, the Why power will nullify any procrastination.

Unfortunately, those were just words on a piece of paper, and the reality is procrastination will always be there to derail you from your intended goal. What is more comfortable going out to complete your five-kilometre run or sitting and spending time on Facebook or some other social media platform. Of course, it is the latter.

We are aware that procrastination is ever-present, so we need to create a way or a habit that defeats procrastination as often as we can. Notice I wasn't foolhardy enough to say 100% of the time, we will beat procrastination because that is probably one of the most challenging tasks known to an aspiring person. We accept that sometimes, procrastination will win, yet we must be conscious to ensure it only wins occasionally.

Your alarm goes off at 6:00 a.m.; you placed your alarm far enough away, so you must get out of bed, jump out of bed, switch off the alarm, and guess who is waiting next to your device "yes" straight away procrastination is waiting for you.

So, the moment we wake up, we begin the battle against that thing called procrastination. It puts us to our very first test, and through our day, you bet that procrastination is there waiting to derail you.

Let us call procrastination one of your mind monsters. You have a mind monster on one shoulder, and you have a mind Angel on the other shoulder. The mind monster will always try and lead you along the wrong path. The mind Angel is there to correct you.

Just jump back into bed for another 15 minutes, shouts the mind monster. The mind angel reminds you that you need to do your purposeful morning. You need to get your day off to the right start because otherwise, you will never catch up.

But the mind monster is still shouting, and the angel mind is trying to be reasonable.

If you have set meaningful goals, your mind angel will win most of the time. This is why we must read and see the goals. Read them or think about them, every time the mind monster rears its ugly head. You see, what we need to understand is that the mind monster or the angel that wins is the one that we give most airtime.

If we keep jumping back into bed for the extra 15 minutes snooze, which turns into a 30-minute nap, this is a habit that we form, and this habit does not serve us well. If we get into the habit of always jumping out of bed, switching off the alarm and then starting our purposeful morning process, this is the habit that will form.

Here's the trick. The alarm goes off, and you jump out of bed; the mind monster tells you to jump back into bed for a 15-minute snooze. You then start counting backwards "54321".

5 - 4 - 3 - 2 - 1

"54321 I am going to get up and start my purposeful morning".

Just those valuable 5 seconds to give your conscious part of your brain sufficient time will remind you why you are doing your purposeful morning. A reminder of why you are engaging in this daily method of operation, and during those 5 seconds, what will happen is your subconscious mind will flash images to remind you of your goals.

When you say "54321", this doesn't want to be timid either in your mind scream out "5, 4, 3, 2, 1" in fact if I can remind you of another programme that you may have watched as a youngster think about Thunderbirds and the starting theme tune of that fabulous programme.

Your big challenge is the mind monster and what we need to do is we need to reduce that screaming and shouting and loud mind monster into a small timorous beastie. One with extraordinarily little vocal time and one that if you wanted to listen to it, you really would need some form of hearing aid. We want to create a mind angel so that whenever we set a task, we've pushed forward and done it without even thinking about it.

Remember creating new habits that serve us are all art and part of the continuous and never-ending improvement process.

So, our mindset right at the start of this process is an "I can" mindset with the ambition of defeating the mind monster. We are declaring war on procrastination.

With an "I can" mindset, you will defeat procrastination in many of the battles you engage in. Remember you don't have to win all the battles to win the war.

I have a friend who has been overwhelmed by his mind monster. The tricky and devious mind monster has got so deep into his subconscious mind he doesn't know that he has been deceived. This friend of mine is such a nice person; he will do absolutely anything to help anybody, yet he is locked in a cage by his mind monster. This mind monster is stopping his growth.

He has things he knows that he needs to do daily to generate income. But that devious mind monster had him trapped.

But what is so dramatic that is stopping my friend from excelling and being the person many of us know he can be?

Ironing and housework.

He will not engage in work-related tasks until every item of clothing in his household has been ironed or until every room in the house has been cleaned.

Only then will he feel satisfied enough to move onto another area of his life. The next thing will do the next thing to go for a nice long walk.

Then he will have some food watching the income reducing box, that he calls television.

Some days he doesn't even engage in business-related activities, but he needs to put food on the table. He is living in rented accommodation that is beautifully kept and his clothing superbly ironed, but he is locked in a cage of his own doing.

Once he understood that this was against the norm. After regular sessions with him, he realised that even his wife didn't want to live in such a clinical environment. He believed what he was doing was good unnecessary. The fact of the matter was his wife wanted him to do more work to contribute to the household income and that they could eventually buy their own house.

It took over three months engaging in the living your life on purpose process to defeat the mind monster. To this day, he cannot wash an item of clothing and put it away without it first being ironed. We had to shuffle about his daily activity so that the clothes weren't thrown into the washing machine until early evening.

He had already undertaken his business-related activities and all his fitness goals and therefore was not distracted by this chore.

It turned out that my friend had not consciously slipped into this ironing and household chore routine. It just became his safe place, and the safer he felt, the longer he stayed in that zone.

Now that he is aware of this zone, he is taking active steps to grow other parts of his life in the wheel of life. I comically suggested that if he loved ironing and cleaning, it might be the right course of action to set up a new business in that profession. He didn't love it that much, and this was another nail in the coffin of those habits.

Sometimes the things we have ingrained in our minds are so powerful that we cannot eliminate them but what we can do is we can move the order in which we do them throughout our daily method of operation. The stronger the "I can" mindset is, the easier it will be to breeze towards our goals. We must place some order into our daily tasks; we must first prioritise the most important ones.

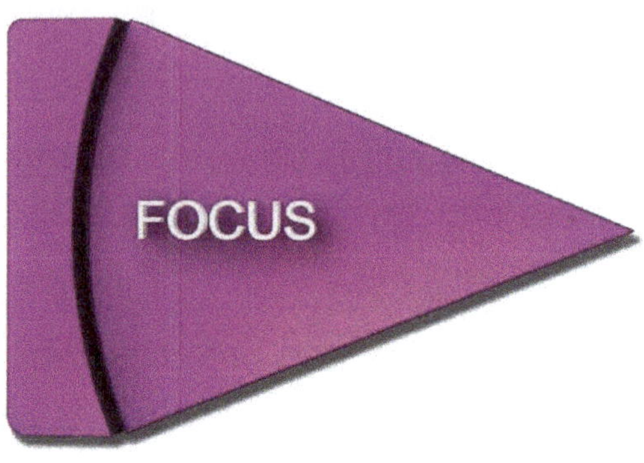


# Focus

In this world, it is becoming increasingly hard to focus.

There are just so many distractions.

The smartphone with all the notifications ringing, buzzing, vibrating, or just the habit of picking it up is one of the main and new distractions.

In a study, Microsoft found that the average distraction within the workplace was 15 minutes. If someone was on a task and distracted, it took a further 15 minutes to re-engage with the job.

Their analysis found that the average amount of distractions in a working week was 28 per person. Meaning 420 minutes or 7 hours a week was lost to distractions. That is one full working day. How crazy is that?

If we can reduce the number of distractions that we each have during a day, we would focus more on the things that do matter. Living your life on purpose requires focus, and focus is an essential mindset of the whole philosophy of success orientated people.

If you have a five-year goal and write down a whole list of actions required to help you achieve that five-year goal, how easy would it be to focus on all those actions necessary?

It wouldn't be easy at all. Your brain could not compute or focus on the magnitude of the time and all the actions required for you to attain your target or your goal successfully.

In line with our mindset and goal setting principles, we set ourselves a big goal, and then we break that big goal into smaller, more achievable, and meaningful goals.

I was once taught that focus stands for:

**F**ollow

**O**ne

**C**ourse

**U**ntil

**S**uccessful

Each morning we create our things To-Do List in line with our daily method of operation. We have some triggers to remind us when to start each of those actions, to ensure we complete that task or the activity in that time.

Contrary to belief, nobody, and I'm sorry to the ladies, but nobody can multitask effectively.

However, you can focus on short-term activities without distraction and complete that activity and then move on to a subsequent activity or task and so on. When you are about to start one of these activities, you must be acutely aware of the things that may distract you during it. For example, most successful people switch off the notifications on their smartphone. This way, there's no ringing, beeping, or vibrations distracting you from your task.

When it comes to emails, many people have an autoresponder on their emails. The autoresponder could say something along the lines of:

"Thank you for sending your email, which I acknowledge I have received. To make myself more efficient and effective I generally check my emails between 9:00 AM and 10:00 AM and 4:00 PM to 5:00 PM. If the matter is urgent, please feel free to call me on my telephone."

A critical fundamental element to focusing effectively is understanding that if you receive a text message, an email, or a Facebook message, you do not need to reply immediately.

The world will still go round if you take an hour to reply to that message.

The problem with today's society is that many feel as though they must reply immediately. What happens is for those who do get into the habit of instantly responding to something, the person who sent the message then expects you to reply immediately over time.

It isn't that they even require a reply immediately. It's just that they become used to you replying directly, so they expect such an instant response.

A phrase on face value does not sound nice, but if you delve deeper into it and understand it, it makes more sense.

**"The person who needs the other person the least has the most power".**

So, start to take back power by not responding instantly to daily messages. There are so few life or death occasions that a response is required immediately, but we have now become tuned to react quickly. It is now such a destructive habit that works against us.

To improve our ability to focus, we must eliminate as many distractions as possible, and you can identify your distractions by merely taking stock of them each day. Then work out ways to stop them from being distractions.

Years ago, your mum or your dad or husband or wife did not contact you whilst you were at work. They knew that you were at work, and they knew that you were being paid to do a job, and your bosses expected you to work when you were in the workplace.

Today people are receiving and reading or writing messages that are not even work-related during work time. Many believe this to be theft.

They are at work and are paid to work. That is what the wage is. It is a trade where you accept money, and in return, you give back the time and skills to justify the money you are earning. If you are doing something alternative to the task you are being paid for, you are stealing time or money from the person who is paying you.

You can debate that as much as you want. Still, the fact of the matter is some organisations that are improving employee production give their employees 10 to 15 minutes an hour to participate and engage in their social media or replying to messages.

As far as mental happiness goes and productivity for the company, the employee is happy because they are getting a designated extra 10 or 15 minutes an hour. Still, the reality is the employer is not giving anything away because the mind can only focus for a certain period, so having some downtime for the brain too rest and repair make business sense.

But we are stealing from ourselves all the time. Forget the dramatic statement that I made about employees stealing from their employers; no, the travesty is far worse.

We are all people on this planet and, once we understand this, we all have equal opportunities. It doesn't matter your age, sex, ethnicity, or where you are from unless you allow it to count.

If you are from any walk of life, are there any reasons whatsoever that would discriminate from you getting fitter or healthier? No, of course, there isn't.

If you are from any age group, are there any reasons that would stop you from developing personally? Of course not.

In this world of abundance, are there any reasons whatsoever, irrespective of what group of people you come from, would stop you from becoming financially independent and debt-free? Of course not.

Irrespective of your age, your sex, your religion, or your ethnicity in this world of opportunity, are there any reasons that would stop you from being a phenomenally successful businessperson?

No, you can be as successful as your neighbour of different sex, of varying religion of differing ethnicity and differing age.

Whenever we doubt whether we can do anything, we must first return to our good old friend the jammy doughnut and then look at our own beliefs. If you write down your goals and your targets and these are "SMART", and you engage in the regular activity consistently, there is absolutely no reason you cannot be successful.

Seriously, no matter who you are or where you come from, you can succeed on your terms.

**If it is to be, it is up to me.**

Those ten two-letter words are so powerful and are entirely correct.

You've written down your goals. You get up each morning and partake in your purposeful morning. You have a daily method of operation, and you have set yourself smaller, clearly defined goals within the larger plan.

Then it would help if you focused on each of those tasks or activities daily. You will move forward in the right direction towards your goals, and you will undoubtedly win in the game of life.

We know the practice makes progress, and we know that when you first start to do something, whatever it may be, there is a high chance it will be hard to do in the first instance, and it may well be extremely uncomfortable. With practice making progress principles, the more we do it, the easier it will become, and then we will allow this to be one of those habits that serve us well.

Therefore, focus is of paramount importance. Focus is what will be the making or the breaking of your achievements in each of the segments in the wheel of life.

It seems so dramatic that I am saying this, but if you are lazy in improving your life and living your life on purpose, there is an extremely high chance that you will not achieve your intended target.

Focus every day, focus every morning, focus on writing down the list of the things you need to do and focus on ticking those things off every time you do them in your journal.

Focus on congratulating yourself for each of the activities or tasks you complete and focus on your dreams and aspirations.

Visualisation is a critical element in the focus process. Some of the most successful sportspeople in the world, such as golfers, will practice, and they will make progress just like you will do.

They practise so hard, and they don't practise to get it right. They practise so they cannot get it wrong. Professional sportspeople have their own daily method of operation, and they are successful because of the focused application of their own systems.

Sports people who are highly tuned to their discipline take focus to an entirely different level. If you were to speak to Tiger Woods, Phil Mickelson, Rory McIlroy, or any of the world's top golfers, ask them about visualisation.

They will tell you before they stand up an address the ball, they look behind where the ball is sitting and look at the intended target. Next, they visualise how that shot will play out.

They then stand up to the ball they line up and hit it. Most times, the ball goes in the direction that they visualised it. But it wasn't the standing up and just hitting the golf ball or the visualising that allowed them to do it so effectively. No, something far more critical happened before they ever played that shot before they ever stood on that golf course on that day before they even arrived at the venue.

Many people understand that we have a creative side to our brain, and we have an analytical side to our brain.

Fewer people will have heard of the way sportspeople divide their brain. Instead of being analytical and creative, sportspeople may divide it into their brain's practice side, which is the analytical side.

When they compete and pull up to execute, this would be the creative side that they use on that brain.

When they are in their practice mindset, they will think analytically about their swing, the swing speed. All things analytical occur on the practice ground. Each time they are on the practice ground, they will swing that golf club. They are thinking analytically about how the shot should play out.

They practise incessantly using the analytical side of their brain. On the golf course, they no longer use the analytical side of their brain to execute that shot. Instead, they focus on their game. They focus on the visualisation of each shot they are going to play, and when it is time to play the shot, they allow their mind memory to take over and let the fluency of the swing hit the ball sweeter to the directed target area.

You can hear countless interviews post-competition when the interviewer asks, "what you were thinking about when you were over that ball"? Nearly all the replies are along the lines that they weren't thinking anything. They just got themselves into the zone, so they focused, and they visualised the shot and then played the shot.

Keeping with the golfing analogy eliminating distractions is a skill that these golfers master. If you watch any of their events when tens of thousands of people walking around the golf course, don't think that could be distracting?

On the first tee of any major event, hundreds of people are lining along the tee box. The professionals stand over the ball and focus. The next job is to eliminate any distractions; these are the people alongside the tee box; they visualise where that shot is going to go, and then they hit the ball, and they get applause from the audience.

Some of these top professionals don't even hear the applause. Nor do they hear the clicking of the cameras or that twig that was broken when somebody walked over it. They have 100% focus. They have eliminated distractions that could be the thief of their chance of success.

Back to our couch to 5K run. A fantastic goal and well worthy of doing. Those who complete this goal will feel fantastic and congratulate themselves for doing such a fabulous feat.

Focus is paramount for the successful attainment of that goal. It all starts when waking up in the morning. By engaging in their purposeful morning, they complete their first routines and solidify their daily operation of method.

They have set aside time to go for their walk and combined run, and yet there is a drizzle of rain, and it is 15 degrees Celsius. The distraction is the rain, and the distraction could be an excuse.

I will wait until tomorrow could be the response. But we all know that tomorrow never comes, and we also know that once you've gone past a certain time point, you will never get that time back. We also understand that the compounded effect of seemingly insignificant things done repeatedly over time becomes a habit and moves us closer to our goal.

Having an excellent focus on your goals will ensure that none of these little distractions gets in the way. If you can embrace habit stacking, as we mentioned within the habits chapter, you will automatically move from one task to another as part of the habit stacking process. Let us run through some habit stacking examples and how your focus can ensure that each of your tasks is completed.

I like to run somewhere between 2:00 PM and 4:00 PM. It does sound strange, but when I compete in my Ironman triathlons usually, I will get off the bike around that time in the afternoon. I like to have my training runs roughly when I may be running when I'm doing an Ironman event.

If I'm going to engage in a daily method of operation, my afternoon activities will have habits stacked in place so that I go through each of those tasks and then I will naturally move on my running.

Habit stacking sheet - Remember this is just part of a whole series of tasks during the day, and after each job, there will be a huge, big successful tick.

| | |
|---|---|
| 12:30 to 1:00: | Lunch. |
| 1:00 to 1:15: | Call prospects. |
| 1:15 to 1:30: | Follow up from previous prospects. |
| 1:30 to 1:45: | Send information to prospects to evaluate. |
| 1:45 to 1:55: | Drink water before run and get changed into running gear. |
| 2:00 to 3:00: | Run 10-kilometre training session. |
| 3:00 to 3:30: | Cool down, drink more water and have a protein shake. |
| 3:30 to 3:45 | Check messages and emails and reply immediately. |
| 3:45 to 4:00 | Send three messages to three people within my focus 15 bubble to let them know I have completed my daily tasks. |

| | |
|---|---|
| 4:00 to 4:30 | Listen to some professional development on audible. |
| 4:30 to 5:00 | Prepare next day's daily method of operation and things To-Do List. |
| 5:00 onwards | Relax and recuperate. |

Throughout the day, you could have a series of habit stacking sheets and what happens is that you sequentially move from task to task without overthinking about it but following your predetermined course of actions. The focus element here is to avoid any potential distractions.

I do not switch on the income reducing box (or the television) as most people refer to it until I have finished everything that needs to be completed.

It sounds strange, but I might have some lunch, it would be so easy to switch on the television, but I get lost in a world of interest, then before I know it, I have lost some time.

The income reducing box has been the thief of more of my time in the past.

Now though, I would have my lunch somewhere without distraction and somewhere without noise so the mind can get clarity or chat with my wife, undoubtedly far better than the television's distraction.

Have you noticed within many chapters of the book that we are habit stacking the book's contents?

We are continually referring to the jammy doughnut. We frequently refer to beliefs or the need for constant and never-ending improvement. We do this because repetition is the number one rule of all learning. The subconscious mind only can accept it cannot reject anything, so garbage in garbage out is a common saying. Therefore, it is essential to engage in regular jam transfusions. Never immediately discount something.

If you hear something or read something, at least using your conscious part of your brain, evaluate the source of this information, and if you deem that this information to be worthy to enter your subconscious mind, allow it to do so.

Accept it consciously and accept it subconsciously, and then keep receiving it regularly to become part of your new upgraded operating system.

Focus is of utmost importance in the jam transfusion in your subconscious mind. It would be best if you always were focused on what you are allowing to enter your subconscious mind on a conscious level. There needs to be a massive alarm ringing if you hear something negative or that will not serve you in the future period of your life.

Remember the GUPTR on the IBE these people will feed your mind with absolute rubbish and unless you have a filter to stop it from going in your subconscious mind will accept it, and you will then allow this to become a central part of your operating system.

We must focus on those habits. Analyse the patterns that are not working for us and highlight the practices that serve us well. We must focus on creating habits that will strengthen our chance of succeeding in our life.

Remember, focus on making sure the habit is easier to do. Before I go to bed at night, I need to focus on getting the bottle of water from the fridge and placing that bottle of water on my desk. Eventually, the habit takes over, and I no longer need to think about getting the water from the fridge. It is just a habit that happens automatically.

Remember, the subconscious mind wants to make as much as what we do during the day a habit that happens without us thinking about it because it saves energy for other tasks.

So, daily we must focus on developing those good habits by using the habit stacker and being conscious in every moment of what we are doing.

Focus on eliminating procrastination. Remember 54321 “Thunderbirds are go”. If you feel a bit hungry, you will walk naturally to the cupboard where the crisps or the biscuits hide. You open the cupboard, and then you focus and say, “no 54321” I will have an apple instead.

We need to be continuously switched on and focussed. It is so easy to slip back to those devilish habits.

Yes, you can do this would be what you consciously need to say to yourself if you are entering any self-doubt phase. Most people have limiting self-beliefs that have been ingrained over such a long period; they are already accepting failure and will not even give it a go.

In the principles of living our lives on purpose and this arena of constant and never-ending improvement, we must always challenge ourselves, and we must always believe that we can do something.

If we had tried to do something before but failed, we need to understand that it was the old you. With this new confident mindset, we will engage in the activity knowing that it may take us out of our comfort zone and yet knowing the more we do it, the better we will get at it.

Remember, though, if you believe that you can jump out of an aeroplane without a parachute flying over 4000 feet, then chances are you will die.

So, don't think you can do everything, you cannot fly!

But you can do the couch to 5K, you can hit your target weight, you can engage in some regular recreation or fun activities, you can develop personally, you can build relationships with your partner with your friends and your family. You can do so much every single day, and you can grow by 0.3% a day every day an improve yourself by 100%.

But it does require focus, and it does require visualisation.

Visualise where you want to be in 13 weeks. Activate that 13-week massive action plan and move towards your goals, your dreams, and your aspirations with focus.

Remember that focus stands for "follow one course until successful" during your day.

Each time you enter a habit stacking phase, you are now entering another thing to focus upon. You do not focus on what you just did, and you do not focus on the next task. You focus on the job at hand, and you complete it.

You focus on your "I can" mindset. You do not listen to negative people or negative forces.

You continuously focus on questioning what you already know, and you adopt a growth mindset that allows you to understand that you can grow ever so much in this world. With your "I can" attitude, you know that not being successful in every single moment of every single task is perfectly okay. That failing in the elements you are looking to improve is just part of success.

Remember, successful people, leave clues if you are looking to do something and you cannot get over that hurdle for some reason, find somebody you know that is good at that task or that discipline and ask for help.

Every morning without exception and sometimes during the day, focus on reading your goals. Successful goal-getters are successful goal-setters, and some people like to focus on the visualisation of their goals by creating a vision board.

Suppose you want to go to Universal Studios in Orlando and stay at the Hard Rock Hotel, which I recommend and love doing myself. Find some pictures of Universal Studios, maybe of some of the rides you'd like to go on with your family and get some pictures of the Hard Rock hotel and place them on your vision board.

Then add lots of the other things that you'd like to achieve in your life on your vision board.

Place the vision board or pictures of these goals anywhere around the house so that you will frequently see them.

Remember, we have five senses; one of them is sight.

If you keep seeing the Hard Rock Hotel, you will remind yourself that it is one of your goals, and your subconscious mind will accept this as a goal. You will feel excited by this goal, and this will cause you to do the activity required to get you closer to your destination.

So, it would help if you visualised all your goals too.

We do know that statistically, most people in this world have debt. We will cover this off and eradicate debt in the finances section of living your life on purpose. But just for one moment, I would like you to visualise and feel what it would be like for you to have zero debt.

> How would you feel to have no debt?
> How much stress would reduce by having no debt?
> If you had no debt, what improvement to your life could that mean?

What could you spend that extra disposable income on if you had no debt?
How would this no debt lifestyle impact your relationships with your partner, children, family, and friends?
What could this allow you to do?

I would like you to focus on those questions. I don't just mean spend 10 seconds or a minute focusing on those questions. Write down answers to those questions.

If you have a partner, ask them to read your answers and better still, ask them to write down the answers to the questions too.

Many people have been in debt for so long that they don't know what it's like to have no debt.

Surely this must be one of the cruellest of all habits allowing the debt to control your life, and yet it is easy to reduce and then eliminate it.

On a scale of 1 to 10, with ten being I want no debt, would you place yourself on that scale?

A four is not going to cut it if you only put a four out of 10 on the scale that means it is a low priority to you, and you accept the debt as a burden of your life. You will continue to have debt throughout the entirety of your life. The closer to 10 you put, the more committed you will be to doing the things that need to be done.

By answering the questions above, and continually reading the answers, what you are doing is you are shouting out to your subconscious mind that they must accept this.

Most people don't want to think about the amount of debt they have. It doesn't bear thinking about, and because it's too scary and because it stresses them out so much, it's better to not think about it.

But with focus and repeated activity in a specific direction, you can eliminate your debt.

With focus and repeated activity, you can become healthier. With a focus on repeated activity, you can have better relationships with your partner and your family and friends.

With focus and repeated activity, you can improve your physical environment, where you live, the car you drive, the material things you own, and the holidays you go on frequently.

With focus, you can improve your business and or your career.

By focusing on developing habits that will serve you and operating in a world of constant and never-ending improvement, and by engaging in regular and daily personal development, you will improve your attitude.

**Your attitude will determine your altitude.**

You need to engage in the wheel of life, and you need to create the habits that will get you moving in the right direction and understand that time will always win out over time.

In fact, with focus, you can achieve anything that you want to do if you have goals blended with goal directed activity, with a mindset that embraces a constant and never-ending improvement, and you understand the laws of attraction.

## The Law of Attraction

One of the most exciting and exciting studies worldwide is on what is known as the law of attraction.

Many years ago, I remember watching, listening, and reading a book by Rhonda Byrne called the secret.

According to Rhonda, the secret to success in life is that most people just aren't thinking their way to success or the attraction of the things that they want in their life.

If you would like some light-hearted professional development with a fantastic message, buy the video, audio, or book, "The Secret".

In this chapter, we will not be covering the content of "the secret". This message is also taught in the book "Think and Grow Rich" by Napoleon Hill. Napoleon discusses the power of autosuggestion. The fundamental premise is, "What you think about comes about."

This book has repeatedly spoken about the subconscious mind and the jammy doughnut theory. Whether you read "The Secret" or understand the autosuggestion chapter in "Think and Grow Rich" or adopt the jammy doughnut ideology, the same rules apply.

Most of the great minds around the world and successful people that live within it understand the law of attraction.

In the habits section of this book, we mentioned a quote by Aristotle:

**"You are what you repeatedly do. Success is, therefore, merely a habit".**

By setting the goals and creating the habits, and overwriting our belief system, when we live our lives with constant and never-ending improvement and focusing, you can attain anything you want out of your life.

When you live your life on purpose, you create a picture of what you wish your life to be.

You then set a course with small, seemingly insignificant goals that lead you along the path towards acquiring the things you want, or the person you want to become or the relationships, fun and recreation you desire.

In the goals section, we mentioned the importance of writing down goals and visualising them. If you remember, we talked about a trip to Universal Studios, staying at the Hard Rock Hotel, Orlando.

The idea of the picture is that you put yourself in the picture each time you look at it. Your subconscious mind understands that is what you want to do, and if you can write the goals in the present tense, the subconscious mind accepts that to be accurate, and therefore you are participating in the rules in the law of attraction.

**Correct goal setting technique:**

"It is the 31st of March 2021. I am delighted to be at my target weight of 82 kilogrammes. Maintaining a good and healthy eating habit and regular exercise allowed me to achieve this goal".

Even if this is the 1st of January 2021, it is vital for the subconscious mind, for the rules of the laws of attraction to work that we say this phrase in the present tense as though we have already achieved it.

When you spend time looking and adding goals that you and your family would love to achieve, such as living in the house of your dreams; earning more money; travelling anywhere around the world and 10s of thousands of other inspiring things; you will be motivated to create plans to achieve them.

As with anything in life, there are rules, systems, or processes that increases the probability of you achieving what you desire.

Simply writing down a goal or getting a lovely picture of your destination is not going to be sufficient to attain that goal.

Before we move on to the rules associated with the laws of attraction and goal getting you to need to: Work out what you want, work out a plan to get there, work consistently, and never quit.

There are lots of essential parts missing from the sentence above. Such as continuous and never-ending improvement and asking for help.

If you are pursuing a goal and are not moving in the right direction and continually failing at some part of what you are doing, don't keep doing it. Find solutions to stop failure and overcome the solution. Remember, in a growth mindset individual, the word fail is a positive word and is art and part of moving to success. So please learn to embrace failure. **Success is 99% failure.**

The mindset needs to be: "I can overcome any small hurdles along the way to the achievement of a goal".

**Rules to increase the probability of success:**

Rule 1: Identify what you want out of life.

Rule 2: Keep thinking about these things from the moment you wake up to the moment you go to sleep.

Rule 3: Write down your goals in a clearly defined manner and read those goals each day.

Rule 4: Put yourself in the picture as though you have already attained those goals.

Rule 5: Break down the big goals into smaller chunked goals and create a 13-week action plan to grow and stretch towards the goal.

Rule 6: Adopt a daily method of operation harnessing the incredible power of the compound effect.

Rule 7: Focus on the actions, not on the results.

Rule 8: Celebrate every success, no matter how small.

Rule 9: Eliminate any negative thoughts and limiting self-beliefs.

Rule 10 Engage in a regular jam transfusion through personal development.

We've identified some of the rules required to attain success in all the segments in the wheel of life.

The real question is: Are you curious about improving your life, or are you serious?

Are you serious within your mind to make a massive change in your life? You must understand that quitters never win, and winners never quit.

You must understand that you must experience despair and failure on route to success in all the segments of your life. This is not negative by any stretch of the imagination. This is a reality.

When you manage your expectations and when you experience disappointment in your life, you accept this as part of the growing pains, and you move on. Therefore, it is vital to find a success buddy, and it is so important to associate with people that are success orientated.

Suppose you go to the GUPTR or the IBE and share with them that you are having trouble in your pursuit of improving your life. There is a high probability that they will say something along the lines of "why do you want to improve? You are good enough as you are."

If you go to a success-orientated person and share that you are maybe struggling in a part of this improvement process, they will discuss overcoming that hurdle. They will explain that they also have experienced similar failures in the past. That was simply a molehill in the pursuit of climbing the mountain.

From the top of a mountain, you can get outstanding views.

**Rule 1: Identify what you want out of life.**

If you have a partner or a family that includes your children, this part of the process is better served doing it together.

It does not need to be an exercise completed in 10 minutes or one hour. This can be an exercise that is always ongoing. But spend some time and switch off all distractions. If necessary, go into a darkened room with a swinging light and spend time without distraction, thinking about what you want out of life.

Using your powers of focus, focus on what you want to have in your life or the people you want to become. Get rid of those limiting self-beliefs. Just because no one else in your family has achieved such high valued goals or that nobody you know has either. It does not mean that you cannot reach them.

Reading or listening to this book means that you are in the mindset of improvement; let us not limit that so dream big.

I have mentioned these words "You don't know what you don't know".

If you have ever watched a movie or a television programme where you see a beautiful house, let us say in Miami just for a lovely location. The house has a gated driveway. It has lovely gardens leading up to the house. The house is large and modern with big windows. It has a fantastic front porchway with pillars. As you enter the house, you walk on marbled floors along the corridor; there are pictures along each wall and top-quality furniture and fittings on either side of the hallway.

There are doors open to the living room with a large modern smart television with tastefully decorated furnishings. You continue to walk, noticing offshoots to other beautifully decorated rooms.

As you walk into the kitchen, you see a modern kitchen with all the modern appliances. You see the central breakfast bar, and all the white goods are clearly of top quality. There are ample workspace and an excellent selection of wine sitting in a wine-rack.

On the breakfast bar is a large bowl of fruit, in the fridge freezer, one of the doors is glass partitioned, you can see the fridge contains good healthy coloured looking foods.

You move through the kitchen into a large dining room, with a large dining room table all set for eight people. There are other pieces of furniture of modern taste, which clearly show quality.

Just off from the kitchen and the dining room, there is an open door to a large Conservatory; within the conservatory are comfortable looking tables and chairs, all tastefully decorated. They look so relaxing.

You open the conservatory doors to a large back garden with a heated outdoor swimming pool, and the groomed gardens perfectly manicured roll down to the water's edge here there is a mooring and a speed boat tied up and ready to use.

Everything is fitted with smart technology. You don't even need to pull the curtains or blinds simply talk to a device. If you are slightly cold, you don't get up and switch the heating on or change the thermostat smart technology takes care of everything. The floors all have under heating, and upstairs all the bedrooms have nothing but the best bedding, mattresses, and furnishings.

With this large five-bedroom detached property costing over 3,000,000 spondoolies, you are living here debt-free with a gardener, a cleaner and someone that prepares your food.

That right as you drove your bright red Ford Mustang up the driveway to your house, you realised that gone are the days when you used to live in a 2-bedroom semidetached house struggling to pay for your bills. This is not crazy thinking, ladies, and gentlemen; it doesn't matter where you are right now. It is where you want to get to that is essential.

Suppose you would love to own a Ford Mustang motor car. Within the laws of attraction, it is vital that you not only write down that you'd like to own a bright red Ford Mustang. You might also want to create a vision board with a picture of that beautiful car. If you can go to a Ford Mustang dealership and ask to test drive that car.

You might very well test drive that car and realise that car is not for you, and you'd rather have an Audi R8 in a beautiful blue colour anyway. Test drive the Audi R8. If it fits with what you are looking for, write down that as a goal.

I am using the house or the car as examples. As a golfer, you may want to buy a new set of top of the range golf clubs and equipment and golfing clothing.

You may not desire any of these material things, which is also acceptable.

Some people who proclaim that they do not want to own such material things. Generally, these are people where that jam in the doughnut has been so impacted, and so dense, that they believe it to be true that they cannot own such wealthy items.

They don't want to have material things because they believe there is no chance on this earth that they will ever get them. It is easier to tell yourself that you don't want something than a stretch to achieve it.

The jam in the doughnut has a lot to answer, and it is the key reason people don't achieve success in their lives. But not you! You live your life on purpose, and you will go and get those goals no matter what. We often hear people say that they are not motivated by money. I can fully understand these statements.

That is an excellent phrase by Zig Ziglar:

**"Money isn't that important; it just ranks right up there with oxygen".**

It does not matter what you do in this world. If you want to buy some vegetables or buy a mansion or anything in between, you need to have money.

Being motivated by money suits others, and if you are motivated by money, one of your goals could be:

"It is the 31st of December 2021, and I am delighted to have 100,000 spondoolies of clear funds in my bank account. To achieve this, I focused on more income-generating tasks and discarded anything that might distract me from my goal".

With the law of attraction, if you said that statement every day and did nothing, you will not achieve your goal. Suppose you wrote down the goal and focused on a system for attaining that money and focused on action and repetition in those income-generating tasks that are identified and needed.

There is a high probability that you can earn that extra money in that case.

If you have never earned more than 40,000 spondoolies, the jam in your doughnut is likely to restrict your belief system and, therefore, will stop you from achieving that goal. If you have lived for 45 years and never earned that amount of money, how on earth can you be expected to do so within one year?

It is to do with limiting self-beliefs and the understanding that other people find earning 100,000 spondoolies a daily routine for them. It is just about knowing that you can get your goals by engaging in goal-directed activity if you employ a system.

You are not motivated by money, and money is not a motivator for many people. Let us say that your goal is to own a 3-

bedroom detached house in a lovely hamlet in the county of Yorkshire.

You would like to buy this house without a mortgage, and the house will cost you 450,000 spondoolies.

You understand the laws of assets and liabilities, and you make an intelligent decision that whilst you would like to buy the house outright without a mortgage, it would take longer than you would like to do so. Instead, you set yourself a target of generating an extra 100,000 spondoolies by the 31st of December 2021. You will then use this 100,000 spondoolies as a deposit to secure the house of your dreams.

This house becomes an asset because the property prices will continue to rise, and you have a sizable deposit. Having acquired the home, you have satisfied your goal. You then create a new plan that you would like to own this house outright.

You decide that you are enjoying your lifestyle and that the extra 100,000 spondoolies can be spread over four years, so you set the goal to own the house outright in four years.

You continue with your income-generating tasks, but you have more disposable income. Following the principles in the wheel of life, you do not commit yourself entirely to that the generating of money because that would upset the wheel balance.

Instead, you focus on other elements of your life to ensure that your wheel is always in balance. The goals don't need to be materialistic, and the plans do not need to be money orientated. The goal could be something health related.

More people, despite having access to millions of pieces of information on health and fitness worldwide, the rates of obesity are increasing and with that, so too are people with diabetes.

After a fantastic Christmas period, you've drunk too much wine and beer and overeaten food. You've put on some extra kilograms, and you look in the mirror and see that you are slightly chunkier than usual.

You've heard about people running from the couch to the 5K, and you see that this would be an excellent way for you to lose that extra weight. You set your goal of running from the couch to 5K within those 13 weeks. And a target weight of 82 kilogrammes.

“It is the 31st of March 2021, and I'm delighted to have completed my first 5 kilometres run without walking and achieved my target weight of 82 kilogrammes”.

This is a great goal that can be scaled up or scaled down, however you want.

What will happen is that when you achieve your goal, no matter how small because you have set and you have completed a plan, you will be more open-minded to set bigger goals that stretch you even further.

Whatever it is you want to achieve, own it, and by acknowledging it and setting out with that desire to achieve the goal, you will satisfy the number one rule and the law of attraction.

**Rule 2: Keep thinking about these things from the moment you wake up to the moment you go to sleep.**

**Rule 3: Write down your goals in a clearly defined manner and read those goals each day.**

You set a series of goals. The next step is to keep thinking about those goals from the moment you wake up until you go to sleep. Within your purposeful morning routine, one of the habits you want to adopt and implement and become art and part of your every day is to read your goals.

Remember you are reading those goals in the present tense as though it has already happened, and you do this every morning. Serious goal-getters are people who don't just read these goals each morning. They say them aloud in the morning, they say them aloud during the day, and the last thing they do before they go to sleep is, they say them aloud again.

If you have got some thick and sticky jam, we've got to do some serious work to get that jam to weaken so we can transfuse it more easily.

Make sure that you are always focusing on positivity. Ensuring that you know where you are going, the law of attraction will work for you.

On that point and the laws of association, you tell one of your friends that you will earn an extra 100,000 spondoolies within the next year. Your friend immediately bursts out laughing and ridicules you. That can be hurtful, and it can be damaging; if you listen to people like this, you may never achieve those goals.

If you do receive any negativity and want to achieve those goals, the first thing you need to do is, once you've received the negativity, go away somewhere quiet and read through your plans and speak them aloud.

We don't want that dream stealing mind monster growing bigger, do we? Remember, whether we feed the mind monster or the mind Angel the most, the one that gets the most airtime will win out.

I don't associate with people anymore that are negative; I found in life that grumpy people hang out with grumpy people. Successful people generally hang out with other successful people.

I made the decision and the type of people that I wanted to associate with.

**Rule 4: Put yourself in the picture as though you have already attained those goals.**

When you put yourself in the picture of your goals, you think that you have already achieved them, the law of attraction starts to gain momentum.

You want to own that lovely house in a hamlet in Yorkshire. You become more specific with that goal, and you want to live in a village called Askham Richard. You've been through the village many times. You love the large weeping Willow tree that leans over to the pond on the village green, and there is one pub and 60 homes. You are literally on the edge of the City of York and within beautiful countryside. There's next to no traffic, and the pace of life suits you just fine.

Your house is detached and overlooks a farmer's field. You have a lovely sized garden, not too big that you can't manage but big enough to have large gatherings at barbecues.

Put yourself in the picture of whatever goal you want to achieve. Let me paint you a picture, and of course, you can edit this however you like.

I'm driving down into Askham Richard's village; I passed through the 30 miles an hour sign. I see some lovely little cottages on either side of the road, as I drive towards my house on the left-hand side is a large village green, I can see the weeping Willow tree leaning over to the village pond that has around 20 ducks and geese swimming in the water to my right is the village pub.

Outside I can see some patrons sitting on the benches enjoying a nice beer glass of wine or whatever their drink of choice is. It's spring, and the cherry blossom trees that line the side of the road are in full bloom. I continued snaking left and then right down towards my house's driveway.

I turn left into the driveway that I share with two other large four-bedroom detached houses. I pull up to my house, open the door and met with the tail wagging chocolate Labrador the beautiful cookie. Today we have planned a barbecue with twenty of our friends and family members.

My wife is preparing the fruit salads and all the other nice little fancy things she enjoys concocting. The meat is marinated, and we are ready to go. The beer, the wine, the prosecco and of course, the soft drinks for those who may be driving are all chilled and ready to be drunk.

I go into the back garden. The grass is cut freshly and smells fantastic. The hedges have been trimmed, and the trees are looking beautiful. The charbroil barbecues are ready to be fired up, the sun is shining, and there isn't a cloud in the sky.

The first of the guests arrive, moving straight through the house into the garden and congregating and chatting, and there's a buzz of enjoyment and excitement as they drink sitting enjoying the rays of the sun.

The food is served, and people are having a fantastic time. Everybody is enjoying this day. It's a beautiful day, and it's a day that's repeated many times over the summer months in the house of your dreams with the people that you love and like the most. This made all the hard work worth it.

Back to reality.

Don't just think of a goal you want to get without delving deeper into why you want that goal.

Own the goal as yours, feel it as though you had already achieved it and think about the emotional attachment of achieving that goal. How good would you feel?

You have one chance to live this life, and you and only you have the choice to make it your way. You live your life on your terms, and if they are exciting, put in the graft and the effort to make it worthwhile living.

Nothing will come easy. You must understand that just thinking about your goals and setting your goals and putting your dreams into your mind as though you've already achieved them will not bring them to life or reality. Not unless you engage in activity directed towards them.

**"If you fail to plan, you plan to fail."**

This is not just a business saying. This is a whole of life saying.

When it comes to the wonders of the world, and this world is a stunning place, how many places around the world would you like to visit if money were no object?

I could write down pages upon pages of places that I want to go to; I did, and the crazy thing is it happens long after you set the goal. Sometimes, even when you forgot about it because it wasn't a high priority at the time.

I remember sitting and watching some soccer with a good friend of mine called Neil. On another television was a programme about some celebrities from the UK walking up

Kilimanjaro. I mentioned to Neil that I'd always wanted to climb Kilimanjaro, and he replied, so did he.

That was the end of that conversation; we continued to chat and watch the soccer.

A few days later, Neil telephoned me, and these were his very words. "I have someone next to me that needs your credit card details".

I asked, "What on earth for?" he said. “I'm just booking us to climb Kilimanjaro”. He wasn't joking, and he knows what I am like, so I gave my credit card details to the travel agent, and we'd booked to go and climb Kilimanjaro.

If it had not been for Neil, would I have ever climbed Kilimanjaro, maybe yes or maybe no? But I did want to climb Kilimanjaro, and I could afford both the money and the time, so we went and conquered that mountain. At the top of the mountain, there is a picture of myself and Neil, and I am crying.

The tears were rolling down my cheek because I had just achieved something quite extraordinary.

Neil was emotional too, but he didn't admit it. We ran down that mountain and enjoyed a curry and a few beers. This is a memory that will never leave my mind. I achieved a goal and thoroughly enjoyed it.

When you associate with success-minded people, it is not uncommon to talk about and share your goals. On one occasion, I was having a chat with a friend called Mark. He pulled out his goal-getting book—an extensive list of things he wanted to do. I passed through the goals and saw many were the same as mine, others were different because he has different interests.

Both Mark and I are keen sports enthusiasts and we both like rugby. He loves rugby. I like it.

He had one of his goals: to tour Australia and follow the British Lions. I saw that goal and told him how fantastic it was and whether there was room for one more to go with him.

It was 2012, and the tour was planned for 2013. He replied instantly, "Of course; the more, the merrier".

I asked who else was coming, and he mentioned that many people from his rugby team were coming along. Great, this is going to be brilliant. The tour is generally seven weeks visiting major cities around Australia.

I was more interested in Australia than rugby, it always had been my goal to go to Australia, so this was an excellent way to achieve that goal. It turns out that whilst lots of people had the idea of going to Australia to follow the British Lions only Mark, John, (another friend of ours) and myself has sufficient passion for investing the time and the money to go and enjoy that tour.

It was a truly remarkable period landing in Perth and going to Brisbane and then from Brisbane to Cairns to Darwin to Alice Springs visiting Ayres Rock, going back to Brisbane then to Sydney down to Canberra where I left and returned to the UK.

Sit down with your partner and your family and write down some exciting goals. Do not die with your dreams inside of you.

Understand in this world of abundance, you really can do, get, and achieve anything, and I mean anything you want in your life.

**Rule 5: Break down the big goals into smaller chunked goals and create a 13-week action plan to grow and stretch towards the goal.**

Paul to Gary

"Gary, would you like to run a marathon"?

Gary: "Yes, I would"!

Paul "Good, I'm doing one next week. See you then".

Gary: "But I've never done a marathon before."

Paul, "It's okay. You just run a little bit and keep running, putting one leg in front of the other. How hard can it be"?

Gary: "Have you ever done a marathon, Paul"?

Paul: "No, I haven't even run 5 kilometres before"!

Gary: "Maybe we should do that first"?

Paul: "Nah, I'm going all-in."

Gary "Good luck. I will build up and start with a 5KM".

Paul makes his attempt and fails, vowing never to run again. Gary has chunked down his big goal of running a marathon into 4 x 13-week massive action plans.

Gary enjoys his personal growth and starts to enjoy running. In truth, he begins to increase his distances and can run the 26.2 miles by the end of the 13 Massive Action Plan period.

That was just a light-hearted scenario of something that happens all the time in this world. People set goals that are not achievable, they are unrealistic, and the time frame is just too short. When you live in this world, embracing the laws of attraction, you can set the goal of running a marathon.

But if you have never run 5 kilometres before, there's an extremely high chance you will fail in your attempt at this goal and likely never attempt to do it again.

In the goal setting, we mentioned earlier of earning an extra 100,000 spondoolies within one year, in your first 13-week massive action plans, your target is not a quarter of 100,000 spondoolies. Your first goal would be something more realistic that motivates you to increase your activity and follow the system you have employed.

For example, your big goal is to earn an extra 100,000 spondoolies by the end of the year; you might set a more achievable target of 10,000 spondoolies by the end of your first 13-week massive action plan. During the second 13-week massive action plan, you may raise your goal to let us say, an extra 20,000 spondoolies.

Logically, therefore, in your third 13-week massive action plan. You might set the target to be an additional 30,000 spondoolies. Now that you have gained momentum and have refined your systems, and become increasingly efficient, effective, and confident, you can set the next target to get you over the line.

You play with these figures how you want to play with them. If you're going to create an extra 10,000 spondoolies in a year, chunk it down so that you earn an additional 1000 spondoolies in the first 13-week massive action plan. And then raise the figure during each period.

In this instant gratification world, people like Paul want to get results now. In the world of the law of attraction, this does not happen this way.

Whilst I thoroughly enjoyed watching, listening, and reading the secret by Rhonda Byrne, I wish in that same material they put an element that highlighted the need for repeated activity over a period utilising a proven success system.

**Rule 6: Adopt a daily method of operation harnessing the incredible power of the compound effect.**

Rule 6 is mighty, indeed, and the problem with rule #6 is that it is easy not to do. This is where we require discipline, and we need persistence. This is where why power comes to the fore. If you have set those goals and are meaningful for you and desire to attain those goals, you will have a greater “why power”.

With greater WHY power, you will be more focused on creating a daily method of operation that suits you, your family life, and your work life.

It is of paramount importance that you do set a daily method of operation.

Sometimes you don't even feel as though you are moving forward, and yet you are moving forward. If you do something once, there will be no real gain, do it twice or three times once again, There's no real visible gain. You aren't even near forming a habit yet.

Around days 21 to days 28 of perseverance and persistence through the employment of this daily method of operation, you will start to feel the momentum.

There's always ups and downs throughout this, but those who continue to persevere eventually reach a point, and that point differs for everyone, but the fact is when they feel, and they sense that they are starting to win.

Once you start to experience that winning feeling and the dopamine circulates through your body. You have been continuously congratulating yourself for your daily activity, you begin to want more of it.

As you start to feel momentum towards your chosen goals, what you find is that some of the distractions that appeared vital to you previously (but were inconsequential) life fade away, and free up more time for you in the pursuit of your goals.

In later chapters of this book or audio, we will share different systems for different segments in the wheel of life. These are just templates to give your ideas; let us call them proforma templates. You can adapt or edit as you wish. It is your plan. It is your life, and you build your goals and live your life on your terms.

**Rule 7: Focus on the actions not on the results.**

In this modern world that we live in, we have mentioned that this instant gratification mindset. That means if you set yourself a target and you do not instantly hit that target, if you're focusing solely on the target, you could become despondent and then start to withdraw from the required activities.

When you set these goals, a top tip is to make sure they are smart. If you have set smart targets, you are under no illusion how long it will take for you to attain those goals.

A psychological trick is to focus on the actions rather than the results.

The definition of insanity is doing the same thing day in day out, week in week out, month in month out, year in year out, and expecting a different result.

It is easy to break back into the habits that served us during the last months and years of our lives. By engaging in this daily method of operation and focusing on the smallest of tasks repeated over the 13-week massive action plan period, we can start to move forward in direction of the goal that has been set.

We have mentioned before that you will set yourself some things to do daily, and for the first week, you will probably experience no benefit. At this point, you could be weak and maybe stop engaging in daily activity. We have also mentioned that somewhere between days 21 and 28 is where you get maximum mental feedback.

Maximum mental feedback is where you are now doing these tasks subconsciously. They have become a habit. You have tracked this activity from day one, and you can see the documented results; therefore, you become increasingly satisfied with your actions.

Maximum mental feedback is where your conscious brain starts to get excited because you can see whatever you are doing is working.

You have set yourself the target of achieving your ideal weight of 82 kilogrammes. At the same time, you decided to start your couch to a five-kilometre run. Each day you are ticking your activity sheet to confirm that you have participated in your activity.

You have also ticked off that you have eaten a healthy and balanced breakfast, lunch, and evening meal. You have also ticked off that you have weighed yourself daily.

During the first seven days of these tracking metrics, there is a good chance you will move further away from your intended target weight of 82 kilogrammes. It is perfectly normal and part of the body's physiology, reacting to increase exercise. As you start to move from day 7 to day 21, you will begin to notice that the combination of the increased activity and the fact that you are eating healthier than your weight will start to mirror what you expect.

Maximum mental feedback is when you look at these metrics, and you see that you are heading towards your target weight, and you are now jogging more than you are walking. One of the metrics to record during your couch to 5 kilometres is how long it took you to do your first one kilometre.

Over the 13-week massive action plan, you may only do one kilometre for the first two weeks, for example. You measure how long it takes to do each of those kilometre distances, and you'll notice that your body is responding to the increased activity. Then you move up to two kilometres, to 3 kilometres, to 4 kilometres and then to your final goal of five kilometres.

You cannot measure what you do not track. Where applicable, do not just focus on doing the daily activity, but always focus on recording the action.

The results will come later down the process.

**Rule 8: Celebrate every success, no matter how small.**

We mentioned that the fixed mindset people love to receive recognition in the mindset chapter. People within the growth mindset don't necessarily seek recognition, but they enjoy it all the same.

I've met so many people who say that they don't like recognition and feel uncomfortable receiving it. I wonder where the jam was infused that meant for the rest of their lives; they did not want credit.

Strange. If you were to think deeply enough about our subconscious mind and how we got so much of our internal operating system created for us without choice, we would probably crack up.

But when you live your life on purpose and stretching yourself in so many ways, please, I employ you to celebrate every little success.

It may not seem like much to put on your running shoes and go out for a walk for one kilometre. But I have seen so many people start by walking a kilometre and then moving upwards onward and beyond, not just being a marathon runner but also being an ultra-runner.

The seeds of success must start somewhere.

If you continue to water those seeds that are in good soil and with the temperature and the environment, it is fair to say that even a little oak seed can grow to a big oak tree!

You complete a task, say well done to yourself. You continuously say well done to yourself for every assignment that you complete.

Eventually, over time and probably sometime after day 21, you will start to receive external validation from those close to you who have noticed a difference in the way you live your life.

They may say to you how positive you look or how healthy you look, or just how happy you are.

When you receive an unsolicited recognition comment, it is like getting 100 of your own. It is such a brilliant feeling when someone sincerely says something positive to you. The toughest of the 13-week massive action plans will be the first. It will take some time, and you will have some false starts. You must focus on the activity and not on the results. You will need to be disciplined and dedicated to completing that activity repeatedly.

In advance, may I say a fantastic well done to you for every single little task or activity that you do in pursuit of creating a better life for you and your family.

**Rule 9: Eliminate any negative thoughts and limiting self-beliefs.**

Negativity surrounds us; negative people are everywhere. When you switch on the income reducing box or follow some social media, something unfavourable is happening. Someone is being trolled somewhere, someone is being bullied, and someone is being ridiculed.

It is such a beautiful world. It's just a shame that there are negative people.

And because we have all been surrounded by negative people and because the subconscious mind only can accept sadly, we all have the disposition to fall into a negative mindset from time to time.

Each of us will dip into the valley of despair and negativity. The winners are the ones that fall in, and as quickly as they fall in, they give themselves a mental electric shock and jump themselves straight back out.

It is practically impossible to eliminate negative thoughts. It is entirely possible to create a trigger in your mind that bounces you back from negative land to positive land sooner rather than later.

In pursuit of this journey and living your life on purpose, living in this world of continuous and never-ending improvement, if we are prepared for the fact that not everything will go as we planned that is a good start. We know that there will be ups, and there will be downs and this is perfectly normal in the pursuit of success.

If you find yourself thinking negative thoughts about yourself or your ability to successfully conquer any of the targets or goals you have set, your mind monster is starting to win.

We want to sap the life out of our mind monsters, and every time we hear it chirping away in the background, we need to shut it up instantly.

To prevent the mind monster from rearing its ugly head, we can do things each morning and during the day that stops it from even getting a chance.

The first thing that we can do each morning as part of our purposeful morning is to go through our goals and be emotionally attached. Read them as though you have already achieved them.

You can go through your afformations, starting with gratitude.

Did you know that desire is the starting point of all riches?

During the day, if you fall into the valley of despair and negativity, simply reminding yourself of the goals and reminding yourself what you are grateful for, it is likely that you will dip out as quickly as you dipped in.

The 13-week massive action plan is hard to do at the start because we haven't yet created a habit for all these changes we are making.

Plus, the mind monster will keep chirping in and will attempt to derail you on such a life-changing expedition.

If you manage your expectations and know that negativity will come along and test you, you can be ready to put that negativity back to where it belongs, and that is not in your mind. The subconscious mind is so powerful that if you allow it to do what it wants to do unchecked, a negative vortex can spiral so quickly out of control it can damage our health, both physically and mentally. We must understand this subconscious mind and engage in the jam transfusion with positive things.

There are millions of people around the world whose subconscious mind goes into overdrive worried about health concerns. There is a clinical and medical term that is called self-induced illness.

People can now go online, enter their perceived symptoms, and read so many false information pieces. These untruths, which are not medically sound, may fit the searcher's symptoms.

They then start to believe that they are suffering from this awful disease and continuously think about it. Their lives will end with this terminal disease, and the vibrations within their subconscious mind are running their body down.

Ask any doctor!

Their patients go into their surgeries and inform them what they think their illnesses are. There is nothing wrong with searching on the Internet if you search on sound websites.

What then happens is that their minds are so consumed about this illness or a variety of diseases they may have, the subconscious attracts illness to the body.

Disease is when your body is not at ease. You may not attract the condition you have researched on the Internet, but because you worry so much, your immune system breaks down and opens itself up for attack. It is the power of autosuggestion!

Some people continuously worry about illness. It is perfectly normal, and it would be inhuman to stop that negative thought process. Instead of looking for the positives in every dire situation, they focus on the negatives and the worst-case scenarios.

The subconscious mind is now always focusing on these worst-case scenarios and how the mind works; it is thinking about these things all day, every day.

The law of attraction does not just work for the things we want out of life; the law of attraction works just like the mind monster and the mind angel.

The subconscious mind is so powerful that people, who have been involved in horrific accidents and told that it is impossible for them to walk again, defy the doctors. Through the power of autosuggestion these people claim that they used their mental strength to repair their bodies.

Using the power of the compound effect, for every minute of every day they transmuted thoughts to damaged areas of their bodies. Months and even years later they walk again.

Some people diagnosed with cancers report the same strategy. They use their mind power to defeat the cancer by FOCUS and DETERMINATION.

Some people rarely get ill, and scientists can prove, that having a good positive and carefree attitude can keep the body at ease.

It is true that a human functioning at a higher level will have a stronger immune system. They will have more protection.

Of course, the most amazing human, will still fall foul to a breath of nerve agent or other malicious elements. But in general, their mindset will help their bodies and protect them from colds, flus, and the like. **Whatever you think about the most and give the most airtime wins.**

Therefore, it is vital to dip out negative thought as quickly as possible.

Another fantastic way to prevent moving into the valley of despair is to start to listen to or read personal development every single day. Even if you read for just 15 to 30 minutes every day, that will make a massive difference.

Another excellent way to prevent entering the valley of despair is to work with your partner, or a success buddy, and to talk to each other each day to say hello and how are you.

Every conversation you have must have a set of rules and guides, and this is that you must always talk positively and never dwell on negativity. Two people who agree on something negative can be so destructive. Remember, this is called emotional contagion.

If you feel a little bit negative, you've read your goals, and you've gone through your power of gratitude, you've spoken to your success buddy, and you still just aren't getting to that happy place, do something that will distract your active mind.

I like to put on some happy music, something like “swing when you are winning” by Robbie Williams or “Mr Blue Sky” by ELO.

Comically, if you have watched Guardians of the Galaxy, one of the Marvel adventure films you saw Groot, one of the characters dancing to Mr blue sky, you can't help but smile.

You could go for that walk admire the countryside, and the sound of it, the smell of it, does anything to distract yourself and when you are in this distraction zone start to think about the good things that you have in your life. You might not dip out quickly, but eventually, you'll come round, and you'll realise that life isn't that bad.

Have a "go to" person that you can celebrate your successes with and who you can rely on to be that extra hook to drag you out of the valley of despair. Find a success buddy.

As you go through your journey, living your life on purpose, when you start to tick off the goals that you set, as you walk over all those pennies to get to the spondoolies, you will begin to build up a wall around these mind monsters until eventually they are caged in like Fort Knox.

You can make the change and be the winner you want to become. There is no doubt ask any winner if they ever hit the valley of despair or negativity.

They did, and they understood that this baseline was a place they didn't like to be in, and as quickly as they could, they want to warp speed themselves out. The same rules in this universe apply to you, and you are no exception.

If millions of other people around this world can change their lives, so can you.

**Rule 10: Engage in a regular jam transfusion through personal development.**

Listen to any successful person around the world carefully, and you will hear that they say similar words to other successful people. They never stop learning.

There is a great film called "Sliding doors". Each of us has thousands of sliding door moments during our years. We are always making decisions. Shall I go this way, or shall I go that way?

The subconscious mind and the way we are wired would always automatically go to the path of least resistance. When you engage in your 13-week massive action plan, there are going to be times when you are going to feel as though you really cannot be bothered. It will be so much easier to switch on the income reducing box and eat some crisps and some cookies, than putting your shoes on to go for that walk and jog.

Every moment of the day, your subconscious mind is working filtering things, so that you don't need to worry about them, and that is super good if your subconscious mind has had a good and regular jam transfusion.

To do this, engaging in the reading or listening or a combination thereof of personal/professional development is advised. Not just once a week but every single day. With Bluetooth technology and the ability to download things onto our smartphones and all this connectivity surrounding us, listen to some personal development when you get into your car.

If you are on public transport, put your earphones in and listen to professional development.

One of my favourite authors was Clive Cussler. I love the action films where the hero saves the day and where the world is protected. I could honestly say I read every one of Clive Cussler's books in my early years.

Give me a choice now to read a Clive Cussler book or to read a brand-new personal development book written by a well-respected author, I would choose the latter 100 times out of 100 times.

Indeed, I haven't read a fiction novel for over double-digit years. I hadn't even thought about that until I wrote this book. You see, I just got used to reading or listening to personal development. It wasn't a conscious decision. It just became a habit, but whenever I wanted to buy something to read or listen to, I would automatically be drawn to the personal development section.

My subconscious mind is taking it easy, not doing too much work and just basically saying, "Gary, this is the genre that you like let me point you in this direction".

And without even fighting against it, I move and make my decision based entirely on the jam transfusion values accumulated over double-digit years.

Engaging in personal development, though, has a far deeper purpose. I'm not sorry to say this, but you don't know everything. You know far from everything, and a large proportion of what you do know might not even be correct.

Okay, so that was a bit direct, but the fact is it's true, and I'm not here to massage your ego or your feelings. Living your life on purpose is a personal development book or audio designed to transform your life.

As you look through the vast libraries of excellent material and start to listen or read these daily, you will soon understand it is a brilliant world to be in, when you are open-minded.

Every minute of every day focuses on ensuring that nothing, but positivity, moves into your subconscious mind. Overwrite any negative thoughts you have with positive and forward-moving goals.

You are what you always think about! Ensure that you start putting yourself in the picture as though you are already successful in any of the areas you choose to do so.

The law of attraction does not switch off during the day; it works 24 hours a day. Even as you sleep and dream, the subconscious mind is still working for you or against you.

# Family and Friends

Your children, loving partner, mum, dad, brothers, and sisters should be the most important people in your lives.

Even though they are the most important people in our lives due to our busy lifestyles, many people are spending less time having a nice meal with their family or communicating with them at all.

Your mum and your dad are the people who brought you into this world; they looked after you and nurtured you. The chances are they gave you everything they could. Even at the time of their passing, they will have set a goal themselves, written or just a combined thought between the two of them, that they would leave you some form of legacy.

If you are a parent yourself, you will also be thinking along these lines. It is the way we have been programmed. It is a nice element of jam within our doughnuts and one that I certainly would not recommend you remove.

Our brothers and sisters would have supported us in some way during our growth phase, even if it were the odd beating, whilst having that play fight or a game of monopoly, where they always cheated.

These people are so important in our lives and many of us fail to appreciate it until they're gone from this planet. One of the main regrets of the dying is that they did not spend enough time with their loved ones.

That's right; there are books about the regrets of the dying.

In each of these books, people near the end of their lives have been interviewed and asked quite simply what regrets you have in your life.

**Making more money never enters any of those regrets.**

Here are some of the regrets of the dying, in no particular order:

Regret 1: I worked too much and never gave my friends and family enough time.

Regret 2: I wish I had lived my life the way I wanted to, not the way I thought people expected me to.

Regret 3: I wish I had taken better care of myself.

Regret 4: I wish I hadn't taken time for granted and lived my life to the fullest every day.

Regret 5: I wish I had taken more risks in my life instead of staying in my safe bubble.

Regret 6: I wish I had taken more responsibility in my life rather than blaming others.

Regret 7: I didn't share or express my true feelings to those I loved or liked most in my life.

Making money was never listed as one of the dying regrets. Yet, they spend their entire lives chasing higher lucrative incomes. Many people later state they should have been focusing on their life and work balance.

Living your life on purpose is entirely that. To help and coach people to live their lives on purpose, focusing on that life-work balance.

In the organisation section of this book or audio, we mentioned the importance of using the LYLOP Journal. Sad as it may seem, mastering the mundane is a critical element in your success in living your life on purpose.

Set aside time in your diary for your family and your friends. Pre-plan a month, two months and even three months in advance of dates and times that you'd like to share the good times with your friends and family.

By planning these enjoyable occasions, you can ensure that you retain and restore balance within your family and friendship circles, whilst also ensuring that any of your income-generating tasks can also be diarised accordingly.

Ensure that you always make time for your friends and family, and by placing these in the forefront of your monthly, quarterly, and yearly diaries, you will never let them down.

Do not let the sands of time slip by because you never get that time back again. You just don't know what is around the corner.

It may be a generational thing, but I Always recall seeing my mum have a calendar pinned to a corkboard in the kitchen and on the calendar; she always pencilled in the birthdays of every single family member or friend that she had.

Therefore, she would always ensure that these valuable people of her inner circle received at a birthday card.

Many people have now stopped the habit of sending Christmas cards to their loved ones. When you live your life on purpose and wish to ensure that your wheel of life is imbalanced, why not ensure that you always send out birthday cards and Christmas cards?

There is a common expression, worded differently but means the same; if you give, you get back, it works. It is called "GiveBackWorks". Others call this "What goes around comes around".

Under the guise of blame or responsibility, we have all agreed that we would accept 100% responsibility for everything going right or wrong in our lives whilst participating in this programme.

We have decided that we will engage in constant and never-ending improvement in the future, and that assuming responsibility is empowering.

When it comes to a relationship, a marriage, or something similar, we assume 100% responsibility for our part in the relationship.

Ordinarily, if you ask anybody what level of responsibility a couple should take within that relationship, many immediately respond with 50 - 50 per cent. **Each partner needs to assume 100% responsibility and no less.**

Spending time with, speaking with, and communicating with via birthday cards and Christmas cards is a great way to improve mental health.

Just the actions of sending a text message or a joke that you've received from somebody else and forwarding that on to people within your inner circle is a start. Building the relationship and making sure it is strong and loyal is your responsibility.

You will find that if you take 100% responsibility for your part in any relationship with family members or friends and give unequivocally expecting nothing in return over time, you will start receiving much more.

You took the initiative, and you took the responsibility to get the ball rolling wherever you can to arrange that valuable time with your loved ones. Wherever you can, be the first person to communicate or send something, you will then remind these people how helpful you are to them and will reciprocate.

We mentioned how your subconscious mind automates everything we do within the habits section. It does this to preserve energy because irrelevant of the task; if you consciously think about it, the same amount of mental energy is used. By automating these tasks, your subconscious mind saves so much energy.

You are conducting so many thought processes every minute of every single part of your day, that it is just incomprehensible for you to be conscious of all that is going on around you. Relationships that break down, therefore, are not generally caused on purpose.

As our lives continue to get busier, we lose focus on what matters. Our days become a series of automated routines. If the relationship is not consciously prioritised, slowly but surely, the passion and enjoyment fizzle out.

Because we have not consciously thought about our friends and our family, if we get too busy, a week, a month, a year may pass by without even communicating with them.

We did not intend this. Just time seems to accelerate through life.

It is incorrect when people say the older you get, the quicker time passes. The scientific reason why it seems that time gets quicker, the older you get is simply because your subconscious mind has automated more of those normal daily functions, so you don't even think about it. You are not using as much energy, so you are not consciously focusing on these things.

Therefore, by diarising events with your friends and family and putting them to the forefront of your mind, your subconscious will not do that dastardly trick of forgetting them.

When we employ the rules of association, we like to understand the importance of associating with at least five people who are success orientated.

Over time some of your friends that are negative may self-select themselves out of your inner circle. They are still your friends but maybe friends you could spend an hour with every so often. However, other friends that are more positive you could spend a day, a week or even longer together.

Whilst you can choose your friends, you cannot choose your family. Some of us may have negative family members, family members with a fixed mindset, and people we don't want to associate with too much.

That is entirely understandable. But when it comes to your mum, your dad, your brothers, or sisters, or worse still, your children, it is vital to understand these are the fabric of our lives and means so much to us.

We can still do our duties as the responsible loved ones, and we can still diarise times to spend with these family members, but of course, we don't need the time that we spend with them to be uncomfortable for anyone. It may be an hour or two a week; it may be an hour or two a month having a bite to eat some civil family conversation. But never regret losing that time.

This book's attitude chapter discusses different personality traits for people within our world. The fortunate thing is that even though over 8 billion people are on this planet, they can generally be separated into four main personality traits.

You will fall into one of these personality traits where you will have a primary attribute blended with some of the other characteristics.

Once you understand that we all have different personality traits, you can be more forgiving to those whose personalities do not match yours.

For example, I have people within my inner circle who are highly analytical. On the flip side, being analytical is not one of my key traits previously; I would have been quite impatient with this personality group.

| Direct | Indirect |
| --- | --- |
| Competitive | Caring |
| Demanding | Sharing |
| Determined | Encouraging |
| Strong willed | Patient |
| **Analytical** | **Expressive** |
| Logical | Social |
| Cautious | Dynamic |
| Precise | Enthusiastic |
| Deliberate | Persuasive |

Now that I understand the different personality traits, I can compose myself more, and before I get impatient, I recite “5, 4, 3, 2, 1”. I pause and think, and then realise it is their mindset and personality trait.

# 5 - 4 - 3 - 2 - 1

In effect, I have bounced from the circle of concern into the circle of influence and recognise that I cannot influence their personality trait, so it no longer concerns me. I could, of course, direct them to this book, "living your life on purpose," where they could learn to understand my personality traits.

Just because one of my friends or family is analytical does not make them worse or better than myself; we are different human beings, making this world such a fantastic place. Imagine how dull it would be if we were all the same.

Besides, we need the analytical people in this world; otherwise, society would be a complete and utter mess.

To improve relationships, we take 100% responsibility, and we acknowledge that each of our contacts has different personalities. We understand that we are not perfect, far from it, and we take the time and the patience to ensure that our relationships improve rather than become destructive.

If you are reading this book as a parent and now understand that you play an essential part in your child's subconscious mind's early stages, you can now use this knowledge to your advantage. You can ensure that your children grow up with greater harmony within the family household.

Suppose you can encourage your children to go through some of these segments within the wheel of life and understand the different personality traits. In that case, they will integrate within society far more effectively than most.

You see, they will become more tolerant of the different personality traits. They will be able to communicate with all the other personality traits. The attitude chapter of this book will help you to understand the different personality traits. The trick is to become a chameleon. Meaning, if you identify somebody as having one of those personality traits, you can mirror the way you communicate with them to be on their level rather than your default level.

If, as a family unit, each family member understands the different personality traits within it, you can become more accommodating to each other. Armed with this new knowledge, the children can go to school and become better equipped to deal with different personality traits.

Why on earth this isn't treated as an essential learning factor within school stuns me. Just because somebody does something different from how we perceive it should be done does not mean that they are doing it wrong. It just means they have a different angle of approach.

Failing to understand somebody's personality trait in the school environment can lead to bullying, leading to an adverse effect on that person's mental health.

As a parent, you want the best for your children. By sharing this personal development material with them from an early age, you can give your children the greatest gift of all.

The gift of continuous and never-ending improvement is so valuable and can give your children a massive head start. Remember, when it comes to a fixed mindset, this mindset group believe that they are naturally talented and gifted.

Suppose we can encourage our children from an early age about the importance of continuous and never-ending improvement, that it is perfectly OK to fail, and that it is encouraged to speak freely. In that case, they will develop into more rounded human beings.

We briefly touched on the new category of young people commonly referred to as the "Snowflake" generation. It is fantastic that the younger generation seems to be more open to sharing their feelings.

As a parent encouraging your children to share their feelings, their worries, and their dreams, goals, and aspirations with you are vital for their growth.

If they live in the family unit's nest environment and feel as though they cannot share their emotions or feelings, they will turn to other communication routes.

Some of these routes may be along a darkened path, falling in with the wrong crowd. The rebellious young person feels in tune with their fellow rebellious associations. This then becomes their new norm. They will become withdrawn from the family unit and are increasingly unlikely to share anything with their parents or siblings.

The big problem is when the parent comes from the "Hailstone" era. I just made up this hailstone idea, but I quite like the snowflake generation's fabric. It does not mean they are weaker than previous generations; they probably are stronger.

The hailstone generation, however, does not like to share feelings. They believe that sharing feelings is a weakness, and they become so entrenched within this thought process, that their subconscious mind creates this as a habit, and they are never fully able to express their true feelings for loved ones or friends.

With the older generation, the world was very much a heterosexual society. If you had feelings for someone of the same sex, they were suppressed and hidden, and they went underground. Coming out became the new buzzword.

In the hailstone generation, the man would earn the daily bread; the woman would be at home cooking the food and ensuring the house was tidy. The man went to the pub for a pint, and the woman did her duty staying at home.

Thank heavens those days are gone.

In any relationship, whether it be heterosexual, same-sex, or any mixture thereof, it is fantastic that there is equality within it.

If you were born into the hailstone generation, this was no fault of your own, and the jam you received was simply the jam that your parents and their parents understood to be normal.

There is no point in being secretive about who you are. There is no reason you cannot share every emotion with your friends and family. There is no reason why you cannot be honest with them.

They will still love you!

Not saying I love you to friends and family members is one of the other key regrets of the dying.

As a parent encouraging your children to be free with emotions and their worries and speak to you with that freedom without judgement is brilliant parenting.

If they share something with you that raises alarm bells, remember "5, 4, 3, 2, 1". Pause within the moment and evaluate what your child has just told you.

5 - 4 - 3 - 2 - 1

Do not fly off the handle because you will cause their subconscious mind to react to your emotional outburst each time you do. They become less likely to share anything with you.

That is a good sales technique that can also be used in such circumstances.

It is called the **feel, felt, found** technique.

It is all about empathy and a way to agree with somebody and give your validated reply.

Your 13-year-old son asks if he can watch the latest horror movie. Instantly you may say “No, of course not” and shun his request away immediately. The fact of the matter is if he wanted to, he could go away with all the latest tech and earphone and watch whatever he wanted.

As a parent though you can turn this to your parenting advantage.

You could maybe reply something along the following lines:

“I know how you feel about watching this horror movie, and I felt the same way when I was your age.

I will never forget my uncle Peter allow me to watch Nightmare on Elm Street. You know to this day I cannot watch horror movies. Son, when have you ever heard of us as your parents watch these films?

I don't mind admitting that watching that film left a negative imprint in my memory at an early age. That's why the governments set age limits on things like this. You know that I will only ever give you the right advice and whilst you may want to watch that film how about we watch a comedy or an action film together”.

Of course, this may or may not work, depending on how headstrong your child is. A couple who are my friends were amazing when they brought up their children Andrew and Aileen.

They realised when their children were young that they wanted to create an environment that was devoid of any devious distractions. By that, I mean they wanted to create an environment where their children did not associate with people that would maybe smoke, drink alcohol, or worse, still engage in taking illegal drugs.

They would actively encourage Andrew and Aileen to bring their friends around to the house, go on walks and hikes around the countryside, go to one of the beautiful lakes in Dumfries and Galloway, where they had a boat. I know that most people do not have a boat, but both Olli and Sandra, my friends, invested their money to buy this boat purely to ensure that both Andrew and Aileen would grow up loving the outdoor life.

I will never forget the day speaking to Andrew, who was 19 years of age, and his dad said that his local high school did not have a drugs problem. Andrew quickly responded that it did, but that he and his friends saw no interest in any illegal activities, so he did not feel the need to speak about it.

Today, many parents are letting their children go and do whatever they want whenever they want. The fabric and relationship between parents and young child are being stretched and tested.

As a parent, if you want to ensure that your children feel loved and part of the family unit, create a non-judgmental and fun environment where they want to spend time with you, where they feel empowered to invite their friends into your household.

In the long run, by becoming excellent parents and giving your children the time during the early phases of their life, time will win out in your favour.

As they progressed through their teenage years, they will have the intelligence to make their own decisions. They will know the right and wrong path, and they will understand that being seduced by the dark side is not a path that they will decide to take.

With the hailstone generation, we were **told** not to take a particular path. With the newer generation, we can discuss why most people do not go along the dark path in an adult way. Conversationally, that causes the child to feel part of the decision-making process.

When a child is encouraged to communicate freely within the family unit and shares things naturally, that family unit will grow, and trust will be retained.

Understanding that there is no need for instant gratification, that it is good to fail and that it is good to set goals and targets, and it is good to work towards those goals will be some of the best parental guidance given.

In our modern society, our children are brainwashed to believe that they go to school, get a good education, leave school, go to University, and leave University to get a great job. This is the pack of lies that our parents shared with us and the same pack of lies that their parents shared with them.

This is the system of control engineered by all governments and conditioning of our children within the school and education process.

Worse still, we are all conditioned to believe that our lives' purpose is to work in a job that we probably do not even enjoy until retirement age, which is looking increasingly like 70 years of age.

There is no such thing as a job for life; in modern times, more people are falling within the debt trap. In modern times more people are becoming distressed and depressed because of the forces placed on them within society.

Yet, we live in a world of abundance opportunity. As parents reading this book "living your life on purpose", the greatest gift we can give to our children is to encourage them to live their lives the way they want to, not the way society expects them to.

If they chose university and a career path – great it was their choice.

If you are reading this book and you are already within the conditioning system. Through continuous and never-ending improvement, understand that you don't have to play a part in their game.

It may take time for you to find your route or your path, but you can do anything you want in this world.

Family and friends will be the pillars of support that allow you to become whoever you want to become. Whatever you do, please make sure that you create time within your busy schedule for your family and your friends. Share the way that you feel about them.

It does not have to be a grand declaration of love for these people, and if you don't feel as though you can verbalise it, there are so many friendly ways to communicate these days. I like to send cards with lovely messages written within them;

one of my good friends just started a brand-new business called kind words. The idea of this business you go online typing what you want to say about somebody, and it gets sent to them in a very nicely presented fashion.

You could easily send a text message with some kind words, but whatever you do don't, be scared to share your feelings.

Go one stage further using the diary on your smartphone. Why not diarise triggers to remind you to communicate with your family or friends?

It seems alien that we should need to diarise something, but incredibly, in this frantic world, time passes by before we even know it.

In the book's habits section, we mentioned the strategy of making habits easier. Setting a diary date that creates an alarm is a brilliant trigger to remind us to do something.

Even making a new habit of sending out birthday cards and Christmas cards would be a fantastic way to build bonds with your family and friends.

**The little things do matter.** This sounds bizarre, but if you are in a relationship with someone and live together, the smallest of things you do make the most significant differences.

Some people are lazy in their relationships, and some minimal subtle activities make the relationship more enjoyable.

Doing the dishes, making a cup of coffee, offering a drink, helping with housework, and taking a share of cooking food, to name just a few.

When one partner sees the other making an effort, they first appreciate it and, secondly, reciprocate it.

The whole point of setting these triggers is for us to be conscious about the things that matter to us. Our subconscious mind is already busy with so many automated tasks.

Unless we start to consciously complete new tasks or habits for our subconscious to think about, they will never naturally occur.

When we think consciously about our friends and our family and every aspect of our lives, balance and happiness follow.

Ever since we were young, our minds have been cultivated by our environment. Our subconscious mind only can accept.

By living your life on purpose, you start to question some of the things consciously in your life that you thought were true.

Think back to times when you were a child and think back to the things you can vividly remember. Consciously and with an out-of-body experience were the things that your parents, aunties, and uncles, and even your teachers preached to you, correct?

We seriously need to validate everything we hold to be accurate, and if we know that what we thought was to be true isn't right, we need to engage in some jam transfusion consciously.

Think about your parents and some of the closer members of your family. Are you turning out to be just like them? You love them but do you want to be replicated like them?

During your infancy and growth years, you were effectively taught the rules of control. Go to school, get a good education, and get a good job. Most people do this, so you think that this is normal, and therefore you follow the path that has already been predetermined for you.

Alternatively, your parents run a family business, and they actively encourage you to move into the family business. They are so adamant that you will follow them into the family business that you apply yourself less at school.

As you go through school, you will have so many life experiences. How you react to them may have a lot to do with the jam in your doughnut.

Yes, the jam that was injected into your doughnut by your parents, media, teachers, friends, and siblings.

The way we were raised in this world plays a large part in our current self-esteem.

What we think of ourselves and what we believe we can achieve in this world is initially created by our early environments.

**Who are you?**

If you have been repeatedly knocked down as a child, psychologically, I mean, there will be a tendency to operate within a safe zone. If, on the other hand, you are always encouraged to grow and experiment, you have different comfort zones.

If your parents drank too much alcohol during the week and fought like cats and dogs over the most trivial things, it may be a fair assumption for you to grow up in this environment and think this is normal.

Thankfully, we are in a more accepting society, and now the rules of the older generations are being left behind. If, as a little girl, you observed your mum being submissive and obedient to your dad, the jam in your doughnut could be that as you grew up to a lady that this is the way you should act with men.

On the flip side, if as a young boy you witnessed your mum being submissive and obedient to your dad as you go into a relationship as a young gentleman, you might believe that this is the way to treat women.

It is vital in today's modern society to understand that the old rules no longer apply. We are all equal in this world, and we all should assume 100% responsibility in all our relationships.

Always challenge and always look to grow. We live in a world of continuous and never-ending improvement, and by living our lives on purpose, we are looking to grow in every segment of the wheel of life. We want to become better parents, partners, friends, and colleagues etc.

This growth may be uncomfortable, and it may challenge you in so many ways. It could be emotional, and you could quickly retreat to your typeset.

I can tell you now whatever negative things you are thinking about yourself and whatever you think you can achieve in this world is a fraction, of what you really can become and what you really can achieve. You are a remarkable individual, and you have total permission to grow and become whoever you want to become.

The main issue is that we still hold on to the beliefs and values that we believe to be true from when we were young boys and girls. Through time as we have evolved and grown, and you can change your value set.

When they integrate into society, many people put up a mask, an outer defence to conform in the way we think they should. Remembering the laws of association and the fact that you will become equal to the average of the five people you associate with the most, take stock of the amount of time you spend with your family and friends.

Then start to think about whether these associations will help you develop to become the person you want to become or have the things you want.

There is an extremely high chance that some of our friends are really good fun, and we love being with them because they do not threaten us in a way that makes us feel uncomfortable. They don't challenge us to grow because they don't want to grow. So, these friendships have become more of a habit.

There are so many people in this world that could be your friends, and there is no limit to the number of friends you can have.

Just start to be conscious of your associations and always be on the lookout for other people that resonate with your values and beliefs. When you find these people, look to build a relationship with them.

During your conversations with these people, do not be guarded about where you want to go, be proud that you are of a cheerful disposition. When you engage with these people, find out what drives them, find out more about their early years, be intrigued by their mindset and where they want to go.

**You don't know what you don't know.**

The sentence above is such a profound and deep statement. You need to think about it; since birth, we only know what information has been passed to our subconscious mind.

We operate using our five senses.

For example, some families don't communicate at all about the future and personal development. Other families regularly communicate about these subject matters. If you have never spoken within your family unit about such positive matters, you may not even know that other people do. It might be alien to you because you've never experienced this, but if you were to ask a successful person where they see themselves in five years, they would ponder the question. Then they will reply to your question. When they respond, there is a high chance that it will include an enhancement and an improvement to their life from where they are currently.

Ask the same question to people who have no real ambition, and they are likely to either ridicule you or say that they would expect to be in the same place as they are now.

So, spend more time with your family, with your loved ones, and choose your friendships wisely. Understand that your personal growth will be determined by who you associate with the most.

I remember delivering a goal-setting session that formed two different parts. We spoke about goals during the first session and taught how these goals could be achieved. The second session several months later was a refresher training to ensure that these goal-getters were on track.

On one of the returning sessions, we asked a lady about her goals. During the conversation, it became apparent that her esteem had improved considerably; she had already moved forward in her life and were indeed a lot happier. We asked about her relationship with her husband, to which she happily replied that they had split up.

Being quite shocked at this, we gave our sympathy, but she replied even happier by declaring that she realised that her husband did not fit into any of her goals during her goal-setting process. At this moment, I should declare that we are not advocating changing your loved one but instead suggesting you consciously think about who your lifelong partner is.

During the process of living your life on purpose and living an abundant and happy life by engaging with this process with your current partner, you can achieve so much more. It does come with a relationship warning.

If you have been living with a partner who lacks ambition, and they see that you want more from your life, it could create conflict within your relationship.

In this scenario, we hope that your partner buys into your positive mindset than you into theirs.

If we have one time on this beautiful planet of ours, we cannot live it properly unhappily with an anchor.

The beautiful part of living your life on purpose and looking for balance in your life is that if you have a current partner and learn to communicate with open conversation, there is a remarkably high probability that your partner will engage in this process.

Suppose you currently do not have a partner. In that case, the great news is that by developing on improving your self-esteem and becoming more confident about who you are and who you want to become, you are likely to find somebody that mirrors your ideal mate.

The first thing you will do if you are looking for an ideal partner is to disregard anybody who is negative or saps the life force out of people.

Do they lighten the room when they enter or when they leave? Are they fun, and do they embrace life? Do they want to achieve more, do they fit into the criteria you have set for yourself?

If you want to travel the world and experience so much that it has to offer and yet you have a date with somebody who never wants to travel, it is a simple elimination process.

You can set yourself a conscious task to write down a list of attributes and characteristics you would like to have from a partner or a new partner. With the law of attraction working for you, if you write down what you want, you will receive the partner of your choice because your reticular will be looking out for them.

Be considerate of who you are looking for as an ideal partner. Do not let your ego or vanity determine who you choose.

Your ideal partner may be eye candy but have little in the world of charisma or ambition, and whilst there might be some short-lived enjoyment of hooking up with this partner, in the big scheme of things, it is likely to be a short-term relationship.

Dig much deeper into what would you like them to look like, the colour of their hair, the eyes, colour, or tone of their skin; we all like people of different shapes and sizes, which are all perfectly normal. Write down the physical attributes that you would like your partner to have.

Also, write down what things you would like your new partner to do as hobbies or interests. Are they wholly independent people or are they going to be dependent and clingy?

If you meet somebody and get a gut feeling about something negative, do not pursue that relationship. If in the early stages of the relationship, if part of it is abusive or doesn't feel right, end it.

You have a blank canvas, and you can create the ideal person you want to spend the rest of your life with. You may idolise your dad or your mum, and you may love them to the tenth degree. But even the people that we love, such as our parents, have weaknesses that we would not like to have in our future partners.

Ensure that you do not write these weaknesses on your wish list.

During the process of living your life on purpose, as you start to experience these small and yet seemingly insignificant wins throughout different segments of your life by default, you will grow as a human being, and your self-esteem will improve.

There is something called impostor syndrome. This is where somebody starts to grow and achieve things in their life, and then they begin to feel threatened by their success and are not worthy of that success.

Imposter syndrome is entirely due to the jam in their doughnut and from the transfusion of jam from when they were a young child, and therefore, they believe they have exceeded their expectations.

The same rules may apply when looking for your ideal partner. You may start to write down or to dream of the type of person that you'd like to spend the rest of your life with. Then imposter syndrome kicks in.

"Why would a person like that want to be with a person like me"?

In life, we create an image of ourselves and settle on a partner that matches our perceived self-worth. Ludicrously this self-worth was predetermined as a youngster due to the jam that was put into our doughnuts.

If this jam were put into our subconscious mind as a youngster, it is right to understand that these subconscious thoughts, values, and beliefs could be incorrect as we had no choice to accept them.

If we can consciously accept that the blank canvas we were as a child has been designed by people who were not good artists, we can rewrite that design.

Think of it like an undo button in a word document. Something was written, and we didn't like it. So, we undid it!

When you look for the ideal partner, think, "Is this what you want or what you think you can only achieve"?

I'm ugly, I'm stupid, and I'm fat, and I'm not a genuinely lovely person.

Just a random statement that I'm throwing out there. There are so many people in the world as they were growing up; they will have heard these statements not just once throughout their early stages, but time after time after time.

If they have heard these statements or multiples thereof, if at a later stage in adulthood somebody says one of these words, they revert to being the boy or girl that they were when they first were insulted and abused by them.

It is a sad indictment of life, but if somebody told a young child that they are stupid, for example, this is merely a mirror reflection of what they think about themselves. Instead of keeping that within their mind, they reflect this via anger onto somebody else that is defenceless.

They do not even know the damage they are doing to that young person's mindset, and because the young person is defenceless, they keep applying the same punishing language. The young person hears this often enough; they deem it valid.

Mum and dad quite enjoy doing nothing literally. They eat lots of food, engage in no fitness and drink lots of alcohol. They are obesely overweight, and they have significant underlying health conditions. As a young child growing up in the environment for the first eight years of your life, you think it is perfectly OK to be in the same shape as your parents, engage in the same habits of your parents, and therefore you at an early age become obese yourself.

Due to being undervalued and not noticed as a child, you could start to do things to get yourself noticed. All you want is recognition from somebody that you love the most. Because you're not getting the credit you wish to, you start to rebel against what they want. They punish you, and now the downward vortex of despair is upon you.

Your self-esteem becomes damaged in any of these scenarios and starts to become even worse. Thankfully in today's modern society, more and more people recognise that this mental abuse when they were children, does not determine who they will be in the future.

When you are picking or looking for your life mate, understand the self-talk you give to yourself consciously; every moment and every single part of the day will determine your transmission of who you think you are.

If you are transmitting who you think you are, you need to become that person mentally. Remember the phrase fake it until you make it.

This is not about lying about who you are, instead forward-thinking who you would like to become and then everyday acting as though you were already that person.

Every day, act as though you are the person that you want to become consciously, making those decisions. Having written down what you would like your ideal partner to be, and by faking it until you make it, you will naturally grow into the person you want to be.

**When you are the person that you want to be, you will then attract the person that you wanted to attract.**

Think deeper into yourself, think more profound into the person you'd love to spend the rest of your life with. Take this task seriously and spend time.

If you already have a partner, do not start writing down a target of another partner. Speak with your partner that you currently have and discuss where you would like your lives to go and who you would like to become.

There is no perfect human being on our planet, including you and any partner you may have or any future partner. So, if you find any of the things that are those imperfections, and they are causing you annoyance or grievance if they are small, learn to adapt to them or speak with your partner to identify them to him or her.

Some people have habits that they do not even know they're doing, and if you have created a relationship environment where you can speak openly and freely, it might just surprise them that they are even doing it.

**For our children**

We all have an enormous duty to ensure that our children's development occurs to the absolute best of our ability and our resources. But there is no manual on how to be the best parent to give your children the best start in life.

It is one of those passed down through generation experiences, where you raise your children either in a similar way to how you were raised or by following your new, improved idea of parenthood.

Design your life on purpose. Engage in constant and never-ending improvement. Understand that wherever you are in your life right now does not determine where your children are heading; you can get them off to a fabulous start.

As children can comprehend things at different ages, you could implement living your life on purpose with various strategies.

You can demonstrate your continuous and never-ending improvement with your growth mindset for the young children so that this naturally passes down to them. Don't get into the habit of being dismissive with your children because you are busy at work.

The wheel of life is all about bringing balance to every area; the first few years of your children's lives are the years that some parents regret never seeing or participating in.

Some parents were so hell-bent on that business or their careers that they disregarded the critical times with their children, their loved ones, their friends, and family. This is mostly not out of design, but because they feel contributing to the family unit generating more income for the family was the best thing.

You cannot buy memories with money, that you did not personally experience.

Instead, with our young children, just spending some time with them every day, playing with them, and encouraging them would be the best love a parent can give.

Of course, your children will do something wrong. Of course, your children will attempt to push their boundaries. Anger or irritation may enter the equation. If these young people experience irritation every time, they try to express themselves or grow, it will restrict their growth from an early age as they won't like the feeling of being reprimanded.

If they do something crazy wrong, they need to understand there are boundaries.

Children learn most in their life when they can play without fear of being reprimanded. As we grow into young adults, we start to lose the playing mentality because we must become serious.

Interestingly people who play longer develop better. In George Torkildsen's book child's play, he demonstrates that even as adults, we should attempt to revert to the mentality that we learn more through play. Why did the world become so serious? Why did the world make life so dull? Why did the world make us work so hard and get so stressed out?

The world did not do any of this, so don't blame the globe. It was the way our parents brought us up. It was the way our parents were brought up. We think this is what we need to do. Everybody falls into the system of control. The job for us, the little ants, is to work away and contribute to the growing society. Or, putting it plainly, pay more taxes!

You want the best for your children, but what does the absolute best for your children entail? It is time to start thinking profoundly and think about how best we can help our children develop.

Irrespective of where you feature in society within this beautiful world of ours, even if you feel your boat has sailed away, it does not mean the ship for your children has. In a world of abundance, if you understand the laws of attraction, you can instil the belief that they can do anything they want and become anyone they want.

To your children, you can spend the time passing down your wisdom and directing them to the path of absolute happiness.

That is a fantastic song which Cher sang "If I could turn back time, I would find a way".

I wish that I could turn back when my son was a young child. With the wealth of wisdom and knowledge I have now, I would have been a different parent. I was not a bad parent, and I like to believe that I was a good parent.

But I was not the best parent I could be. Armed with little knowledge on how to communicate with my son, I followed my father's teachings. My father was not a bad dad, quite the opposite, but he was a disciplinarian. He was and still is one of my heroes.

I was replicating my father's parenthood in my son's early years. It is so fascinating, and I am sure that many of you will echo what I am about to say. My father now is so horizontal he is laidback, and he is relaxed.

As I passed through my 40s, I became more relaxed and laid back myself. If I had my son now with this more laidback and more world-savvy approach, I am sure that I could have been a much better parent.

If you have children and you are participating in living your life on purpose and have young children seek wisdom from maybe grandparents. Understand that any of the pressures that you hold within your mind will be transmitted to these young Beautiful Creatures.

You don't know what you don't know. Let your children grow and express themselves. They will find their purposeful path if they can follow their instincts and the things that they enjoy doing. Right until they go to school, the teachers will strike to impose their beliefs that they need to get a good education.

When your children are going through school and maybe the teachers, because they want to get better pass marks, so their schools can pass governmental inspections, are placing pressure upon your child to get better grades. As an understanding parent, you can de-stress the whole situation.

As you grow and learn within the live your life on purpose community, you will pick up new skills from other people who are sharing their wealth of knowledge.

One of the top things you can do is not to put pressure on your child to become a straight “A” student. If you do, you will force them into a fixed mindset, and you will be causing your children to be good at regurgitating information to pass the exams. Sometimes your children will infuriate you with some of the seemingly silly things that they do. Being silly is all part of growing up. Remember, they are just learning about their own lives.

Some parents want their children to be straight “A” students for their own kudos. A friend’s daughter worried throughout her exam year. Stressing and became ill with those stresses. She was so incensed on getting her “A”’s. She eventually did and her dad (her hero) told her that the only time he saw three “A”s together was when he bought batteries.

She had put so much pressure on herself and it was unnecessary.

Try to control your emotions, and if your child does something, do not instantly respond. Try the 5, 4, 3, 2, 1 approach. They do something your brain goes into alert mode instead of instantly reacting. Countdown from 5 to one, and during the countdown, compose yourself an evaluate your response. Maybe you might have to countdown from 10.

For the slightly older children, share the "living your life on purpose" philosophes and the fact that you are involved in a continuous and never-ending improvement programme. They like to mimic their heroes. Yes, you are their hero, well, right up until you start to dismiss them.

You may even want them to read the book or listen to the audio.

As your child grows and develops their own personality, remember that they could fit into one of the other four personality trait categories. They could be red, blue, green, or yellow. More about the colours in the Attitude chapter.

If you are a green personality and then quite analytical, your child is a blue personality and loves life and does not like data, learn to communicate with them in a way that they understand. If they have already been taught the different personality traits, they will also understand why you speak how you do to them.

This is top-level communication and understanding. If you can work with your children and treat them as intelligent beings, and share secrets such as personality traits, there will be so much more harmony within your household.

They understand your personality trait and why you act the way you act, and contrarily, you know their personality trait and then comprehend why they act the way they do.

It will become a source of humour within the household. You can start to joke that it's OK being a blue all the time, but sometimes you need to drop the blue personality trait and squeeze into a little bit of green, red, or yellow. Teaching somebody to become a chameleon in the personality traits so they can adapt to the different colours means that they will become better equipped when they go through life.

With some of their school friends at school, if something occurs, the person with maturity and understanding the different personality traits will respond differently to a conflict situation.

Indeed, better still, the person who understands another person's personality traits, will become a chameleon and mirror that person and therefore diffuse any likely conflict, because communication will be at the same wavelength. Knowing why somebody else is communicating how they do to you becomes a more enjoyable experience because you do not feel as though there is any abrasiveness if they are a green or a red personality, for example.

Your child going through school will be able to relate to why the different teachers communicate with them. It is not about forgiveness. It is about comprehension. It is about understanding why somebody communicates the way they do. It is just a different communication style!

Having passed through the education system, your children will then be thrust into employment. Here they will meet people with the four personality traits, and because they are well equipped to become that chameleon, they will be seen to be mature for their years because they have a grasp on diplomacy.

We will speak about business and career in another segment in the wheel of life. Sufficed to say that if you take the time with your children and share with them not just what you are learning through living your life on purpose, but from your involvement and engagement with personal development, you will shape them to be better people than you are.

**Your legacy will be that you will give them a 20-to-30-year head start to what you had.**

Over the next years of your life, you will experience your most significant growth phase if you can follow the simple philosophies and principles of continuous and never-ending improvement.

Spend time with your family, spend time with your friends, and develop sound, meaningful relationships with all the people you love and like.

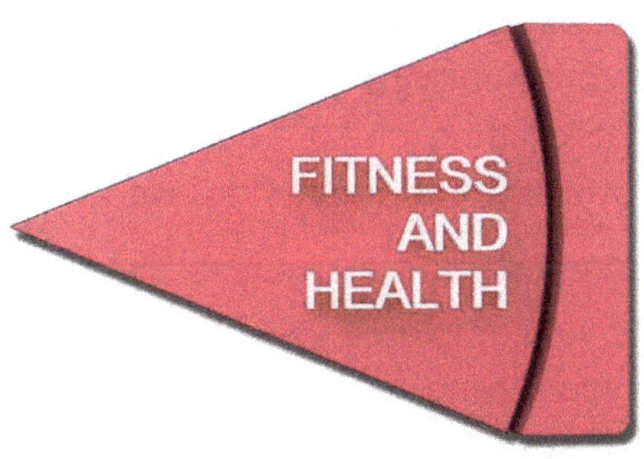


# Fitness and Health

This chapter will run through some top tips and techniques to help you become healthier and fitter.

We aren't going to suggest you eat lettuce all day, nor are we going to recommend you shatter yourself every day with gruelling exercises.

Quite the opposite!

Harnessing a good diet and light to moderate exercise regularly, you can become a happier, more content person.

Eating tastier food that must be good - right? Feeling better with ourselves both mentally and physically, that's got to be good - right?

So, let us throw away any stigma and, in this chapter of the book, embrace the good things in life and understand that the bad things in life, whilst enjoyable, don't need to be discarded either.

At this stage of living your life on purpose, you will have completed your first wheel of life exercise. On a scale of zero to 10, you will have graded yourself appropriately when it comes to health and fitness.

During the next days, weeks, months, and years together, we will work as a community to grow from wherever you graded yourself to that grading of 10. There is no rush; if we are continuously growing and improving, we are heading in the right direction.

If you have not yet completed your first wheel of life exercise, please go to your living your life on purpose Journal and complete that first task. We need to track where you are now and continue to track monthly. Remember, we want to make sure that your wheel is in balance or, more importantly, your life is in balance.

One of the good things about you reading this book is that you don't need convincing you to improve your life.

When we go through our lives and focus just a little bit on improving our health and fitness, these small conscious decisions can extend the length of our life quality.

Being fit and healthy does not mean you have to abstain from the luxuries you enjoy treating yourself to; it does not mean that you must be able to run a marathon in under 3 hours.

Being fit and healthy is a choice, and here in this segment on the wheel of life, we aim to improve your balance so that you can live a long, happy life and hopefully disease-free.

There should be no doubt that if you are fitter and healthier, both mentally and physically, it will serve you presently and in the future. In the classic, "you don't know what you don't know", if you have always been unfit and unhealthy, you won't even understand or appreciate the difference in the quality of life if you were to improve.

Within this segment of the wheel, we want to contribute to your growth in several different ways:

1. Mental health and fitness

2. Physical health and fitness

In a world where you can access information on anything, there should be no reason to have unfit or unhealthy people. We are aware of the ramifications of being unfit and unhealthy, yet why is it that so many people within Western society are on the edge of obesity, if not obese?

I do not think they deliberately became unfit or unhealthy, they just got caught up in the compound effect of deteriorating activities.

When it comes to mental health and fitness, some people might believe you cannot become mentally fit, which is fine because they don't know what they don't know.

The mind works best open, remember just like a parachute. Our mind is like a muscle. The more you work the muscle, the stronger the muscle becomes. When it comes to physical fitness, what happens to build the muscle is that you break the muscle down, and it rebuilds bigger and stronger.

The same happens when we talk about mental fitness. Using the jammy doughnut analogy, we break some of our thoughts' legacies, rebuilding with a new thought process. The more we engage in learning and personal development, the more our mind starts to accept this new fitness regime.

In later life, those who have not engaged in continuous and never-ending improvement or continued to use their brain these people are likely to suffer some form of mental disease. Besides, it is fun learning, and it is brilliant growing as a person.

One of the critical facets of living your life on purpose is to help you with your mental health. One of the travesties in this world is that most people don't understand the need for mental growth or direction within their lives.

They wake up each morning, and they engage in the same daily habit and routine. Nothing is taxing their brain too much, and they go about their daily business pretty much on autopilot.

Forty-five years later, having engaged in the same routine during the week and then pretty much the same pattern at the weekend, they can retire and then they are screwed up.

They don't know what to do. They are confused, which is so sad.

When you live your life on purpose and set stretching goals and targets and set your mission to harness the tremendous power of the compound effect, and you are growing daily, life just started to improve little by little. Every single day you are celebrating your successes. Every day you stretch yourself and push yourself just a little more.

In all the segments in the wheel of life, you are improving, and that is what living your life on purpose is all about!

If you wake up in the morning and have a purpose for that day, you will actively engage in that purposeful agenda. At the end of the day, you can celebrate your activities, and then the next day, you can re-engage with purpose.

When it comes to mental fitness, make sure that you read or listen to a good book for 15 minutes a day. There are so many fantastic authors worldwide with such creative and mind developing content that you will never run out of books or audios to read or listen to.

As you enrich your mind, your knowledge will improve. Your mental fitness will allow you to communicate on an entirely different level. Through the power of associations, you, and the people you communicate with regularly start to have meaningful conversations.

You form what is called a mastermind group. A mastermind group is where people come together for mutual gain. This ordinarily is a structured gathering where, maybe, they meet once a week or once a month—some of the people who participate in my mastermind groups joke that it is like a book club.

Within the mastermind group, you can organise and set yourself up to meet at whatever frequency you all agree upon. Each time you meet, you can have open discussions in a safe environment. Whatever is discussed within the mastermind group stays within the mastermind group.

When it becomes your turn to table the subject discussed in that week, you can choose any life-enhancing topic you want. It could be business-related, and you could be asking the mastermind group to share their combined brainpower to help you with a business or a career problem.

You might like some advice or guidance on a problem that you are envisaging is happening within your Child's life. How should you react, how would they react, what is the best way to approach my child issue?

**Birds of a feather flock together.**

To grow your mind and grow as a person, find people with the same mindset and ideology. You may not even know that mindset groups exist but if you go onto the Internet and put into the search box mastermind group, be stunned.

So, within the living your life on purpose community, we have a platform where you can join a mastermind group. We are setting mastermind groups up all the time. Because of the beauty of web-based communication tools, it doesn't matter whether you're in Perth, Australia, Los Angeles, America, Berlin in Germany or York, England.

We can all meet once a week for two hours and share life experiences and grow together with the mastermind's power.

**Physical Health and Fitness**

Let us revisit the couch to 5K and the target weight of 82 kilogrammes. You can set any goal you want regarding your physical health and fitness. To demonstrate, let us assume that the above plan is the couch to 5K.

In this scenario, we are setting a 13-week massive action plan. We cannot run for one kilometre, and now we are 89 kilogrammes in weight. We want to plan on how we can complete a 5-kilometre run within 13 weeks and achieve the target weight of 82 kilogrammes.

Please remember and note the target is not to lose 7 kilogrammes in weight. The brain will work far more effectively if you set the target of 82 kilogrammes, so you focus on reaching that target weight. This is not a weight loss goal; it is a weight attainment goal. We want to achieve a weight of 82 kilogrammes.

Through our daily tracking that you can find in the living your life on purpose Journal, you will track your new weight. If we are 89 kilogrammes on day one, there is an extremely high chance that the weight will be either higher or like 89 kilogrammes on day two.

As we continue to weigh ourselves daily, after we get through the initial zone of a shock to the body, the wait will slowly start to aim towards your target of 82 kilogrammes. On day eight, you might weigh 88.8 kilogrammes. You jot this into the Journal, and you celebrate that you are on target for 82KG with a lovely big tick next to the activity.

With the same recording in the Journal on day one, you may walk 500 metres. Having walked the 500 metres, you jot down 500 metres in the Journal and put a lovely big tick next to the activity.

To help achieve this goal, you have understood that just doing the exercise will not be enough for you to get to your target weight of 82 kilogrammes. You have decided to implement a healthier eating regime. Each day you eat healthy for breakfast, for lunch and your evening meal, and once again, you jot down in your living your life on purpose Journal that you have successfully had a healthy day for eating and place a lovely big tick next to the activity.

We repeat this every day for 13 weeks. As you complete your sheet, you will see lots of lovely big ticks. Let us not be naive. You will have days when you do not record one of those beautiful big ticks, which is fine.

If there is a day when you do not complete the activity that you wanted to achieve for that day, you cannot put a tick but what I would like you to do is just to put a dash. Please do not put a cross because psychologically, unless it's a kiss, we don't like crosses because it reminds us of our school days when we got something wrong.

Suppose you eat healthily as often as you can, and if you work towards your target of couch to 5 kilometres, you will naturally also start to move towards your target weight of 82 kilogrammes. Let us now discuss healthy eating in more detail and how you can upgrade your daily fitness activity in a physically non-damaging way.

So, let's press on and help you to get physically and mentally fit.

**Manage expectations.**

This will be difficult for some; it will be challenging. Moving from the couch to 5 kilometres, aiming for 82 kilogrammes in weight and eating healthily could be a reality shock.

Therefore, we want to track the progress daily so that you can see those seemingly insignificant wins and ticks. Each time you see a success and a tick, your subconscious mind will enjoy that, and it will release some of dopamine through your body.

I call on you to be persistent, and I call on you to persevere for the first 21 days of the target. Days 1 to 7 of this goal will be challenging. During this first week, temptation will find a way to persuade you not to do what needs to be done.

Remember the mind monster and the mind angel?

Let us not give the mind monster any more airtime. To make this habit easier, if you have any naughty foodstuffs or alcohol in your house, give it to a friend or a family member to look after for the first week at the least.

Remember, to break a habit, we need to make it harder, and by having none of the tempting bad, destructive, and yet gorgeous food and alcohol in the house, we limit the chance of distraction.

In a world of instant gratification, we want to get rid of the spare tyres around our waist immediately, we want to be able to run the five kilometres on the first day, and we want to hit our target weight within the first week. Hello! That is not reality, so managing our expectations and understanding that time will always win out when mixed with the right exercise and the proper eating habits we will get to our chosen targets.

I will probably ask you to eat more than you usually do in a bizarre twist. The difference is that you will be eating more of the good stuff rather than the unhealthy super processed, or fatty foods.

Understand that we all have different physiology and differing physiology determines the speed at which we can achieve our targets.

When it comes to achieving that target weight of 82 kilogrammes, do not compare yourself with somebody else. Comparing with others would be counterproductive as your Physiology is different from the person who is achieving their targets quicker than you. This is not a race with anybody else. The race is with you and with you alone.

Here are some of the factors that influence results:

**1: Hydration status.**

What I mean by this is how much water, coffee, or alcohol do you consume during the day?

If you are drinking entirely water, your hydration status will be higher. If you drink alcohol and coffee, these are dehydrators, so you basically must subtract the coffee and the alcohol you drink from your water intake.

The higher the hydration, the better the body performs, which is a critical contributing factor to achieving your weight target.

Aim to drink at least three litres of water a day. Have you noticed that if you have consumed alcohol in the morning that you crave water? It is simple mathematics. The alcohol has worked against you.

**2: Gender.**

Men and women have different Physiology, so do not compare what you're doing with somebody of other sex.

**3: Age.**

A young person's body works in an entirely different way from an older person's body. Once again, do not compare with somebody more youthful or more senior than you. Of course, if you are whipping somebody's backside that is significantly younger than you internally, enjoy that win.

**4: Sweat.**

Does your body sweat a little or a lot? There are so many different bodies in the world that somebody could walk for 500 metres and experienced no rise in temperature. Their pores do not open, and therefore they do not sweat. Other people may walk briskly for 500 metres and get a good sweat. If you are somebody who sweats quite a lot during physical activity, you will likely lose weight quicker than somebody who does not sweat.

It does not mean that when you are engaging in an activity, you need to do a sweat test by rubbing your forefinger on the back of their neck to determine whether they are sweatier than you or not.

**5: Competency.**

Whilst engaging in the task. Irrespective of what activity we do, we want to find the optimal form or technique. Someone with bad technique is more than likely to overexert than somebody with good form or technique. It may sound crazy, but there is a technique of walking and running effectively. There is a technique to riding a bike effectively. There is a technique of swimming effectively. Always look for good form.

**6: Support**

From family members or friends. If you have a loved one or family members or friends supporting you unequivocally during your task of improving your health and fitness, they will give you encouragement and motivation.

If, on the other hand, you have a partner or family members that ridicule you for attempting to improve your life, this could be a distraction, and this could be an excuse for you not to live your life on purpose. Remember the rules of Association that these people are like the GUPTR' s all the IBE's.

**7: Management of your time.**

In the "getting organised" chapter of this book, we discussed the importance of creating a "things to do" list. Diarise the time that will do your activity in a time slot that works better for you and your family, and never let other distractions get in the way.

If it means getting up an hour earlier or doing your activities whilst your friends or family members are watching the income reducing box, then so be it.

**8: You!!**

Be committed to each of the goals and targets that you have set. Brief your mind that this will be a difficult task at the start and that it will become easier. Remind yourself why you are setting these goals on these targets and go about your daily business on purpose.

Remember “winners never quit, and quitters never win”. You need to adopt a winner's mindset because you have the opportunity right now to win in every segment in the wheel. By entertaining this multi-pronged attack to achieve your goals, your body will come to realise this is not just a temporary measure. You hear all the crazy fad diets helping people lose 1 kilogramme a day or become super fit with the six-pack abdomen. These fad diets are not sustainable, and as soon as you get to that weight by losing crazy amounts in a crazy period, as soon as you stop that diet, you go back to your original weight.

If we use weight loss as the terminology through this process, we will be looking to lose weight, maintain that weight and stabilise that weight.

You don't need to engage in any crazy fat diet or go on some crazy over the top physical exertion. Instead, we blend in a moderate physical fitness level with a healthy diet where we eat healthy food each day.

Caveman Jane and John. They didn't have any fad diets. They ate single source foods. It was meat, vegetables, or fruit. None of their food had been processed. They did not have cars or televisions. To get their food they had to hunt.

"Hey, caveman John"

"Yes, caveman Jane"

"John, I notice your BMI is a bit high, maybe you should stop eating those Burgers and Fries that you wash down with beer", "John, I also suggest you try a couch to 5k".

This conversation 100% never happened back in those days. Why?

They ate healthy single ingredient foods, and they were not lazy. Originally our species would graze during the day.

The modern 3 square meals in the morning, noon and evening doesn't serve us well really.

There will be no massive yoyo in weight using this process, and there will be no massive loss of physical fitness. Of course, we will have periods where we don't do any fitness, and we are going to have periods when we don't eat healthily.

I cannot remind you enough of how much I enjoy those Five Guys burgers and fries. I will eat that without any guilt, I will drink Marlboro region, NZ Sauvignon Blanc, without any shame, and I will go through days without engaging in any physical activity without any guilt.

I urge you to join this mindset that life is for living, life is fun and enjoyable, and through this process, we will engage in an improvement to our mental health and wellness and an improvement to our physical health and fitness.

**You might have a Ferrari body, but with a Citroen engine.**

Do not get phased out by the shape of other people's body, by the fact that they look physically impressive. Having the Ferrari body does not mean they have a Ferrari engine under the hood.

I will never forget when in Lanzarote, I was about to take part in that Ironman event. It is perceived to be the world's hardest Iron Man. Lanzarote is incredibly hilly, incredibly windy, and deceptively warm.

The day before the event, I saw a man walking along the poolside and don't mind admitting that I got “man envy”. This person had the most fantastic body perfect pecs, ripped abdomen, and leg muscles to die for.

I managed to speak to him, where we worked out that he was taking part in the same Ironman invent that I was. He had set himself a target time of ten and a half hours; I was looking at that body, thinking there was no doubt that he could achieve his goal. I realised that this was his first-ever Ironman event during further conversation.

It is important to note that this was to be the first-ever Ironman event, and he was going to do it in a fabulous time. A time that a professional Ironman athlete would be satisfied.

Following the day of the Ironman event, I saw him at the poolside excitedly. I asked him if he had managed to do his target time. Sheepishly he stated that he did not finish the event. It transpired that he had not even completed the bike element. He only got to the 90-kilometre point, which was halfway.

He proclaimed that he suffered from hypothermia. I was amazed that you could suffer from hypothermia at a 30-degree Celsius temperature. I asked him if he had eaten whilst he was on his bike. He replied that it was too windy to eat.

At this point, I diplomatically reminded him that it's essential to eat nonstop on the bike, taking on gels, drinking the right fluids and eating something. I also mentioned that as he had zero body fat, this would contribute to him losing his energy and feeling unwell during this event.

So, whilst the bodywork was like a Ferrari internally, the engine wasn't up to competing in this Ironman event. It would have been a lesson learned for him. I suspect that he did not manage expectations appropriately and did not give this race the credit and respect it deserves.

An Iron Man invent entails a 3.8-kilometre swim, followed by a 180-kilometre bike ride and then finishing with a 42.2-kilometre run. I am confident that this spectacular image of a man went too hard, too fast and paid the price of overexertion over the hilly route of Lanzarote.

Please ensure that you manage your expectations.

We have all got different body types, and there is no right one, and there's no perfect one. However, if you watch the media, you want to be 6 foot tall if you're a man with bulging pecs, abs, and biceps muscles everywhere, and if you are a woman, you're going to have long gorgeous hair, slim, with nice-shaped boobs and a nice-shaped butt, but that's not most people.

Most of us are normal, and we love being normal, and we accept our body and our looks for what they are. The happy people in this world take their body and shape, knowing that if they were unhappy with certain parts, they could do some toning up exercises get to their ideal weight, but in the main, they are happy with who they are.

If you do find a success buddy to train with, do not compare your body shape with their body shape or how they may be getting to their target quicker or slower than you.

**Food glorious food.**

We will simplify the type of foods to eat and the type of foods to avoid. I say avoid what I mean is avoid as often as you can. We need to get inside our body protein, fat, and carbohydrates.

The fat, protein and carbohydrates digested into simpler compounds. Fats are used for energy after broken down into fatty acids. Protein can also be used for energy, but its primary and first purpose is to make the hormones, muscle, and other proteins. Carbohydrates are used for energy.

The average calorific value for a man per day is 2500, and the average calorific value for a woman is 2000 per day. We would recommend that you do not need to calorie count. If you engage in a regular activity routine, eat healthier and reduce the intake of those naughty foods and drinks, that will suffice.

In simple banking terms, calories are put into the body. During the day, the body will naturally burn up calories.

Suppose you are engaging in regular activity.

It may be that you eat to a calorific value of 3500 calories per day, and you might be burning 3500 calories per day. In the simplest of terms, you would not have a gain or a loss in weight. But you may have a toning up of muscle groups that are being worked during the exercise.

Think of this as a bank. If you put in fewer calories than you burn, you will likely lose weight. If you put in more calories than you burn, expect to increase weight.

Therefore, we do not recommend you worry too much about calories. Eat healthily, do some activity, and reduce the naughty stuff. It isn't rocket science – it is common sense.

If you have a target weight of 82 kilogrammes and your current weight is 89 kilogrammes, in simple banking terms, you need to ensure that the calories that you put in are lower than the calories that your body burns.

Remember, this is not a Sprint, so there should never be a time when you go hungry. If hypothetically we are burning 2500 calories per day and are engaging in a regular exercise programme if we are eating 2000 calories a day, we are 500 calories short of our daily recommended intake, so the net result is a minuscule weight loss.

When you repeat this over some time, the weight loss will be gradual, and more importantly, it will be easier to maintain due to your new and improved habits.

If you are somebody who engages in a lot of physical activity, you could very well be consuming 5000 to 7000 calories a day of the right food and still losing weight.

If we want to lose weight, tone up or both, that will determine the amount of protein, fats, or carbohydrates that we put into our daily food intake.

In basic terms, the correct percentage of each of these food groups is as follows:

1: 45 to 65% of daily food should come from carbohydrates.

2: 10 to 30% of daily food intake should come from protein.

3: 20 to 35% of daily food intake should come from fats.

What are carbohydrates, protein, and fats, and what do they do?

**Carbohydrates.**

Carbohydrates are essential nutrients that are the primary source of energy, measured in calories. They deliver power for the body and is also the preferred fuel for our nervous system and the brain. Carbohydrates increase a person's blood sugar level depending on its amount within the food that we consume.

Essentially carbohydrate comes in two forms these being sugar and starch.

Sugar is a simple carbohydrate and is found in milk, honey, desserts, juices, and fruits. These simple sugars provide quick energy.

Starch is what we would call a complex carbohydrate, and this can be found in foods such as pasta, rice, flour, vegetables, cereals, breads, and legumes.

Foods that are high in starch are the ones that provide that longer-lasting energy.

**Protein.**

Protein is an essential nutrient made up of building block chemicals that you may have heard called amino acids. Protein provides energy and is needed for the body to create new cells and maintain and rebuild muscles. Protein also carries other nutrients to other parts of the body and supports the immune system.

The primary protein sources are poultry, meat, fish, dairy, eggs, soy, grains, and nuts.

**Fats.**

Fats are the nutrients that give you energy, and they have nine calories in each gramme. Fats help absorb vitamins A; D&E are either saturated or unsaturated. Foods generally that contain fat will have both types of saturated and unsaturated, although typically there is more than one kind of fat than the other.

Saturated fat, also known as solid fat, is mostly found in animal foods such as milk, meat, and cheese. Poultry and fish have less saturated fat than red meat. You will also find saturated fat in oils such as palm oil and coconut oil.

Saturated fat can increase your cholesterol levels.

Unsaturated fat is liquid at room temperature and is mainly from plants. Eating unsaturated fat instead of saturated fat is likely to improve cholesterol levels. Try to eat more unsaturated fats.

You can break the unsaturated fats down even further into monounsaturated fat, found in avocado, vegetable oils, nuts, and olive. When you eat high monounsaturated fats, these may help lower your cholesterol.

Polyunsaturated fat is found mainly in vegetable oils such as sunflower oil, Sesame oil, soybean, and corn oils. Polyunsaturated fats are also the primary fat found in seafood. Once again, eating polyunsaturated fat in place of saturated fats may lower your cholesterol.

The polyunsaturated fats also contain Omega 3 and 6 fatty acids.

Within the living your life on purpose community, we have a whole raft of different recipes and meal selections to save you from overthinking about them.

Enjoy your food and enjoy its selection and ensure that you maintain a healthy share of each of the three primary component parts fats, proteins, and carbohydrates.

## FOOD PLATE BALANCE

**MAINTAIN**
-or-
**MODERATE WORKOUT**

50% Veggie/Fruit
25% Protein
25% Starch

**GAIN MUSCLE**
-or-
**HEAVY TRAINING**

33% Veggie/Fruit
33% Protein
33% Starch

**LOSE WEIGHT / LEAN OUT**
-or-
**REST DAYS**

50% Veggie/Fruit
35% Protein
15% Starch

**Nutrients needed by the body and what they are used for?**

| Type of nutrient | Where it is found | How it is used |
|---|---|---|
| Carbohydrate (starches and sugars) | • Breads<br>• Grains<br>• Fruits<br>• Vegetables<br>• Milk and yoghurt<br>• Foods with sugar | Broken down into glucose, used to supply energy to cells. Extra is stored in the liver. |
| Protein | • Meat<br>• Seafood<br>• Legumes<br>• Nuts and seeds.<br>• Eggs<br>• Milk products<br>• Vegetables | Broken down into amino acids, used to build muscle and make other essential proteins for the body to function. |
| Fat | • Oils<br>• Butter<br>• Egg yolks<br>• Animal products | They are broken down into fatty acids to make cell linings and hormones. Extra is stored in fat cells. |

**Physical Fitness**

Physical fitness is often a misunderstood term. I guess it goes right way back to when we were at school, and we were all forced to take part in physical education or PE, as they called it in the UK.

Wherever you are in the world, your school will have had some form of physical education class. I find it quite comical that it is called physical education because I don't ever recall being educated on physical exercise benefits during my time at school.

All I recall was an underqualified teacher in charge of a sport that they were either interested in or the teacher that was not interested in that sport. They had drawn the shortest straw or weren't good at any sport and were left with the discipline that nobody wanted.

As is the way around the world, millions of school children just before every PE class would produce a sick note from their parent highlighting their exemption from that class. No wonder there was no education, and for those who did not like sport, there was undoubtedly no enjoyment.

Fortunately for me, PE was the release from the boredom of sitting in a classroom. I mean when I was ever going to use Pythagoras theorem or such like? I needed a sick note from the rest of the school curriculum!

If we had been educated from an early age and understood the benefits of physical activity on our physiology, we would probably have engaged a little more. The jammy doughnut reveals itself again in the world of physical activity. If your grandparents didn't enjoy physical fitness or your parents tried to skive off pe then guess what you are likely to have followed?

The legacy of school can be quite damaging, especially in physical activity. If you remember being forced to go cross country running in the middle of winter when you didn't enjoy running, then chances are you have a total disdain for that sport.

If you were fortunate to have swimming lessons as a young child but during the swimming lessons you found it hard and were not supported by the teachers or by your fellow school pupils, there's a chance you didn't follow that sport either.

On sports days, if you could play football, or rugby or cricket or if you are in America American football, basketball, or baseball if you were good at these sports you enjoyed them. If you were interested in the sports but did not receive the right level of support and coaching, your interest in the sport diminished.

The rate of obesity creeping upwards in most western civilisations can be contributed wholly to poor nutrition and lack of exercise, except medical conditions.

Here in living your life on purpose, we are not looking to help you become a super fit athlete. One that may dedicate 3 hours of your day to the sport of your choice. If you are out of balance in the wheel of life regarding health and fitness, just improving that balance would make a living your life on purpose a roaring success for us.

The strategies that we will employ can work for somebody who never does exercise, already participate in light to mediocre regime and even that fitness fanatics—the main agenda to get onto the path of improvement to their physical wellbeing.

**Physical fitness is a way to improve mental wellness.**

In this section of the book, we would like to share tips and techniques to go from trepidation to the enjoyment of your chosen sport.

In our community, rest assured you will receive a lot of support and encouragement, and we are with you all the way. Within you're living your life on purpose journal start to record the activity that you engage with daily and remember don't walk over the pennies to get to the pounds.

Suppose you have never run 5 kilometres in your life, but you have a hunch or an interest to do so. In that case, we can do this together in chunked down seemingly insignificant activity where we increase the duration and the distance slowly. I want you to imagine that you know someone exceptionally large indeed, and they carry a lot of weight. They express an interest in completing their very own couch to five-kilometre run.

Walking 300 to 500 metres for them is a tiring a stressful exercise. It is tiring and stressful because the bodyweight they carry around with them suffers from a power to weight ratio.

This rule will apply irrespective of what weight you are. For this scenario and ease of understanding, let us assume that our person in the spotlight is significantly overweight. Wherever you are on the weight/fitness spectrum, the same rules apply.

On day one of their 13-week massive action plan, they wake up and start with their healthy eating habits. They go out for a 500-metre walk around the streets. During this activity, because they carry so much weight and are not used to this distance, they will increase their heartbeat and burn up calories. On day one, there will be no amazing change in their weight or body shape. They will be flushed around the cheeks, and they will know that they have engaged in physical activity.

During that first day, they ensure they hydrate properly by drinking plenty of water. They eat only those single-ingredient foods—for example, chicken breast, vegetables, fruit, and any of the others listed in the charts above. They refrain from eating any of the bad things they enjoy so much, because they have hidden them from sight or reach, and they have made that habit harder to do.

On days 2 to 7, they continue to walk their 500 metres. It is not getting any more comfortable, they are sweating just as much, and they are good with their discipline with their eating habits.

At the end of week one, there is still no noticeable movement of their current weight towards their target weight. This is perfectly normal; the ones with a weak mindset could very well quit at this point. You know by now that the most apparent results will not start to occur until between days 21 and 28.

With physical fitness and the movement towards your target weight, if you manage your expectations appropriately and understand that nothing will happen with noticeable gain until days 21 to 28, you will not quit in this challenge's early phases.

On day 14, our friend is now easily walking 500 metres; they walk without sweating profusely, but they're still getting hot under the collar. They have done so well by falling foul of just a few of the bad things they enjoy during those two weeks. Each day they have made a record of their activities in their journal and can see more and more ticks are evident on the page.

They can start to see something happening with their weight. They are beginning to move towards their target weight, filling themselves with more encouragement.

Under the bonnet of their body, the muscles in their legs are now strengthening and because there is a weight reduction, the power to weight ratio heading in favour of the muscle groups.

This means they exert less effort and, therefore, not overheating or over sweating.

On day 15, our friend decides to extend the distance to 1000 metres, they are still walking, but now instead of walking at an average pace.

They are slightly speeding up to try and get around 1000 metre route quicker.

Another tick in the book and another success to congratulate themselves on.

Remember, in any segments within the wheel of life; we are not seeking instant gratification. Our friend will continue to improve daily. If the target weight is lower than their current weight by engaging in these good eating habit exercise habits, they will start to see and feel noticeable results.

Slowly but surely, they continue with their 1000 metre circuit. After another week, they decide that they're going to drop back down to 500 metres for the next week, yet for these 500 metres, they will run for 50 metres and then walk 50 metres, run for 50 metres, and walk for 50 metres.

On completion of their first walk and jog, they will be shattered; they have put more stress on their muscles, and they will have burned more calories. They are heading in the right direction.

You can see where this is heading, and our friend will complete their couch to five-kilometre run within 13 weeks because they have staggered their increased activity over a long period in bite-size increments.

Whatever you wish to achieve and wherever you are on the fitness scale right now, don't try and do any intergalactic jumps.

If you have not run 10 kilometres for over two years, do not put on your running shoes an attempt that distance. It will have a damaging effect on your muscles; you are likely to spend days afterwards recovering, and the torture will leave a scar mentally, and you will probably not want to repeat that.

This sounds quite bizarre; as a 15-time Ironman athlete with three more events planned for this year during the winter, I tend not to run that often.

To get me back into running mode, I would go for 3.2 kilometres.  I probably don't even enjoy that first run, yet I still celebrate that I have completed it at the end of it. It seems relatively trivial that I'm celebrating a 3.2-kilometre run, but seriously it is such a rewarding thing to do for yourself to celebrate.

Over the next three weeks, I may increase my running gradually to 6 kilometres and then to 10 kilometres.

The same rules apply no matter how physically fit you are - increase in small increments.

While I am focusing on this couch to 5-kilometre challenge, there are many ways to engage in physical activity.

Running has the worst reputation; so many people mentally discount that activity within a second. In terms of ease and terms of reward, running is by far the best activity you can do.

If you don't enjoy walking or running, consider improving it by adding some music to your exercise. Having a run partner, a success buddy, will also encourage you to go out and do your daily activity. Do not compare yourself with anyone else because this is your race, and no one else is.

Running, if done correctly, can be a thoroughly enjoyable exercise and can allow people to hit their target weights quicker than any other activity. It is also a fantastic sport for strengthening the core muscles and leg muscles.

To entice you to engage in this sport that you have hated for most of your life, or you feel as though you will never enjoy, Build in some form of reward plan. Do the task earn a reward.

Maybe at the end of your first month, treat yourselves to the most delicious top of the range Five Guys burger with fries and beer.

They say you cannot track what you don't measure. We can, of course, write down the activity that we have done, for example, completed a 5-kilometre run, and we can also record our weight on that day, so we are measuring what we are doing.

Another good innovation is the GPS tracking apps you can get for your smartphone or smartwatch.

I refer to our friend, overweight but ambitious to reach a new target weight—one of our friends in our living your life on purpose community. We do want them to succeed.

Our friend downloaded a fantastic app onto their smartphone called Strava. On day one, they started Strava as they went out for their first walk. During the walk, Strava recorded the activity, and at the end of the walk, that activity was recorded and uploaded to the Strava website. Our friend could see the route they took and the time it took to complete it.

Each time our friend engaged in the physical activity, it was uploaded and recorded for them. Our friend could see that they were getting slightly quicker each time they made their loop.

Then something fantastic happened, some of their friends and family, or members of the living your life on purpose community, saw that they were completing their daily activity, and they pressed the thumbs up and gave kudos to them. Some people even took the time to make a comment congratulating them on that activity.

Strava is an excellent supporting app. Each time you do an activity, you can guarantee that somebody will give you kudos. I know this is sad, but when I complete my 3.2-kilometre first run of the year, I seek kudos. I feel so delighted when I get the first person to give me that little bit of recognition and congratulation.

For those who invest in a smartwatch, you can sync your smartwatch to your smartphone and upload Strava onto the watch, and your activity will be recorded when you return.

Ask you go through each of your daily activities, your body will start to respond, it will be strengthening, and you will begin to become more toned, and if weight loss is your target, you will begin to move towards your target weight quite quickly after your first 21 days. Your muscle groups will be strengthening, your cardiovascular system will be more responsive, and your confidence will start to soar.

Create a Plan B exercise just in case the weather elements prevent you from doing your planned outdoor exercise. You have committed to doing your daily activity, so don't let a 3-foot dump of snow stop you from doing it! Or, in my case, a drizzle of rain!! Yes, I am a fair-weather sports enthusiast.

If I go skiing, I am dressed to ski. I love the cold, and I love to ski. If I am in Yorkshire and it starts to snow, I don't like the snow and won't go out and exercise.

Therefore, having multiple exercises in the training programme is beneficial. It is recommended that you include numerous exercise disciplines anyway because continually running, or regularly cycling, or always swimming will not have the best effect on your muscle groups and physiology.

I look to alternate my exercising daily. One day I will run, another swim and another cycle. If it is my day to go outside and run, but it is raining, I will default to indoor cycling. If it is my day to do indoor cycling and I missed a day running because of the bad weather, I will drop the cycling and go for the run.

Having multiple activities will stop you from making an excuse to give it a miss!

YouTube has an abundance of good, keep fit programmes that you can follow inside. From light tempo up to the insanity programme. There are so many different types of fitness programme out there.

I would suggest that you find one that harmonises with what you enjoy. Do not be misled by programmes that claim they will turn you into a beach Adonis within 90 days. These will wreak havoc on your body and likely cause permanent mental scarring and physical damage.

Find some exercise programme, dependent on your physical ability that will last for over 30 minutes. Look for something that will raise the heartbeat and cause you to sweat a little bit. If you are energetic, obviously work for more than 30 minutes at a higher tempo.

When you plan your next week or next month or the 13-week massive action plan activities, try to mix and match your workouts so that you do not rely on just one. If you can mix in multiple activities, that is even better.

For example, you could implement a run, a cycle, a yoga class, and an online fitness class. Not only does this break up the monotony of just one exercise activity, but it is also perfect for your muscle groups and for your cardiovascular system to mix things around.

When I was younger, I was fortunate to join the British army. As I loved my physical fitness, it didn't take long before I was drafted into the gym to become one of the regiments, physical training instructors.

When you go through the British Army and train to be a physical training instructor, there is much emphasis on learning anatomy and physiology. There were even six weeks of doing gymnastics.

Part of the learning when studying and training to be a physical training instructor in the Army is to encourage the soldiers of all ages and all abilities to pass a basic fitness test.

Part of the basic fitness test was to run and walk a 1.5-mile route and then run back along the same 1.5-mile route as quickly as possible. The second stage needed to be completed in 11 1/2 minutes or less.

Every soldier in the British army must complete a basic fitness test, and if they fail that test, they must go on remedial physical exercise training.

I would like to introduce the concept to you of a basic fitness test and a 13-week massive action plan fitness assessment. It is not a competition. It just forms another part of our tracking and measuring process.

We are not Going to set a generic basic fitness test that fits all. It is a good idea to create your fitness assessment. Something that you repeat once a month as a barometer of your progress.

Suppose you are working with a success buddy or are participating within the living your life on purpose community. In that case, you could set your tests with somebody of a similar fitness threshold.

I want you to start enjoying exercising, and by choosing your track and testing, you will buy into it more.

Here is a guide that you can use, edit, or add other things too:

1: Run and walk 1.5 miles in a 30-minute session. Then run that same distance as quickly as you can.

2: In your home, office or at your gym, set yourself some timed activities to do and record these activities. Within 2 minutes, record how many:

Press-ups that you can do.
Sit-ups that you can do.
Star jumps that you can do.
And how many shuttles runs you can do throughout around 50 to 60 metres.
After the shuttle runs, record your heart rate.

At the start of the press-ups, if you need to get onto your knees and do the press up in that position, absolutely no problem.

The sit-ups form and technique is vital. Never place your hands interlocked behind your head when you are doing these. You are better to place your right hand on your right temple and your left hand on your left temple. Do not jerk into the sit-up. Take it smoothly, remembering to exhale as you go into the sit-up position and inhaling on the way back down.

Please make sure that you are nowhere near anything that you can break with the star jumps. If you do not like star jumps, replace them with burpees or any other similar exercise.

Remember, the games aim here is not to be the top person doing press-ups, sit-ups, star jumps or shuttles, and it is not to be the person that runs the fastest 1.5-mile run.

This is just a way to benchmark your improvement. Aim to do your basic fitness test in your 13-week massive action plan fitness assessment every four weeks.

At the end of the 13 weeks, having also engaged in the daily activity, I promise you will be stunned at your improvement and achievement.

But what is physical fitness? Physical fitness is not a super-fast runner; it is not the strongest person globally; it is not a world-class soccer player.

Don't get me wrong, these people are fit and talented, and I applaud every person who accomplishes professional status in any sport.

Physical fitness is just precisely that making sure that we are fit physically. This means that we don't want to be too heavy, we don't want to be too light, and we want to make sure that our internal organs are adequately nourished.

People who are physically fit focus on 5 elements. Speed, strength, suppleness, skill, and stamina.

When designing your fitness programme why not use your initiative and look to incorporate the 5 elements above in some of your sessions. It will break up any monotony and you will become fitter physically!

When all our muscles are toned, and all the connecting ligaments and tissues are in good health, we can deem ourselves physically fit.

Throw in that we are nourishing our minds with continuous a never-ending improvement through the constant intake of professional development; we become both physically and mentally fit.

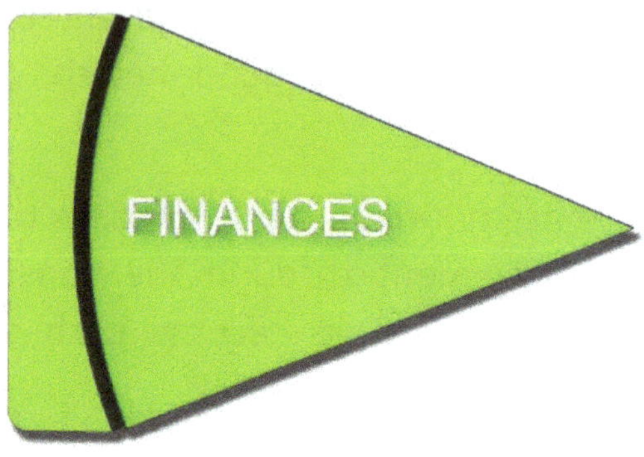


# Finances

**"Money isn't important; it just ranks right up there with oxygen". Zig Ziglar**

You can't buy things with self-esteem and the fact you've got a cracking smile. It's just the way of the world we need money.

Poor people may say that money does not bring you happiness, and of course, they are right. It does not bring you happiness; what you can do with it can.

It is just one of those self-defeating phrases when said means you do not have to go and earn more money. It is a way of making sure you don't fail. I bet we all could do with some extra cash in our lives.

Do not be seduced to think that if someone is earning 100,000 spondoolies a year or earning 30,000 spondoolies a year, there is a massive difference to their disposable income.

The amount of money that each of those homes is left with after all the expenditure is considered is probably the same.

Sound fiscal management is essential to ensure any home or business thrives and survives, and that is precisely what we will be going through in this segment.

When you live your life on purpose and focus on each segment within the wheel of life, you can make a transformation and enhancement to your life.

The finances section of this book will show you how to significantly reduce stress, improve your lifestyle and feel healthier as a direct result.

At this stage, you should have completed your first wheel of life and marked yourself accordingly in the finances section.

Throughout this chapter, we will give you some top tips on how to improve your financial status.

Each of us is in different stages of our lives, so if you are reading this book or listening to this audio and have not accumulated any debt, hopefully, this will serve as a reason you should not.

If you have already accrued debt, you will be able to use the tips in this chapter to increase your wealth.

First, though, it is essential to understand that most people worldwide have been caught in a system of control. We will call this the debt trap.

Once you understand the debt trap and why the banks want to keep you in debt, and the cunning little strategies they employ to keep you where they want you, you can break free. Most people in the western world are in debt of some description.

It has been designed that way. Some who are not in debt learn to employ careful financial management from an early age or learn the tricks to escape the debt trap.

The most powerful institutions in the world are not governments. They are the banks and financial institutions.

Three main sectors borrow money from the banks:

1: Governments.

2: Business Owners.

3: The People.

Let us put the banks in the middle of this graphical demonstration. Using the UK as a benchmark model, however, every other government have the same debts.

Here in the UK, the government is in debt to the tune of 2.1 trillion spondoolies.

Each year, the government borrows more and more money and is therefore getting into more significant debt.

The result of the COVID-19 pandemic accelerated the amount of money governments around the world borrowed. Year after year, governments borrow more money than the previous year.

The government is in debt, and it must repay that debt and the associated interest. But how will a government repay the debt?

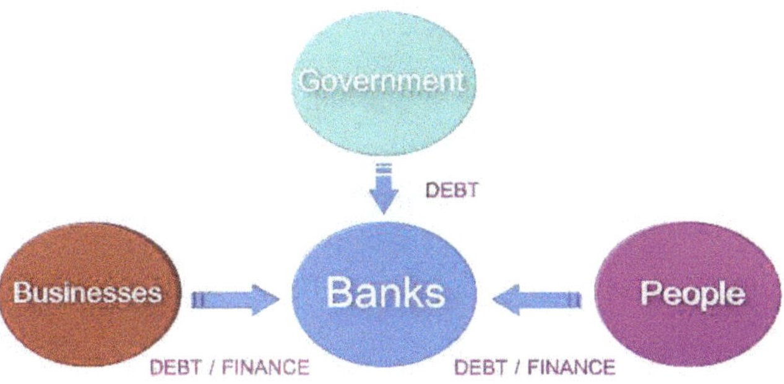


Logically it will raise taxes. The government will tax two different Stakeholders: business owners and the people.

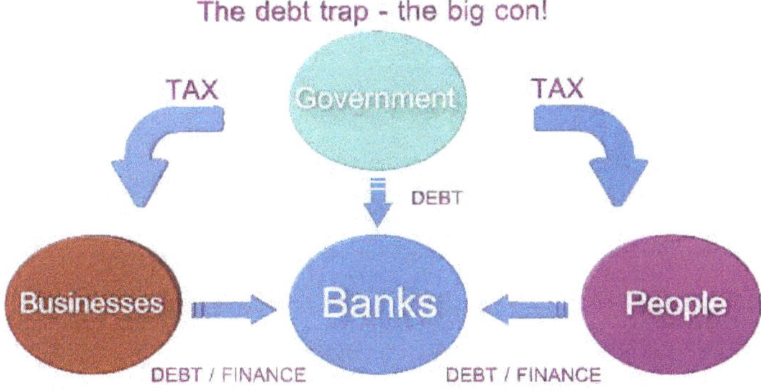


The business owners are likely to have their debt already, and when they are taxed more if they wish to retain their current profit margins, the likely scenario is that they will raise their prices. The public, the poor people of those lands, are now being taxed more by the government, prices increase, and they already have their debt.

Their disposable income reduces even further, and their reliance to acquire more debt increases.

The average debt in the UK Is around 55,000 spondoolies per household. The average debt for a qualifying adult over 18 is in the region of 28,000 spondoolies, an increase of 790 spondoolies from the previous year. This does not include mortgage payments.

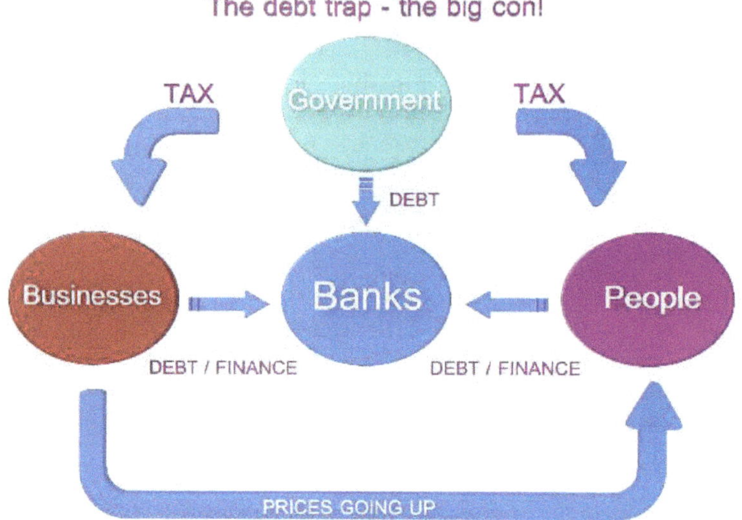


The figures generally fluctuate depending on the source. Still, the matter is that debt levels are increasing for the people, businesses, and governments, which is why banks are the most powerful institutions globally.

As a personal debt increases, the ability to pay it off quickly reduces every month. Many people are paying off more interest than the debt they owe. **The financial institutions want us to not only get into debt but to keep us there!**

This is why it is called the debt trap. Once you are locked in it, unless you decide to get out of the trap, the monthly payments made to pay off your debt just become part of your monthly expenditure.

Financial worries are one of the main burdens for people and their relationships. Their quality of lives is downgraded. They cannot afford to go out and enjoy themselves because they are so laden with debt.

Other expenses could be reduced too, and we will cover this later in the chapter.

Our purpose and strategy in this section are to show you how to eliminate your debt within five years or less. Irrespective of your debt, we can employ strategies to eradicate the debt.

The bigger the debt, the more we will need to do. Understand that it is possible to eliminate your debt as quickly as you want if you are prepared to do what others are not prepared to do.

I would like you, just for a moment to think of the amount of debt that you are paying off every month. Instead of this being money that you are paying off and never seeing, let us just for one moment pretend that this money is now either being spent on doing things you've always wanted to do or saving up to buy a deposit for your very own home. Or that fancy bike that you tell your wife only costs £1000 but costs £5000! 😊.

Let us assume you are paying 300 spondoolies a month to a credit card and other associated loans. If you had an extra 300 spondoolies each month to spend as you wish, what would you spend this on?

You could save 300 spondoolies a month for a year and buy a holiday somewhere exotic. Where you paid it upfront and did not hit the credit card again! Now that would be a change.

Maybe you want to treat the children to more days out, to invest more in some of those fashionable items they crave so badly, and perhaps just eating where you want to eat rather than where your purse or your wallet requires you to buy your goods from. When they go into a restaurant, many people read the menu from right to left. They look at the price and then scan left to see what the food item was. Have you ever done that?

We all have, and it does not need to be that way. By making some simple shifts in the way we live our lives daily, we can free up more money to pay off our debt more quickly, and by paying off more than we usually pay off, we will reduce the interest payments and more of the debt will be paid promptly.

If you do not make a change in a positive direction, you will be in debt for the rest of your life unless you get a lucky break, you get made redundant, or you just get plain old and finish paying off your mortgage. Once you ended paying off your mortgage, you could start paying off all your other debts.

This doesn't read right; look back to how many years you have worried about money, how many years you have not been able to live the life you wanted because you didn't have enough money?

Or the number of times you made the decision, just one more time, to put something on a credit card.

That is not the right way to live, and it doesn't have to be this way; the problem is we all like our worldly things, and we all want to keep up with the Joneses. This world of measuring up against one another is bad for our health.

You can feel temporary enjoyment and getting something on credit, and yet that feeling will pass you by in no time at all. Then you feel discomfort for years and years after that for just a flavour of temporary comfort.

How about we change the status quo? To do this, we will pay the price and pay the price means we will pull the belt around our waistline a little tighter. We shall forego the little luxuries in life for a short period so that we can enjoy the lovely luxuries of life for the rest of our lives.

We now know, or you should now have realised, that you have been duped. You have been deceived just like billions of other people around the world. We think that we can trust the banking institutions, yet when we look at them and hear the profits that they announced every year, we can surely not be that naive to allow them to get away with this.

It is time to turn the tide. It is time to put the shoe on the other foot and kick those banking institutions where it hurts. There is a shift occurring right now, which will diminish conventional financial institutions' power and decentralise how wealth around the world is distributed.

The banking institutions will do whatever they can to ensure that these new ways of doing business financially are put to bed. We are talking Crypto here, by the way!

You have no loyalty whatsoever to your current bank, they have been fleecing you for as long as you have been with them, and now it is time for you to give them something that they don't want! The banks don't want you to have money in them. That sounds quite bizarre. The banks earn very little if you have money with them. The only way the banks make money is if you have a debt to them, and then you are paying exorbitant interest rates.

So how are we going to kick them where it hurts? We will reduce the amount of money you owe them and, consequently, the interest payments, and then we will move your bank balance from a negative figure to a positive model.

The next exercise I ask you to do is not pleasant. But please go into your living your life on purpose Journal and go to the finance section. Take some time to do this exercise properly because we will chase down your debt.

Now go and find your credit card statements, loan statements or store card statements. Don't worry about how much debt is outstanding. The amount is irrelevant to our exercise.

Go to the most recent months statement and write down the amount of interest you are paying off for each of your debt elements. Not the % but the actual spondoolies dedicated just to the interest.

Jot them down in your Journal and understand that physical fitness and financial fitness follow the same rules.

We will employ some relatively simple strategies to drive down your interest payments. These are not going to drop instantly, and at the start, just like getting physically fit, it will appear that the interest payments are only reducing slowly.

Our key priority is to drive down the amount of interest you're paying monthly, which will drive down your debt.

Rule number one that people don't appreciate or fully understand when taking out debt is that when you agree to debt, the banks will recover the interest you have agreed to pay on top of the debt first.

As a very rough example, let us assume you have taken a loan for 10,000 spondoolies, and the bank has calculated that the interest on that loan. Over 48 months is 4000 spondoolies.

For the first year or even more, you will be paying very little to pay off the original 10,000 spondoolies; instead, you will pay more to pay off the interest first.

The same rules will apply to a credit card or store card debt. By working out a strategy to overpay on the obligations, you can reduce the interest element quicker, shortening its time to eradicate the debt.

In your living your life on purpose Journal, you should have recorded the interest element of any debts you have. It may not look very healthy, but in reality, you have done this exercise means that you are serious about eliminating that debt.

People respond in different ways to this confrontation of their debt, and you may, at this point, be feeling slightly sickly or even depressed. Do not worry; you will get rid of this horrible debt.

We have identified the interest payments that you will reduce. What we need to do now, though, is to determine which of those interest payments are harming you the most.

Spend some time and now work out which of these debts has the most significant interest percentage. In our new strategy, we will focus logically, and we are going to look to drive down the interest of the highest % first.

By focusing on this debt with the highest interest percentage, you will drive down this one quickly, and once you have eliminated this one debt, you can then focus on the second-highest interest percentage.

This may sound remarkably simple, and indeed it is. Far too few people consciously think about the interest payments that are harming them the most.

Therefore, we do not focus on the debt and more on the interest percentage. You are going to make your money work for you better. After all, you worked hard to get it!

Even if the debt with the highest interest percentage is the lowest of the debts you owe, we still want to eliminate that debt first. Many people fail to take stock of what they are spending their money each month. This failure means that some are haemorrhaging money to unnecessary places.

In your living your life on purpose Journal, allocate some time jotting down what you spend monthly. Take this right down to the number of coffees you buy from Starbucks or something similar.

Write down how much you spend on alcohol, tobacco, and those cheeky little takeaways from time to time.

Go through all the subscriptions that you pay every month, such as Netflix, Amazon, or the sports channels.

Yes, we need to document how much money we're spending on those things we enjoy doing, such as chocolate, wine and five Guys burgers. When I first did this, I wasn't traumatised, but I was quite surprised at how much money I wasted on nonsense.

Once you have spent time writing down all your expenditure and you have also added what your take-home pay is each month, you will be able to subtract your spending from your income.

It can be quite a sobering exercise, but if you spend a good hour on this and do it properly, it will be worth the reality check in the long run.

The next phase of your personal finance scrutiny is putting an Asterix or a tick next to the expenditure you think you can do without and what you think you can improve on.

If Gary wanted to clear his debt in five years and all it took was an extra repayment per month of drinking less wine, eating less Curry, and losing his subscription from a sports channel, would that sacrifice be worth it in the long run?

Only you can decide what is worth paying the price for, but the more price you pay, the quicker you can become debt-free.

Subtle changes to how you spend money can make quite a big difference. If you have the habit of drinking alcohol during the week instead of consuming it on the weekdays, drink only at the weekend. It sounds quite surreal but dropping one bottle of wine a week could save you around ten spondoolies a week. Paying off 40 spondoolies a month extra onto your debt reduces the period considerably.

Then add on those cheeky takeaways that you have now replaced with good healthy food and the sports subscription. It wouldn't take too long to be repaying over 100 spondoolies a month extra from your debt.

Once you have worked out what you could sacrifice or stop spending money on for a while, you can look at other ways to reduce your household expenditure.

You could always shop around to save money on your home telephone, Internet, mobile or cell phone, gas electricity, and insurances.

Don't be fooled and be lazy by going to a comparison website. They move people from deal to deal, and they get a kickback from the company that they recommend, so they are not acting in your best interests.

If you look around and take the time, you could easily save yourself over 100 spondoolies a month on the right deals.

Another way you can save a lot of money is not to be fooled by the newest mobile phone handset. This locks you into a longer-term contract, and you pay a monthly subscription. Just do with your current handset. You can make use of it to make telephone calls, send messages, take pictures, and surf the Internet. Let us face it you aren't using it to its full potential now!

When it comes to shopping for your household food and groceries, do this online. Online shopping is a great way to avoid the temptation of buying those treats that we don't need. If you are going shopping, maybe look at other shops that offer the same quality products but are not a premium brand supermarket.

If you have the option to collect any form of cashback using a card, or award points for shopping in a store collect them whenever you can. It seems relatively trivial, but even collecting discount vouchers and using them will go a long way.

Look at the type of cars you and your partner are driving. If you have two fancy cars on the driveway, do you need them? If you do have these cars, there's a high chance you're paying for them on some form of lease deal, and they will never be yours. If you are coming close to a lease deal's renewal, do not go for a newer vehicle; continue the current agreement with your existing car.

The automobile, the mobile phone and television are three ways that the bling factor seduces people. Seriously nobody cares if you're driving a three-year-old car, using a three-year-old mobile phone, and don't have the latest television technology.

Also, be mindful before you purchase anything of note, do you need it, or are you buying it just as a luxury.

You think it matters because it massages your ego and lets people believe that you live an extraordinary life. Nobody cares about you! They have enough to worry about themselves.

Sometimes people buy an item and then immediately after that experience buyer's remorse. We have spoken so much about being consciously in the moment. If you are looking to purchase something, don't take the knee jerk reaction and buy it spontaneously. Check out what you want to purchase and then go and have a break, a cup of tea or coffee and evaluate whether you need it.

Just being more conscious in the buying phase of your life could save you that buyer's remorse.

We are not asking you to go shouting through the streets that you are looking to eradicate your debt within five years, but if you did tell some of your closest friends, family members, and colleagues you were doing, it would be a great way to declare your goal.

You never know you may even help them aspire to the same financial freedom.

What will happen is each month, you are going to track your interest payments. You will see that these interest payments are reducing every month as those interest payments start to reduce every month, the amount of desire to eliminate the debt increases.

By tracking and measuring this critical interest on your debts, you will start to become fuelled, inspired and, for some people, addicted to reducing it from whatever it is to zero.

It is like doing the couch to 5K but in reverse. Days one to seven of the couch to 5K aren't the best. Months one to 7 of eliminating your debt are not the best. But as time goes by, and remember, time will always win out; there becomes a tipping point where you see the light at the end of the tunnel. You need to be disciplined, and you need to understand that your persistence in eliminating your debt and the activity surrounding this vital. Do not give up.

We can engage in a process where we reduce our expenditure, and we have the target of eliminating debt within five years. You can also look at other ways to speed up becoming debt-free.

One such way is to increase household income. I am not talking about doing overtime at your job or taking out too many dividends from your business because it could be detrimental to your business.

There may be no more overtime available at your job or dividends available from your company.  But there are so many other ways to create an extra income.

Here are a handful of ways to create extra income alongside your job or your business. Remember, this is additional income, and this extra income can accelerate the reduction and elimination of your debt.

Within the LYLOP community, we will have a section specifically designed to show you multiple ways of creating extra revenue:

Join a Network Marketing company.
Start Drop shipping.
Try Print on Demand.
Make Money with Affiliate Marketing.
Monetise a YouTube Channel.
Become an Influencer/trainer on social media.
Create an Online Course.
Publish an e-book.
Consider Freelancing.
Create an App.
Become a Writer.

Create Side Gigs.
Do Translation Work.
Sell Your Stuff.
Become an Online Tutor.
Drive Your Car – Uber or the like.
Become a Virtual Assistant.
Invest in Stocks or Crypto – high risk.
Sell Your Photography.
Sell Your Designs Online.
Review Websites, Apps, and Software.
Get a Part-Time Job.

You just need to make a shift in your mindset. We have talked a lot about the need for a jam transfusion, and we have mentioned several times that you do not know what you do not know.

We are creatures of habit, and many people worldwide have a fixed mindset.

One of the top tips I can give you right now is to drop any ego. There would be no loss of credibility if you were to go away and do something extra to improve your life. The stupid people do the same thing day in day out, week in week out, month in month out and expect a different result!

You are different, and you are in pursuance of improving your life. That is why you are reading this book.

We spoke about the GUPTR and the IBE.

The generally unsuccessful people talking rubbish and the instant bleeding experts. I do chuckle when I mention those phrases, because there are so many stupid people globally, and the sad thing is that these people influence others and stop them from attaining their success. There has never been a more excellent time to create extra income for ourselves in this wonderful world of opportunity. Working out where those income sources are is merely a matter of investigation.

Through your jam transfusion, do not discount all the different ways to create extra income.

There are lots of ways that you can partner with a successful company involved in the industry of network marketing.

Network marketing has got a bad rap, and the reason it has a bad rap is that people do not understand it.

My take on network marketing is quite a simple one. If you are prepared to put in five to ten hours a week part-time on top of your current job or business and follow the system outlined by that company, you will generate extra income.

Much of this is about managing expectations. Within this finance section of our book, we have set an initial objective of eliminating debt within five years. It will be less, but five years could be a good target for some.

Forget about the riches you may hear that can be earned by partnering with a network marketing organisation. Some people make significant earnings; many people aren't interested in the significant gains, which is a large misconception of why people join such organisations.

You may have no interest in joining a network marketing company and may have no interest in their services or their products. But if you are serious about eliminating your debt and creating a better lifestyle for you and your family, sometimes you must do the things you don't want to do to get the things you've always wanted. Let us say you join a network marketing company, and you invest a nominal fee for starting.

In this scenario, you generate an extra monthly income of 200 spondoolies.

In literally any of the network marketing companies I have researched worldwide, earning an extra 200 spondoolies a month is instantly achievable.

**What would an extra 200 spondoolies a month do, to lower your interest on the debt you are carrying?**

We have already worked out ways to pay more towards those bad debts by reducing our expenditure or awareness. We could always work part-time on another business and create another way to drive down the interest of those debts.

The reduced amount of time it takes to eliminate your debt by adding an extra 100, 200, 300 or 400 spondoolies a month is staggering.

To put this into some form of perspective, let me give you a real-life example of a company that shares with its customers how they can reduce their debts even further.

It is a bank, and they have a Repayment Calculator that shows how quickly debt can be repaid by paying a little more each month.

This could shock you but demonstrates why being stuck in the debt trap is merely a choice.

Suppose you have a credit card debt of 10,000 spondoolies and have an interest rate of 18%. Paying off just the minimum amount each month would take 37 years for you to satisfy that debt. The interest that you will have paid off in this exceeds 18,000 spondoolies. The monthly repayment figure in the region of 237 spondoolies.

Did you read that? 37 years!!

For the same debt, if you increase the monthly payments by 100 spondoolies to 337 spondoolies, the amount of time to repay the debt now is five years four months. The interest paid would be 2978 spondoolies.

Increasing that payment again by a further 100 spondoolies to 437 spondoolies per month Would reduce the repayment time to two years four months and the interest paid Down to 2116 spondoolies.

You may now be able to appreciate just how you can eliminate your debt within five years. Let us say you have a debt of 50,000 spondoolies, and we want to reduce this to zero within five years. In this scenario, your minimum payment would be over 1000 spondoolies a month, but if you were to increase that to 1300 spondoolies per month, you would eliminate this debt in four years eight months.

We can't magically make an extra 1000 spondoolies appear, but we can live our lives on purpose, creating an additional income stream and reducing expenditure to create an extra 1000 spondoolies a month.

You could become an eBay seller; you could be creative and start to make things at home that you can sell, you could get a part-time job. For ease, though, don't forget the network marketing company. They have every ready for you to plug into and earn money.

To pay the price is worth it, and their reward is so great that it is justifiable. Many people with the wrong mindset believe that they do not have time to create an extra income stream. That is just so wrong and lazy, and they need to have a mindset shift.

We can all agree that there are 168 hours in a Week. Let us assume that you work for 70 hours in that week; you sleep for the regulation 8 hours a night, which is 56 hours. When you subtract the 70 and 56 hours from the 168 hours, you are still left with 42 hours of spare time a week.

Most people don't work 70 hours a week, so I've exaggerated that. But if you are left with 42 hours a week, and you were to spend 10 hours a week building some form of extra part-time income, you would still be left with 32 hours a week to enjoy. You will create an inner sense of satisfaction when you put in extra work for a veritable goal.

If you can eliminate debt of 50,000 spondoolies in five years, what can you do with the remaining years of your life? You could create such an abundant life by simply changing your habits, focusing on improving your financial fitness, and reducing stress associated with debt.

**If it is to be, it is up to me.**

If you were to grade yourself from a zero to a ten and had eliminated your debt, what grading would you give yourself?

If you had generated more extra income with your part-time business than you were earning from your full-time job or your business, how would you grade yourself?

Think it is impossible, and you are right. Working with a growth mindset and preparing to think outside the box and give it a go, you have a chance.

I have seen it happened so often that people start working a part-time business on top of their job or regular business to see the income that they earn overtake their other revenue and live an extraordinary life. If it can happen to them and hundreds of thousands of other people worldwide, it can happen to you. Just don't listen to the GUPTR and the IBE.

## Physical Environment

It is not an accident that the chapter Physical Environment follows the Finances chapter in living your life on purpose. Our physical environment is likely to be determined by our financial status.

The physical environment will include the place that you live, for example, the County or the Country. It will also include the home you live in, the school that your children go to, and the place you work.

The physical environment includes the things that you have in your life that are tangible.

If we go back to the jammy doughnut scenario and where your parents lived when you were growing up and where their parents lived, a trend may start to form. Many people still live in the same area or the same type of dwelling house they did when they were children.

It may be full of more modern gadgets and up to date decoration, but the actual building itself is likely to be in a similar neighbourhood. If your parents lived in a three-bedroom detached house in a relatively modern estate, there is a higher probability that you live in something similar.

This is a broad sweeping statement and, of course, may not relate to you at all.

When we look at our physical environment, we can assume that where we live also determines our health and fitness. Where we live can also define our employment status or the type of business that we run.

But how can living in an apartment in a slightly lower demographic in a large city be any different to living in a semi-rural location in a mid-demographic area, with an abundance of nature?

We have already discussed that by living your life on purpose, you will now have made meaningful choices in your life, and you are better equipped to grow physically and mentally. If you take stock of some of the advice in the finances section and become wealthier, you will have the ability to improve your physical environment.

Where you live right now does not need to be where you live in the next three to five years and beyond.

We are not saying that where you live now isn't a nice place, I am sure you have made it homely, and the surrounding areas are lovely.

For a moment, dwell and consider where you are currently living. With open eyes, scan around your house and then look at the area immediately surrounding your home, for example, your garden.

Then scan to a slightly wider perimeter and look at the location that you live. Then go even more expansive with that perimeter. Are you living in a city that you like? Then widen even further are you living in a country that suits you? Each of us has differing needs and wants, and none of us is wrong.

Some people like to live in the countryside, and some people like to live in the city. Some people like to live in apartments whilst others like to live in houses. Some houses are detached, semi-detached or terraced.

In this chapter, we would like to spend some time evaluating other ways to live, other places you could live and what it could do for you and your family.

Being conscious of your surroundings and then ambitious about where you want to go gives you a mental image, and that WHY POWER continues in the habit, you are forming on the attainment of your goals.

I have some friends that live in the City of London; that place is crazy, it is full of the hustle and bustle, it is full of so many noisy and polluting vehicles, and people don't seem to want to smile at one another. Yet my friends that live there think it is brilliant.

I could think of nothing worse in my life than living in a city like London. It would go against all my values and the way I like to live my life, and I am sure it would harm my mental and physical health.

The cost of living in this city is extortionate. People pay way above the national average for their accommodation and their food, and any other luxury they may treat themselves.

I am not for one moment saying that people who live in a city are wrong. I'm demonstrating that this is their choice, and many of them like it. Many of them don't like it, but they need to live there because that is where their job or business takes them.

On the other hand, we live in a rural location just three miles away from the city centre of York. If you research York, you will find that this is a quiet historic city. Our little village has just over 60 houses, one pub, and a pond with a large weeping Willow tree drooping into the water.

We live in a lovely house, a four-bedroom detached house for myself, my wife, and our chocolate Labrador. Our gardens are of adequate size, and we have farmers' fields behind us. All the people in the village say hello and we smile, and we talk to each other it is a wonderful and friendly community.

My friends in the city could think of nothing worse than living in a small rural village where the bus service operates just two times a day, where we have a rush 5 minutes in the morning, and the afternoon, when the local primary school picks up and drops off.

Inside our house, we have comfortable furniture. We do nott have any state-of-the-art audio or visual gadgetry. Our main passion is getting out into the countryside where we can cycle, golf, run, and even paddleboard down the local River. We drive comfortable cars, and we have nothing extravagant in our lives.

You could say that we live simple lives and yet very happy. We love our holidays and enjoy experiencing what those Holidays bring. Sometimes your perfect place and your happy place don't have to be exuberant and way out expensive. It is your place and your place alone. That was a brief description of our physical environment.

Are we where we want to live, yes and no! Would we like to have some of the up-to-date tech? Probably yes.

Would we like to drive better quality cars? Only ever so slightly. A car is just an object to move me from A to B. It must fit my golf clubs, my bikes, my paddleboards, and a tail-wagging chocolate Labrador dog.

I've owned some luxury vehicles in my past, and as I matured, I soon realised that I held no respect for the car at all. Irrespective of how much the car cost, it was treated the same way.

I was never one of these people that would vacuum the inside each weekend and clean the exterior. Quite the opposite, I would throw things in and out of the vehicle. It would get cleaned on the outside once a month and inside every quarter.

I soon realised that a vehicle is an item that we may need, and it is one of those purchases that people make for them to look better within their society and circle of friends. Buying a vehicle just because of its manufacturer can be just a materialistic and egotistical buy.

As you mature and get slightly wiser, you soon realise that people do not care what type of vehicle you are driving. They don't care if you have the latest golf clubs or a top of the range bicycle.

The people who matter and the people you associate with are the people who take you for what you are and who you are, where you live, and not by what you have. They don't expect you to do anything for them that would cost you financially.

The modern era's curse is that people seem to want to invest their hard-earned money, or money that they borrow via a credit card or loan, to keep up appearances of success.

When goal setting, I must admit that some of my goals include owning properties abroad. Living in Spain, for example, suits us because of the incredible weather, proximity to the United Kingdom, and the fact that we love our sports. Living near the sea and an abundance of golf courses would suit us superbly. New Zealand is one of my favourite places in the world. I would also love to have a property on Lake Taupo's banks.

If you ever get the chance to visit New Zealand, jump at it! If it is not on your bucket list, put it on as soon as possible. The scenery in the countryside is phenomenal, the people and the culture lovely. I love the idea of owning a property in Lake Taupo area because we could visit there whilst the northern hemisphere is wintering as the southern hemisphere is in the summertime.

We would also love to buy a Villa in Orlando, Florida. More specifically, in a place called the villages. We visited there several years ago, and that place is impressive. Imagine having 50 odd golf courses and several villages built around the golf courses.

Imagine a community with lots of recreation centres and swimming pools, and just pathways for golf carts to whizz along. Over 60,000 golf buggies are racing around these tracks to and from the shopping centres, restaurants, golf courses and recreation centres.

This is a brilliant place to live if you have an active lifestyle and want to relax at the same time.

Hopefully, you now have an insight into goal setting within the physical environment. Set yourself some goals and some targets of things that you'd like to have in your current physical environment, and if you desire it, the type of house you would like to move to, in the area that you'd like to live with all the amenities that you always wanted.

Moving to your ideal physical environment can also be beneficial to your health.

I hear from so many people that they suffer from ailments such as arthritis or asthma. To name just two, I listen to people moaning about their illness, and they live in North Yorkshire.

Here in North Yorkshire, we have the most beautiful County in the United Kingdom, and I would urge anybody to visit this place of beauty. But as with many of our beautiful areas in the United Kingdom, the weather plays a part in its beauty.

We have colder and wetter winters than the South of England and other parts of Europe. If someone has arthritis or asthma, they often tell me how much better these conditions are when they go on holiday and are in warmer climates.

In my mindset, I cannot understand why they choose their physical environment to be North Yorkshire rather than Costa del Sol, in Spain.

They may have perceived reasons why they should remain in this country, but for a better and healthier quality of life, there are only a few reasons why you need to be in a location that doesn't serve your health. You may think that your family need you to stay where you are because it makes you feel better.

If they knew that you were moving to a warmer climate for health reasons, most of your friends and family would applaud you for making that move, and they would support you.

It would also give them an excuse to visit you in this warmer climate.

As you design your physical environment, think about the ramifications on your health and your family's health.

Do you think living in a large city with a vast quantity of polluting vehicles would be beneficial to somebody who has asthma or respiratory-related problems? Do we believe that these conditions caused those health issues?

What can people do if the area they live in does not suit their health? They can move!

Here in the UK, the middle classes gravitate to areas where schools have the best grading.

I find that quite comical that parents think that their children will have a better education, and a better future by moving to a school that has been graded higher by government authority.

You will know from recent chapters that my personal belief is that the school education system is flawed. They are merely teaching our children to regurgitate facts to pass exams. The purpose of passing exams is not for the benefit of the children. It is merely for the use of a better-graded school. The cycle of life in this scenario is absurd.

People choose their physical environment, where they live, on the virtue that they want their children to go to a school that has a better exam conversion ratio.

If you were to live your life on purpose and were to engage in the wheel of life and the philosophy that you live your life with continuous and never-ending improvement, what you pass on to your children will be far better than any education system around the world.

I am not saying it is wrong to move to an area to put your child in a school with higher grading. As it happens, many of the schools are in a physical environment that is very pleasing. So, by virtue that you are going to move to that area is good progress.

We're talking about balance in the wheel of life. If you examine your current physical environment, think about things that are in it, that don't serve you well, and think about things within it that you would like to have. If you have children, choosing your physical environment will have a massive impact on how they grow up. Many people who live in the cities, I mean the largest cities, do not understand the different environment with living in a smaller city, town, or village.

Children are at their weakest when they are growing up and approaching or going through their teenage years. Peer pressure is now more significant than it ever has been. If you fly with the crows, you get shot with the crows. Birds of a feather flock together.

**You become equal to the average of the five people you associate with the most!**

The risk of falling in with the wrong crowd is significantly higher in an inner-city lower demographic area. The more rural you go on a sliding scale from a large city to a village, then mix in going from a lower demographic to a high demographic will determine the child's associations.

As adults, remember you don't know what you don't know. If you are seriously engaging in this philosophy of living your life on purpose and improving many aspects of your life, one of the significant elements you can improve is the physical environment where you live.

You may live somewhere that is perfectly comfortable and has everything you need. All your friends and family members surround you, and it is great for convenience. If you are looking to develop yourself, take a close view of this environment and then, without any malice, decide whether the people around you are going to help you and your family in your growth.

If you have the ambition to live in the house of your dreams, in the location you desire, you must set about working towards those aspirations. In this world of opportunity, you can create your physical environment, and everything contained within it. There is no limit to what you can manifest.

Spend some time researching different places to live and other things to have. Go for drives around your local area or areas you always wanted to live in. Look around the physical environment, take into stock the place's feel.

If you see somewhere you like, take some photographs, and place them on your vision board. Once you have identified where you want to live, think about what you would like in it. There is nothing wrong with this goal-setting phase. Enjoy this process. It is fun and can be quite enlightening.

Once you have chosen the house of your dreams, think about the furnishings and the fittings. What type of living room furniture would you like?

With your loved one, go to the type of shop that will sell the things you would love to buy. You may not be able to afford these things just now but visit some places that sell the things you like.

Do some window shopping, even in the department stores or shops that you don't usually enter as your wallet or purse cannot afford. People go into shops, look around, and walk out without buying. For you, this can be an enjoyable fact-finding mission!

Did you know that some people from specific demographics have never walked into a shop because they think they don't fit in the shop? They believe that the shop is above them!

I remember being fortunate to win a company competition with a prize of a night at the Ritz in London, with a lovely meal and a West End show.

I flew from Scotland, where I was living, and as I approached the Ritz hotel, the doorman stopped me in my tracks. I was wearing denim jeans, and this doorman looked me up and down in a rather condescending way. He asked if he could help me, and I replied, “Yes, I’m staying here tonight”.

He looked at me as though I did not belong there. I wondered how much he was earning and where he was living to be the Guardian of this glamorous hotel.

As I walked into the hotel’s reception, one of the managers behind the reception desk looked at me. He then shuffled over to me and took me to one side. Once he realised I had a reservation, he asked me if I could go and change into something that was not denim. I had a perfectly good suit in my luggage, but I decided I wanted to play this on.

I informed him that I had no other clothing other than jeans. He then told me that he would check me in personally, and I was then to take the elevator up to my room and that I was only permitted to move from my room to the elevator and out through the hotel’s exit doors.

On arrival to my room, a champagne bottle was chilled and provided by my company. I looked around the room and saw all this gold and ornate furnishing. Immediately I was not too fond of it, and I would have disliked it even if it weren’t for the doorman and the manager.

This was not my environment. I like to have the finer things, but this was ostentatious and unnecessary. I would go as far as to say that the Ritz hotel in London is the worst hotel I have ever stayed in.

On the other hand, the Hard Rock hotel in Universal Studios Orlando would rate right up there as one of the best I have ever stayed. As you approach this rock and roll hotel, it doesn’t matter whether you’re wearing flip flops, or you are wearing brogues. On arrival, it is instantly relaxing, the staff members are welcoming, and the whole ambience suits me perfectly.

Give me burger fries and a beer anytime over some of the most lavish foods in the best restaurants in the world.

I was fortunate to win a six-star cruise on the Silverseas, Silver Wind around the Caribbean. Part of that also included an evening meal with one of the UK's wealthiest people. Alongside him and his wife were six of us.

The waiter came round and took the food orders with Charles and his wife Elizabeth, the last to order. Six of us ordered from the menu.

When it came to Charles, he asked for "Chicken and fries", Elizabeth asked for the same. Sitting next to Charles, I joked that "Chicken and fries" wasn't even on the menu. He replied, "You are on a six-star cruise ship. You can have whatever you want"!

This brief story reiterates that it doesn't mean you need to turn into someone you don't want to be when you improve your physical environment. Be you!

Charles is the most successful person I know, and ethically he is fantastic.

I went to a seminar once and heard him say some words. I remember them verbatim to this very day.

"I view my success as an entrepreneur, not by how rich or successful I become, but by how many people become rich and successful as a result of me." 20 years later, and he still lives by this mantra. Strange, how he has become one of the world's wealthiest people – eh?

I have a perfect picture of my physical environment, and I choose you to get the perfect picture in your mind. Think about where you would like to live and what you'd like to have, and why you would like to have them.

You walk into a furniture shop, and you see a three-piece suite. It looks stunning in the colour and decor of your choosing. It has reclining elements and places to put your drinks in the cup holders. Wow, everything you need for a perfect relaxing time watching a movie in your favourite home.

You check the price and instantly baulk!

The price of this three-piece suite-only made you react this way because you've never bought anything of this price. It doesn't mean that you never will, and it doesn't mean that this furniture is overinflated. Designing your perfect physical environment opens your mind to what you want within the home, not what it costs.

As you grow as a person and follow the principles of living your life on purpose, some things you think are expensive will soon become the norm.

This is why it is important to visit places that sell the things you want to buy. For many people, this is enlightening because they didn't even realise some of these things existed.

For example, if you like your tech, go to a shop, maybe an audio-visual shop and have a look around. These places will blow your mind. Voice-activated equipment from the curtains and blinds you want to open and shut, heating or cooling down your room, and switching their channels on your television. Tech to switch on table lamps to voice command and even APPS to switch on your cooker remotely.

This James Bond or luxury movie world does exist, and the great thing is these tech things are coming down in price and becoming more affordable, and you can have them.

I can't remember exactly the type of car one of my friends always wanted to buy. It was an Aston Martin. He had always set a target of owning one of these DB7 vehicles. It was a picture on his fridge freezer. Everywhere he went, he thought of owning a DB7 Aston Martin. Fortunately, he was a goal setter, and he was a goal-getter, and he lived his life on purpose.

When he could afford to buy the car and buy the car for cash, he went to the garage and drove the car for the first time. He didn't like the car. He didn't like the way it drove, and he had set the target of owning one of these cars' years ago. He didn't like it one bit!

When you have that level of income, disappointment must be with you just for moments because instead, you go and buy another car with an equivalent value that suits you better.

But if you would like to own a Range Rover motor vehicle, go to a garage, and test drive one. Get a picture of said car and the colour you want it and put it on your vision board or fridge.

I want you to imagine that you are now living in the house of your dreams in five years. You have made some new friends in the locality, you haven't lost the old ones you just now have new ones. Your children are currently playing in the street with their new friends. You regularly have get-togethers with these new friends in this social environment and have barbecues or dinners together.

You feel healthier, you feel happier, and your stress levels don't appear to be with you anymore. You don't owe any money, and you live in the home of your dreams.

If you want to buy something you go and buy it. If something breaks, you don't cry about it.

Things break all the time, and the way we react is mainly determined by how much it will affect us and cost us.

How good would you feel to be living your life on purpose, in the place that you designed, to the degrees of happiness and health that you created on purpose?

Let us then start to design your physical environment. We are goal setting now. It does not matter if you cannot afford to do this now. The whole purpose of goalsetting is to throw magnets into the future, and then we get drawn to the magnets.

Spend some time and go to your living your life on purpose Journal to start the goal-setting process. Start to paint the picture in your mind of your forthcoming life and be excited by it.

## Business/Career

By now, you should have entered your wheel of life where you think you are regarding your business and your career.

In the wheel of life, we are looking to gain balance. If we are sitting at an 8, 9, or 10 in our business or career, is this harming your family life and fun and recreation?

If you are sitting in the lower echelons of the grading for your business, the great news is that by living your life on purpose, the grading will continue to improve each month.

Remember, they say that the definition of insanity is doing the same thing and expecting a different result.

As a person, you will already be improving. By simply following some of the book's techniques, you will be growing personally. You will also have set some goals, and therefore if you have a big enough goal, you will be undertaking a goal-directed activity. But what if your ladder is leaning against the wrong wall? The first thing to understand is, are you doing something you want to do or are you doing it because it is a means to create money?

If you jump out of bed every day, and look forward to going to work, and you treat it as a passion rather than a money-making exercise. You are more than halfway there to success.

If today like every other day, you roll out of bed and lethargically get dressed to go to the job or the business that you do not particularly enjoy, you are doing yourself more harm than good.

I recently had a chat with a physical therapist, and one of the things I like to do when I'm engaged in business networking is to find out what their back story is. Forgive the pun!

As I spoke to this person, I was smiling inside because it was a jam in the doughnut story. This person had grown up with an accountant father who had encouraged him to become an accountant himself. He went to school, then University and then joined an accountancy practise. He then set up his accountancy practise with a partner, and the business was doing well.

By sheer chance, this person went to a job fair and whilst at the job fair, his reticular was alerted to physical therapy. He started to investigate physical therapy, and the more he researched it, the more he realised that it fits in line with his values and interests.

Whilst practising as an accountant, he also started to pass his qualifications to become a physical therapist. On passing his exams, he joined a clinic and now owns his business, partnering with a beautician. You could see the body language difference when he spoke about being an accountant and when he talked about being a physical therapist.

His shoulders and facial expressions drooped, and he didn't look remotely interested in being an accountant. He even stated that he only became an accountant because that is what his dad had done. Yet when he spoke about physical therapy, there was a genuine interest and passion.

Interesting, I thought, my dad was in the army, and so was I!

If you have something that you are passionate about, but a job or a business that you do not enjoy is getting in the way, there are more than enough hours spare in a day to retrain. It may take you a year or three- or five-years training part-time on your passion, and you may have to continue to run your business or stick at your job that you don't like during that.

**Which plan do you want to follow, the 45-year plan or the five-year plan?**

Most people are likely to work for at least 45 years, from leaving school or University to early retirement at that. Why would you want to work for 45 years in a profession that you don't even enjoy?

Doesn't it make sense to retrain if necessary, in a profession that you would thoroughly enjoy than sticking at a life-sapping dull and boring career?

This chapter will cover some things to help you in your business and your careers; however, we have an entirely separate living your life on purpose book dedicated to business owners.

Let us first understand the difference between a job and a career. They are not the same, not by any proximity.

A job is deemed to be more short-term and directly pursued to receive a wage. On the other hand, a career is long term and pursued by somebody who has a passion for that profession or subject matter. We joke that job stands for just over broke, where you do just enough not to get fired, and your employer pays you just enough so that you do not leave.

It is just a joke because there are some fantastic jobs out there. Some are paying a lot of money. That can only be good, if money, is the individual's primary motivating factor.

The money will not bring happiness if somebody is engaged in a job for 40 to 50 hours a week doing something they don't particularly enjoy doing.

The average amount of jobs for a person in the UK is 14.

Many people move from job to job to get a pay rise. Indeed, this is the best way to get a pay rise throughout your life if you have a job mentality. Some statistics show people who remain loyal to their employer earn less money during their lifetime than those who upgrade from job to job.

On the other hand, a career is about finding out what you enjoy doing and then getting paid to do that.

When it comes to a job, just because you are good at something does not mean you need to keep doing it. Take some time and thoroughly evaluate what your job means to you and how it affects your life.

Whether you have a job, a career, or a business, think forward 40 years and feel would you like to be still doing this during that length of time?

If you have completed the wheel of life properly, and, you now internally analyse your enjoyment of your working week. Is it having a positive, a neutral or a negative relationship with other facets of your life?

Do not just have a job, create a career, and do something you are passionate about. If you do not have the skills right now, do not worry; there are plenty of places where you can get the skills and qualifications you need.

If you refer to the finances section of this book, if you have a job, career or business that is not serving you well, you could get a side hustle to generate more income. Then bank that money so that if you wanted to, you could save the money and then go into full time learning to get the qualifications to move you towards your dreams.

Once you have defined your career path, create a concrete plan, and then work on the project. Remember, if you fail to plan, you plan to fail, and living your life on purpose is all about natural progression.

In line with our philosophies within this book, you must start to do something that serves you well and gives you purpose; remember you are in charge of your ship, and you are the master of your destiny.

**Set the sail for your ship and understand that the winds of opportunity blow on all of us.**

By following this book, we have already identified that you will be growing as a person, and you will be engaging in continuous and never-ending improvement. You will become healthier and fitter, and because you are engaging in professional development daily if you have a job or a career, This growth will not go unnoticed.

Through this great energy passing through your body, you will go to work and do whatever it is you do. However, with an improved attitude and the creation of your own new personal brand, your employers will detect an improvement in your personality and an enhancement in the way you are undertaking your work. Many people fail to understand that whilst they may have all the knowledge to complete their tasks for promotion purposes within an organisation, employers don't just look at their skills.

To progress through the corporate ladder, if you are good at what you do and go to work daily and continuously improve and seek validation for that approval from your employers, they will start to promote you into higher-earning positions.

During any annual appraisal, your employers are likely to inform you; they are impressed by your growth and how you are engaging in your work. You can also ask what progression paths there are available for you within the organisation and whether the company would pay for further education.

This is all about creating healthy boundaries to have a successful business or career. It is essential to understand that you cannot please all the people all of the time, and by setting your boundaries and set of rules, you will put yourself in a better position for growth.

For example, you go for an appraisal, and your employer sets out a progression path for you and agrees to fund some education. Your employer understands that you are ambitious and therefore want help to support you in becoming a more valuable member of the organisation.

This is a natural win for you and the company.

On the other hand, during your annual appraisal, you ask what the progression plans are and if they would fund some further education for you, and they utter the immortal words that there is no progression plan because this is dead man shoes.

At this point and in a moment of reflection, take time to work out why you would want to grow in an organisation that is not ready for your growth. You would also need to understand that as you grow, you will outgrow the organisation, and if you are doing something you enjoy doing, for example, it is a career; you may need to leave the organisation to find a fit for you.

My son once told me a funny story that reflected precisely this. Our family is predominantly Scottish. Once my son had finished his degree at the University of Stirling, he got a job in the City of London in the recruitment game.

He loved it in London, the party life, and the working hard, he found that he was good at what he was paid to do. He, however, realised that he missed living in Edinburgh, Scotland. He brought in a lot of money for the company but didn't feel congruent with his environment.

After a weekend of contemplation on a Monday morning, he went to his employer and stated that he wanted to move back to Edinburgh.

"But we don't have an office in Edinburgh", replied his employer. "I know" said my son in reply.

"What you are telling me is that we should open an office in Edinburgh", replied the employer.

"That would be so good", replied my son, and that is precisely what happened. He moved back to Edinburgh, and the company opened an office.

When you grow in value and become an asset to your company, it would be detrimental to them to lose your skillset. Of course, in my son's scenario, the company would not experience corporate failure if he did leave them. Still, there must be a balance, and there must be boundaries within an organisation of healthy respect. If you grow as a person and add value to what you bring to the company, it is only fair to repay you financially or with some other reward.

The most successful people in this world are not orientated by money. Instead, they become good at what they do, and money grows with them. The cash slave is likely to have a less fulfilled life and certainly less happiness.

Far too many employers treat their employees appallingly, and the reason they do so is because the employees don't stand up for themselves.

This is likely to be in places where people just go for a job. For example, you may work in a call centre, and employees' churn in the call centre is remarkably high. The employers know this is the case and therefore pay enough to get people attracted to the job, maybe with extra commission payments.

If an organisation has a high churn of employees, they tend to treat them with less respect than those with a low churn of employees.

Yet even within these high churn organisations, if you have the mindset that you want to have a career within it, and your employers are aware of this, they will start to treat you with greater respect and give you that progressive pathway you require.

By standing up to the people who pay you and asking for a fair return for the skills you are giving the organisation, you will gain more respect from them and they are likely to reward you accordingly. They know that if you are a valuable resource to them, if you don't get what you want, within reason, there is nothing to stop you from leaving.

**Do you enjoy what you do daily?**

It is such a simple question, and most people worldwide, certainly in Europe and the United States of America, will be saying NO to that previous question.

It is a fact that most people don't enjoy what they're doing for a living, and you cannot help but wonder why they are still doing it! There is an abundance of ways to create a career or set up a successful business. Indeed, there has never been a better time in humanity's history to do so.

It makes absolute common sense to do something that you enjoy doing, doesn't it? Getting up every day and going to work and getting paid to do something you enjoy doing. Being passionate not just every so often but every single day.

If you are happy at work, you will be satisfied at home. If you are happy at work and delighted at home, life is much better, and by default, you will be leading a healthier life.

You need to own your happiness, take the blame for your joy, and understand that people will receive this if you transmit that you are in a good place.

If they receive good vibes from you, doors will start to open everywhere.

Running a business in an arena of life that you don't enjoy is likely to lead to severe stress. You will have to force yourself to keep learning and keep up with the turbulent environment that we live in. You will have to compete with people in your industry who enjoy what they are doing, and it will be like a grind to you.

The very fact that you are a business owner and have business acumen means that if you wanted to follow something you enjoyed doing, a passion of yours, you are more than likely to be successful because you already know how to run a business.

Suppose you were to read Napoleon Hill's, "Think and Grow Rich". In that case, he mentions the importance of desire, faith, persistence, specialist knowledge, autosuggestion, and the benefits of being involved in a mastermind group.

Within the living your life on purpose, you can Join one of our mastermind groups. The format is straightforward. We invite 8-10 business owners or people that are on a career path to join the mastermind group.

Over a 26-week period, we meet every two weeks, over a zoom webinar is perfectly fine or face to face in a meeting room. We discuss one of the chapters in Think and Grow Rich at each meeting.

There are 13 main chapters, which is why the mastermind session runs over 26 weeks.

The growth of people who participate in a mastermind group is impressive. By associating with other ambitious individuals that want to improve their lives, you cannot fail to improve your life.

Remember, you become equal to the average of the five people you associate with the most.

During these 26 weeks, you operate in a safe environment and talk freely to the other members of your mastermind group. Each member will help the other within their careers and their personal development.

One of the best things about being in business is that there is no accountability. One of the worst things about being in business is there is no accountability!

By participating in a mastermind group, you follow through a sequence of the chapters, and then you can put meat on the bones of a simple business plan. The mastermind group sessions motivate all that get involved. If you'd like to participate in a mastermind group session, go to the living your life on purpose portal, where we can allocate you to an upcoming group.

Most people who participate are business owners; however, some people with careers also experience.

One of my favourite stories involves such a person who came to the first group I had run. He was a salesperson for a print company. He went around businesses and found print solutions to save them money, but I guess, more importantly, to make money for his company. It did not take long during the mastermind group process to eventually become the top-performing salesperson in the company.

The association with other success-oriented people started a different way of thinking. You see, in a mastermind group, if you have desires, dreams, goals and aspirations, you will be encouraged to precisely fulfil those things.

One of his goals was to learn to fly. With the group's vocal support, he eventually paid for one week of flying lessons in France. He went from Yorkshire to France to get the flying lessons.

He could have gone to a local airfield, but he had worked out that you are more likely to get increased flying hours at the French flying school because they have more stable weather. He went away and passed his flying course and came home and then set a goal of owning an aeroplane.

Not long later, he and a partner bought an aeroplane, and he then fulfilled one of his goals of flying his plane. There was an increased passion within this person; he soon realised that going as a salesperson selling digital print was no longer his calling. It had served a purpose, and he had earned some good money from it, but he wanted more. What happened next totally stunned me!

I had never even thought this person was remotely interested in physical fitness, yet he went and bought a gym. When you speak with him now about running a gym, he can talk non-stop and enthusiastically about how, along with his physical trainers, he is helping people from all walks of life become fitter physically.

I can honestly say I'd never heard one conversation, where he enthusiastically demonstrated he had reduced the cost per click on a photocopier for one of his business contacts. He was happy, and you could tell from his body language and physiology he had found his calling.

Just like the accountant did not want to be an accountant, he didn't want to be involved in sales; he was just good at it.

By participating in a mastermind group, you will be establishing a support system. Within this support system, you will have success buddies, and you will be able to talk freely about anything you want to discuss.

Being in business or being an ambitious career person can be a lonely place to be. You may run a business, and you may go home, but your partner has no interest in your business, so who do you talk to?

You may be career-minded and want to progress through the corporate ladder, and yet if you speak to some of your colleagues about your ambition, they probably will not see it your way, and they could be those GUPTR's or IBE's.

Participating in a mastermind group will remove you from the toxic environment and give you positivity and fuel to fulfil your goals. Have you ever been about to do something and then just as you were about to do it stopped and went no-no-no, and you held yourself back?

You have a fleeting moment of excitement to do something, but that horrible mind monster on your shoulder holds you back? That negative self-talk eats away and then stops you from doing that thing you wanted to do but was beaten by your mind monster.

I am sure that we have all done this from time to time and it is perfectly natural. Did you know that 80% of our anxieties and fears never materialised? Yet, these anxieties and fears keep us within the comfort zone.

By engaging in continuous our never-ending improvement and participating within a mastermind group, your comfort zone will start to reduce your anxieties, and your fears will subside. Consequently, you will do more of what you enjoy doing.

In your career or your business, it is essential to follow some simple rules, and we will go through some of those rules right now. In the living your life on purpose book for business owners, we will explore more and the importance of business planning, marketing, and acquiring more sales.

To be good in your career, job, or business, you need to be ACE. Speak with Authority, Conviction and Enthusiasm.

Authority means that you should know your business or what you are doing inside and out. If you offer a product or a service, know the product and service and its benefits for the people you are selling.

Conviction means that you believe in your product or your service and that you have no doubt that what you are selling will fit the customer.

The last four letters of the word enthusiasm are IASM. This stands for "I am sold myself". If you genuinely believe in the service you are selling or the product you are presenting, you will transmit this belief to the person you are selling to.

When we talk about enthusiasm, it is vital to get that balance. Sometimes, people's spirit can be overbearing. Be cool, calm, and collected. If you deliver a presentation to somebody, deliver it in a sedate way that allows every person you sit with to have confidence in you and what you are selling.

Do not fall into the trap of gushing and waffling and enthusiastically telling people why they must buy from you and why your product is the best in the marketplace. There is a skill to being positive and enthusiastic but allowing your body language to deliver more than the words that leave your mouth.

Here at living your life on purpose, we want you to improve all of the segments in your life. With your business and or your career, we want to get momentum within it.

You are continuously skilling up and learning more about what you are doing, but for a moment, we would like you to imagine that you are the captain of a plane on the runway. The tower gives you the go-ahead to take off. What percentage of power would you need to use to get your aircraft off the ground?

Obviously, you are right, a plane uses 100% of its power on take-off, but it only requires a fraction of the power to reach its destination when it reaches its cruising altitude. Your job, career or business are the same.

It doesn't matter whether you are running a new business or a well-established one; for it to move up a gear, an increased injection of power will create momentum, and this will create small edge victories that compound through time to become massive wins.

Momentum creates a buzz, and that buzz creates more enthusiasm, and more enthusiasm creates more activity. When you focus on the activities needed to improve your job, career, or business, the results will naturally follow because you repeatedly do the right things.

We've already spoken about the incredible power of the compound effect, and we know that if you go to the gym once, do you immediately become fit? Of course, you don't. If you eat a hamburger, once would you suffer from an obesity-related illness? Of course, you wouldn't. Highly unlikely in both scenarios. But if you repeatedly go to the gym for months and follow a proper health and fitness plan described in the previous chapter, you will become fitter.

I'm also sorry to say that if I were to have my favourite burger, you've guessed it, a Five Guys burger for breakfast, lunch and evening meal after a few months, the chances are there would be a significant decline in my health.

Business is the same. Focus on the right things consistently, and there will be a gradual improvement in business results. If the wrong things are being done consistently, well, you know you're going downhill.

The difference is that when you engage in the right business activities consistently, and your competitors keep doing the same wrong things, eventually, you will gain a competitive advantage.

Through our natural growth, we will develop our skills and confidence, and we are now going to grow our comfort zones.

Do you remember how you felt on the first day of your first-ever job? Nervous? Anxious? Scared? Unsure? That's how everyone feels. We didn't know anyone, we didn't know what we were supposed to do, and we didn't want to make mistakes.

But as the days passed and we made friends, we knew what we were doing, and even though we made mistakes, it was all part of the learning process.

We became comfortable in that environment.

Then we go and get another job, and it started all over again, nervous, anxious, afraid, unsure.

Each time we got a new job, the same process repeated until we became happy with our environment. The same rules apply to making changes in your approach to life and business.

You will start to do things differently, and you will begin to feel uncomfortable, but the more you do those things, the more comfortable you will become, and you will be stretching your comfort zone. There is the excitement of something new, the positivity of a potentially life-changing opportunity, followed by the nerves, the anxiety's, the fears, and the doubts.

Remember our old friend, the mind monster! Can I do it? Is it for me? What if I fail?

Success is 99% failure, and there is nothing wrong with failing. In our world today, the word failure is deemed to be negative. In the world of successful businesspeople, failure is art and part of success and is merely part of the process to gain results.

As we pass through and improve our professional development, we will learn to understand that failure is part of the process. Indeed, we will focus on failing more.

Imagine that focusing on failure, worse still, what if we deliberately attempted to fail more. Did you know that you will increase your success rate if you increase your rate of failure?

With your participation in your living your life on purpose mastermind group, you will discuss failure at length, and then together, you will all aim to fail more and grow with this failing attitude.

As time passes by through your powers of association and learning and increased confidence, your comfort zones will expand. Previously tricky tasks will become more comfortable, and acquiring and retaining new business becomes the norm, rather than a challenge.

You then realise that you can do this!

You can be successful, and consistency of activity will earn you the lifestyle you want.

**Rejection**

Here is the thing with rejection; everyone gets it in every aspect of life. It started in childhood when we heard the word "No" thousands of times.

Imagine a young Gary who had a favourite biscuit. More specifically, gingernuts.

"Mum, can I have a biscuit"?

"No"

"Mum, can I have a biscuit"?

"No"

"Mum, can I have a biscuit"?

"No"

"Mum, can I have a biscuit"?

"You can have one!"

Gary devours the biscuit, and as soon as he has done, he asks mum another question. Can you guess what that question will be?

“Mom, can I have another one”?

As a child, you were always testing the boundaries. You were always asking for something. But as we grew older, we learned to stop asking for the things for which we knew we'd get the answer no, and we only ask for the things where we were likely to get a positive response.

This is the classic jam in your doughnut stuff. Our subconscious mind protects us; it protects us so that we don't fail. If we have had rejection as a negative put into our minds from such a young age, the subconscious mind will do all it can to stop us from feeling that horrible feeling.

Conditioning is all in our heads.

We put it there! Our subconscious minds became the controlling section of our brain that stopped us from asking for the things we wanted. It became so powerful that it allowed us to be happy with our lot rather than expand into someone better.

Just opening your mindset to question the things you think are normal will give you an avenue to challenge those thoughts you previously knew to be true. Remember you don't know what you don't know, and the things that you do know that are in your mind, you need to question the source.

As we grew up, our parents, brothers, sisters, teachers, and the media filled our heads with many facts and pieces of information. But what if the source of that information is incorrect? By merely questioning what you know to be right on many occasions, you find out that the source of that information was incorrect and, therefore, your beliefs set was wrong.

Here is a great analogy that just makes sense.

And this has been happening since time immemorial.

How many people do you think have ever walked into a shop, had a look around and walked out without buying something? It's not just a lot of people; it's most people. And you have done it too. Similarly, how many people have walked into a shop, had a look round and bought some thing? Lots, of course. And that includes you too!

So, we are happy with the fact that people go into shops and they buy, or they do not buy. It's normal. The owners of shops know it's normal, so they don't get upset when someone walks in and out without buying anything.

Think of your business as a shop. When you show people around, understand that the same rules will apply. As the great Jim Rohn said, "some buy, and some don't buy, and that's just the way it's always been".

In our other books, we will detail the skills and knowledge to support and grow your career and business.

This chapter of the book is more about mindset.

**Belief... It grows legs!**

It is normal when you start a business, run a well-established company, or embarking on a career path that your belief levels will go up and down like a yo-yo.

At the beginning of any new business enterprise or career, you are at your most vulnerable, and those GUPTRs and IBEs will test your beliefs. Think of your business as a three-legged table. Each leg represents the key areas of belief you need to succeed. Firstly, you need a belief in your company. Secondly, you need to believe in its products or services and the sector you operate in, and Thirdly you must have belief in yourself.

If your number one leg is wobbly and your brother-in-law tells you your competitors are better than you, that leg could give way on your table will fall over.

When Napoleon Hill talks about persistence, he does demonstrate that it is required to grow belief. Suppose you continue to follow the principles of living your life on purpose and engaging in that continuous, never-ending improvement. In that case, you will understand the winners never quit, and quitters never win.

The magical thing about your belief table is as time passes by, and you are tracking your company results, and you see that the results are improving. You realise that your customers are becoming happier with the product or service you are selling them, and you know that you're becoming more profitable. As your successes continue to improve, what happens is that your table grows more legs.

These belief legs are great for your business, and you start to see that this is the business or career for you. You know without a shadow of a doubt that it is. You are doing something that you enjoy doing, and you are passionate about it. Your table continues to grow more and more legs until it has hundreds literally!

With hundreds of legs on your table, even if one of those IBE's manages to make one of your legs wobbly, your table stay solid because it has so many legs.

I want you to imagine setting up a brand-new business. We will open a hair and beauty product business with a High Street presence for this scenario. You will have a launch party, and you spent the time decorating your units, getting the stock in, and the unit looks fantastic. As you stand outside in the street looking back into your shop, you are filled with pride and excitement.mYou will have a launch party and invite your friends, family members, ex-colleagues, and other business owners with a circle of influence.

The launch party is a roaring success lots of people have come in and had a look around your store. They have drunk your champagne and ate your canapes.

At this moment, you believe your business will be a roaring success; everybody enjoyed visiting, and now you will sit back and wait for the sales to come in.

If only careers and businesses were that easy. The purpose of the launch party was to form part of a marketing strategy to announce to the world that you have arrived.

The work starts now. To be successful in any career or any business, you need to learn how to master the mundane.

After your launch party's excitement, now you need to get to work and not rest on your laurels.

By learning new skills, you will take advantage of your new launch by engaging in some form of post-event survey, looking for referrals, ensuring that there was a press release and posting your new launch on social media channels.

Don't be fooled by the moments of excitement in your business or your career. These are just little molehills along your journey of success.

**Seriously, you need to learn how to master the mundane.**

In your job, career or business, research what successful people do, how they do it, why they do it and if you can find out what their conversion ratios are. Find successful people and ask them for help, advice, or guidance.

People will help if you ask, none more so than part of your mastermind group.

If we refer to the compound effect's tremendous power, I'm sure you will understand that it is vital to work out all the things you need to do daily that will positively serve you and your business.

It is also a good idea to highlight the things that will not serve you well. Far too many people follow the path of least resistance, and they employ low pay off activities because these are the things that are easy to do.

Unfortunately, the things that are easy to do are low power activities for a reason, and that is because literally, everybody else is doing the same thing.

When we spoke about habits, we talked about creating good habits sets, and we spoke about stacking our habits.

Within your career or your business, identify habits that will serve you well. You want these to become natural to you through time. You will, of course, need triggers to remind you what you need to do, and you will need to work out ways to make the habit or the task more comfortable to do.

If you engage in repeated activity in a definite direction, the compound effect will win every time. Like flowing water carves a river, you can carve channels through your subconscious mind to improve everything you do.

How long does it take for a river to carve a route through the ground? We don't have that long in our lives, but the metaphor is the same. By mastering the mundane and repeatedly doing the activities you know will serve you well. You will eventually start to get that momentum we spoke about previously.

Once a body is in motion, it remains in motion. A classic example of this, that many of us may have done or observed is pushing a car.

Just recently, a friend of mine asked for some help. They had parked their Range Rover outside the doors of their workshop as an anti-theft measure. People couldn't get into the workshop because the vehicle was in the way.

This is a good strategy until you factor in that he had not driven the vehicle for an extended period due to the pandemic. He wanted to go into the workshop; however, when he went to move the Range Rover, the battery had died. The jump leads were in the workshop!

By chance, I was close by, so we both set about pushing the Range Rover out of the way of the doors. You've probably played a part in this before, and you know the score.

We both put our shoulders against the back of the Range Rover, and we huffed and puffed for a moment. At first, it didn't seem like we were going to be able to move the Range Rover. They are quite heavy these things.

We are applying power through our bodies through the Range Rover, and it seems like nothing is happening. And then we get that first little piece of momentum. The wheels start to turn, and then as the wheels begin to turn, we continue to apply the same amount of pressure. The vehicle starts to speed up, and we get the car out of the way of the doors.

Because we had not generated enough speed, the moment we stopped pushing the Range Rover, it stopped moving forward. But we had accomplished our task, and my friend could get the jump leads out of the workshop. The learning curve from that process was that he now puts the jump leads in the back of one of his cars.

The same rules of momentum apply to your career or your business. By focusing on those seemingly insignificant tasks repeated over consistent daily input, you will start to move your business or career forward.

It may take months before you feel as though you are getting any traction and movement, yet if you keep applying the same pressure, eventually you will gain momentum, and it will continue as long as you continue.

In business, if you are getting momentum and using the Range Rover analogy, if you wanted to accelerate the speed of the vehicle, you could enlist the help of somebody else. In our scenario, three people doing the same task with a goal-directed activity would be better than two.

There are easy things to do, and there are easy things not to do. If you make simple positive steps over time, you will experience an upward curve in your life and your business. When we talk about living your life on purpose, these simple and easy things to do with the right philosophy, attitude, and actions will eventually positively impact your lifestyle.

It will have a positive impact on your finances, your health, your business, your personal development, and your relationships. By taking responsibility and applying discipline and persistence, and being value-driven, i.e. living with continuous and never-ending improvement, these simple disciplines will lead to success. What feels uncomfortable early becomes comfortable later.

You start to gain momentum positively in all segments of your life. Some people though they make simple errors in judgement, and they do not just make those simple errors in judgement once they repeat them time after time.

Remember the fixed mindset we spoke about earlier in the book?

These people do not ask for help, and they don't engage in continuous and never-ending improvement because they believe they know everything already. They blame everybody; they neglect the things that need to be done, and they have an entitlement culture. What happens is they are making the wrong decisions repeatedly over a long period, and they then experience a downward curve in their life and all the factors associated with it.

You can have a prosperous life by merely mastering the mundane.

We must understand that success is not instantly attained in our careers and business. People who live in a world of instant gratification and expect instant results are likely to have a flaky attitude. By thoroughly understanding that success will come directly from positive actions repeated over time, you will not be disillusioned, and you will have managed your expectations appropriately.

But how do you have the best year of your life? You have the best quarter of your life! But how do you have the best quarter of your life? You have the best month of your life!

But how do you have the best month of your life? You have the best week of your life!

But how do you have the best week of your life? You have the best day of your life!

When we went through our goals section, we mentioned that sometimes the five-year goals could be too long, and you can't grasp the urgency of them. Of course, we may set five-year targets, but we want to set smaller, more achievable goals.

**Don't walk over the pennies to get to the spondoolies.**

If you write down the activities that need to be done every day and repeat them continuously, you will be moving towards your target.

With a 13-week massive action plan mindset, everything you do daily will form part of a weekly plan. Whatever you do during the week will fit into a monthly schedule. And the monthly plan will fit within the 13-week massive action plan!

So many people fail to understand the power of repeated activity over days. Instead, they adopt a feast or famine attitude. They may work busy one day and do nothing for the next three to four. They have no consistency within their lives, so their results are inconsistent.

Creating your purposeful morning and setting your specific tasks every day will allow you to remain focused and move forward.

In Brian Tracy's "Eat that Frog", he shows you some sure-fire strategies to make sure you do the essential things first. By engaging in a process where you do the most important things first and focus on those high pay-off activities, you will get higher pay off returns.

Those high pay off activities may test your comfort zone more but remember, the more you do them, the more comfortable you will become. Imagine being entirely comfortable doing high pay off activities that generate high pay off returns!

To be successful with your career or your business, employ systems or processes that will serve you well. For everything you do in your career or business, look to create a system or a method, literally with every part of what you do in your working day.

You have the same hours as everybody else within your working week. By creating a system in every facet of your business or your career, you will maximise your use of the time available.

You will become incredibly efficient and effective, and you will get more done in less time and because you're organised and in control with less stress.

All successful goal-setters will employ a system specific to that goal, and then they will work the system. The habit will be formed by using these processes and engaging in them regularly.

A good tip is to create triggers to remind you that it is now time to move from one system to another during your working day.

Many people fail to follow any method whatsoever, limiting their chance of success. Instead, they spend more time doing the things they enjoy doing, than what needs to be done.

By diarising process or systems and creating those alarm triggers, to move them from one system to another set of procedures, they smoothly flow into the new systems.

You have set yourself some triggers, maybe an alarm in your smartphone. At 11:00 AM, you get reminded now is the time to move into your sales process.

In the living your life on purpose for business owner's book, we will delve deeper into the practical tips on creating a successful sales process and the benefits of systemising it. For this example, let us assume you have created a sales process, and your trigger has set off, and you are now moving seamlessly into your sales process.

I want to introduce you to a Dr Tom Barrett special. He calls this focus 15, and I employ and teach through all my seminars and coaching.

This may seem absurd, but if you were to engage in a focussed 15 minutes of daily activity employing a sales process, you could change your business's successes.

Imagine becoming increasingly profitable, with more customers with seemingly less effort. That is the power of focus 15.

Let us now introduce a sales process to you, understanding that this may not fit your business, but it will give you an insight into how you can employ and create such a sales process. The biggest killer in anyone's business is NEPL. "This stands for Not Enough People Looking".

It does not matter if you are in business by yourself or whether you are one of the large international organisations; if you don't have enough people looking at your business, you are likely to experience corporate failure.

No customers or reducing customers is a big problem for any business.

If the biggest killer in any business is N EPL, it is logical that we need to strive to have EPL. Enough People Looking.

Successful businesses follow a pipeline process. A business pipeline summarises that you get prospects into your channel. You move them through your sales process and get them out of your pipeline with a decision.

That decision will be a yes, no, or maybe.

If you were to leave water in a hosepipe for a long time, it would stagnate.

The same applies to a business pipeline, so when you are working a channel, it is crucial to get people through your pipeline as quickly as possible and for them to decide one way or the other. Potential customers are abundant for you, so do not worry about sticky people in your pipeline. Get them through your pipeline as quickly as possible with a decision.

Let us assume that we have zero people in our pipeline right now, but we want to build a pipeline and want to work it continuously. We need to spend some time ascertaining who our ideal clients are, where they hang out and how we could approach them.

We then create a sales process, whose objective is to show potential clients what we do and how they could benefit from it and buy from us.

The objective is to get sales, but it is essential to focus on the actions and not on the results.

If you do something often enough, a ratio will appear. More on that later.

Having identified our ideal client, we now start to move them into the pipeline.

Here is a sales process that we follow and may give you an idea of what you could use. We employ a rule of three because we believe that three is the magic number.

1: Connect to three of our ideal clients on LinkedIn.

2: Send these three people a lumpy letter. Our lumpy letter includes a Christmas smelling tea bag and a short letter introducing ourselves.

3: We telephone these three people. Listen to the positive paraphrasing of the language and understand that we are going for no. The more people we contact, the more knows that we get, and consequently, some will say yes.

“Hi, is that Jody”?

“Yes, it is”.

“Hi Jody, my name is Gary. We’ve not met as far as I’m aware, but we recently connected on LinkedIn, and I sent you a letter with a Christmas smelling tea bag in it. Did you get it”?

Say this with a light-hearted and humorous tone.

“Yes, I did”

“Curious question did you drink the tea”?

Answer “No, I didn’t”.

In the letter with the Christmas smelling teabag, there was a sentence that said, please find enclosed a tea bag that makes a cracking Cup of tea; even if you don’t drink the tea, open the tea bag because it smells just like Christmas.

“Did you smell the teabag”?

“Yes, I did”,

“Did it smell like Christmas”?

“Yes, I guess it did”,

“Thank you very much for taking my call; and I mentioned it is just a quick call, but I said in the letter that I am an accomplished sales coach and wondered if you were open to having a chat to see if we could work together to increase your sales?

“No, thank you.”

End the call politely and move on.

Notice how friendly and relaxed this telephone call was but how I led Jody along the path I wanted to take her. How many times did she say yes to my questions?

This is where the power of the compound effect comes to your aid. Let us assume that I make three phone calls a day for each working day, I connect to three people on LinkedIn a day, and I send out three lumpy letters a day.

When I make the three phone calls a day, I'm sure you will agree that three phone calls a day five days a week equals 15 calls a week.

Over a four-week month, I will have made 60 telephone calls, and over the year, it works out to be 720 phone calls.

That whole process will take around 15 minutes—a focus 15 minutes of activity that could change your fortunes by its simplicity and by your consistency.

If you do something often enough, a ratio will appear, and if you keep doing it, the ratio will improve.

During a year, I've made 720 phone calls:

With a conversion ratio of 10:1, this will have created 72 new clients.

With a conversion ratio of 20:1, this would have created a conversion ratio of 36 clients.

And even with a conversion ratio of 60:1, this will have created 12 new clients during the year.

But what did you do? You employed a system, and for a focus 15 minutes of activity a day, you engaged in building your pipeline and then moving people through the channel.

In a sliding doors world, Jody said "yes"; she was open to talking about increasing her sales by chance. It is imperative that when she says "yes" that I already have within my system and part of the sales process the next stage. Without going into too much detail, each process will include where I present my services to Jody. Within the process, it will end with Jody being asked to decide.

Jody makes the decision, and it will be either a yes, a no or a maybe.

The more people I show the presentation, the more people will say "no", and that's perfectly fine because we are going for now just like Gary looking for a ginger nut biscuit when he was a young boy. We continuously go for no, and eventually, we get a yes.

A conversion ratio may look something like this 10: 3: 1.

The 10 is that we sent ten lumpy letters to these people, and we called ten people.

The three are the people who accepted the chance to do a presentation with, and the one is the result. The person that agreed to do business with us.

Once you understand your ratios, these are so powerful. If you know that your ratios are 10: 3: 1, you know to get one piece of business, you need to follow your sales process ten times.

Just by making three phone calls a day, you'd effectively get a new client every three to four days. If you wanted to increase your success rate, you would increase the amount of time you spent in the sales process system.

By focusing on the actions, you do not get despondent and "going for no"; you celebrate the people who have said "No".

This then eliminates the fear of rejection because you are going for no.

In their book "Go for No", Andrea waltz and Richard Fenton explain this in a beautiful story fashion.

Some large organisations have the biggest failure award. And most of the sales representatives wanted to win that award. How interesting, they wanted to win the biggest failure award. Interestingly, the person who won the biggest failure award also won the salesperson of the year award more often than not.

Prospecting for customers is like looking for an ace in a pack of cards. The laws of probability dictate that you could technically pick out four aces within the first four cards if someone were to fan out a deck.

The law of probability also, therefore, dictates that it could take you until the last four cards in the deck to get four aces.

We all know that the likelihood is that you're going to pick up an ace when going through the cards sporadically, and there will be absolutely no logic to when you find them. If you adopt a similar mindset that you are employing the laws of probability and regularly applying your activity, you must always find the ace.

It is a numbers game, but if you are unconsciously incompetent and you have not created a proper sales process, you could be the best prospector in the world and never get customers. We need to analyse all part of the process and always engage in that philosophy and mindset of continuous and never-ending improvement.

Always streamlining and always improving the system so that it works. This was an abbreviated version of a sales process and didn't include the necessity to avoid data protection issues where we may have bought data. Hopefully, you get the point that by having a series of systems for each aspect of your career or business, you can become increasingly efficient and effective.

When you are working, your systems ensure that you perform a backup plan that prevents distractions. If you are in the zone of activity for your business, ensure that nobody can distract you from that zone.

Moving away from this section of the book developing an attitude of gratitude will always serve you well when creating a better career or business for yourself.

We know that if you give, you get back, and it works. The phrase what goes around comes around is widespread throughout the world.

**People do not care how much you know, until they know how much you care.**

If you can make a living, moving towards your purpose in life. Look to do it in the areas that you are passionate about. It is a sad indictment of life that many people don't work within their passion areas because they feel they cannot earn enough money.

It is like we have been conditioned to spend money on worldly things to keep up with the Joneses.

Seriously, if you are happy with what you do and live in a lovely comfortable house and drive a nice comfortable car and not stay at the Ritz hotel, nobody cares.

What matters is fulfilment in your life. If you have a life partner that is also congruent to your values and passions, then all the better. You hear so many beautiful stories of so many couples that stay together for life because they have the same interests and passions.

You should employ some habits for a better career or a better business.

Reading and learning every single day is one of these. This should be one of the triggers you have set daily— personal development. In your day, you can just relax, get away from the busy outside world, and reward your brain with some new material.

On the LYLOP website, I have listed the names and titles of authors and books that I would recommend that you listen to. Every day is a school day!

I once heard somebody delivering a presentation, and they asked how much a family typically spent on things like Holidays, cars, eating out and drinking alcohol, closing and unnecessary luxuries.

In this seminar environment, we worked out that the average family spends over 20,000 spondoolies on such things. Twenty thousand spondoolies during a year on luxuries that if you never invested the money on would never be missed.

The speaker then asked a great question. If you're spending this much each year on these luxury items, can I ask you how much did you spend last month on your brain?

Wow, most people had spent nothing on their brain. To buy a good book or listen to good audio, maybe 15 spondoolies a month averaged over a year. In the big scheme of things, that is nothing. So, few people have even heard of many of the titles I've mentioned, let alone Napoleon Hill's "Think and Grow Rich". That book has to be the mother or father of all personal development books.

Once you have created your systems and are engaging in this personal development and therefore engaging in this constant and never-ending improvement, things will start to change in how you think, how you talk, and even the way you dress and present yourself.

You will be conscious of creating your brand, and creating your own personal brand is very important. Do you lighten up a room when you enter it or leave?

Creating the right impression about you is intrinsic to your success. There is a saying that you don't get a second chance to make a lasting first impression, and to some degree, that can be true. Indeed, when we speak to people either over the phone, via a webinar or face to face, we want to get our new relationships off to the best start possible.

So, we need to create the right impression, and your business is precisely that. Your business!

It is vitally important to create a good reliable brand for yourself. Don't confuse this with your company brand.

This is not about advertising your company by wearing all their corporate gear. If your company believed that advertising was the best way to distribute their products or services, they wouldn't need you!

How do people see you? Are you a serious business owner or career-minded professional? Can they trust you?

It takes seconds to create that first impression, so make it count.

> How do you dress?
> Are you punctual?
> Are you genuinely interested in people?

Remember the saying mentioned earlier in this chapter; people don't care how much you know, until they know how much you care.

When you speak with people, genuinely look to find out more about them. Ask them questions that show a genuine interest in them, their family, and any hobbies they may have.

Everyone's favourite subject is themselves. If you ever see a group photograph and you are in it, where do you look first? That's right at yourself!

Developing good people skills is paramount to your continued success and growth. Become an excellent natural networker. When I talk about networking, I am not necessarily talking about structured business networking events; it's just networking with people you meet in your organisation or people associated with it.

Develop that positive attitude and learn to respect others. Don't get involved in the tittle-tattle conversations that are merely gossiping and negative.

Show empathy to people that you associate with. This will create an emotional intelligence where you pause before replying, to engage the right part of your brain to deliver the correct answer.

Through time, we have learned that if you can use interpersonal skills to help people open-up to you and gain trust, you are more likely to develop better relationships within your organisations and create more trusted customers.

When you are looking at your brand, how are you perceived. Are you perceived to be a Hunter always hunting and taking things? Or are you perceived to be somebody that genuinely gives?

For your business and career, always look to improve, learn to master the mundane, and learn to employ systems to help you get what needs to be done finished quicker with better results.

Being innovative and methodical, you will develop your careers and your business. If you operate a hit and hope Harry approach, you will get hit and hope Harry results.

If your competitors are also hit and hope Harrying, you are all underperforming. If you employ systems, you will eventually trump your competitors.

## Fun and Recreation

**All work and no play makes Jack, a very dull boy indeed.**

**All work and no play makes Jill, are very dull girl indeed.**

There is no accident that the chapter fun and recreation follows the business and career chapter.

Many people talk about work-life balance; however, we prefer to reorder this to the life-work balance.

At this stage, you will have completed where you scale yourself on the wheel of life regarding fun and recreation. If you are having too much fun and recreation, you are having a blast of your life. But is this to the detriment of the other segments within the wheel?

When we talk about balance in life, we address some fundamental physiological matters. When we are under too much stress, the body can break down.

This could be why they call it distress!

You will already be aware that within our amazing anatomy's, our body secretes hormones depending upon our mood, the way we feel and how our physical environment impacts us.

Children have the most brilliant time; they do not worry about anything. They just want to go out and play. I refer to the book child's play By George Torkildson earlier within our living your life on purpose book.

Why is it as adults, we seem to think that we cannot play?

Of course, it would be a little weird if an adult of my age played with action man and play cars, for example, but the play element is still essential.

There is a hormone called the happy hormone. We will give it the proper name, serotonin.

When you are doing activities having fun, the brain starts to emit this happy hormone. When you are having fun, your brain forgets about your life's stresses.

The opposite of the happy hormone of serotonin is the stress hormone cortisol.

If we have too high cortisol levels within our bodies, this causes stress within the mind and the body. It is known to reduce cognitive functioning, lower our immune system, and open our bodies up to disease and ailments.

Stress is one of the top five contributing factors to an early death around the world.

Fun helps reduce stress, so this chapter's calling is to encourage you to have more fun and engage in more recreation.

**We don't live to work; we work to live.**

In the previous chapter, we spoke about creating time within our daily activity to utilise processes and systems to become increasingly efficient and effective.

It is a mind conditioning belief that you need to work for 8 hours a day. Why would you want to work 8 hours a day when you can do more in four hours than most do in 16 hours?

There is a belief that you would go to work in our society, for example, between 9:00 AM and 5:00 PM or if you are on a shift pattern engaging in your regulation 37 1/2 hours a week.

If you are looking forward and are implementing the right strategies and process, you will do much more in less time, therefore freeing up more time for you to do the fun things you want to do in your life.

Having fun will make you more effective in your career and business. It is commonly known that if you have fun, your brain gets fuelled with greater positivity, so fun reduces the harmful levels of cortisol and increases the levels of serotonin. If you get more happy hormones going through your body, this will allow you to be more effective in your business or career.

When you combine physical activity, such as the couch to 5K in a previous chapter and combine fun, with the new healthy eating habits, we discussed the synergistic improvement is enormous because this then causes our brain to release more of those feel-good chemicals.

These chemicals improve our health, heighten our immunity levels, so we are less likely to become ill.

We have ascertained that having fun improves your health and improves your ability to function better within your business or your career. You will get an increase in energy levels. Because you lead a healthier lifestyle, the knock-on effect is that you will be more inclined to be active, and therefore your body will benefit.

Living your life on purpose links all of the wheel of life elements. You have set yourself your goals, dreams, and aspirations. You have implemented strategies and processes within your business and career to make life easier. You are adopting a healthier lifestyle and engaging in physical fitness.

Because you are focusing on these elements of the wheel of life, the time you spend with your loved ones, your family, your friends will start to improve. Because you are now more focused and effective, your finances are beginning to improve. If you reduce your expenditure and increase your income, the stress levels will subside, and you will start to feel better.

Through this daily and weekly activity moving in the right direction, what will happen is there will be a natural decrease in those harmful hormones. Over time, your body will start to emit more serotonin than it will cortisol. Your stress levels will begin to drop, and you will become more used to serotonin and other endorphins.

It seems that the modern way of living focuses more on work than it did previously, and our fun and family time seems to be further down the pecking order. It appears that there's no longer time to have fun, or it seems that fun is a premium and rare activity.

When did it happen between childhood and adulthood that we stopped having fun and playing?

Due to the increased stresses associated with daily work, more parents now come home from a stressful day at work and don't prepare a proper nutritional meal. They then fall onto their settee and switch on the television, while their children play some form of computer game.

Many parents blame the fact that their children are playing computer games because that is the modern thing.

It couldn't be further from the truth. Our children need mental stimulation, and if they could get mental stimulation from their parents, they would much rather do that than play a computer game.

There is, of course, time for them to engage in this gaming world that we now live in, but when you speak to young people, who have moved through from childhood to adulthood, the one thing that they miss was time spent playing with their parents.

It is so easy to blame modern society and our children on why we are not spending more time with them. But if you were to create an environment that was so much fun and so enjoyable, not only will your children, if you have them want to participate, they will want their friends to come along to.

Of course, you might not be bothered with that, and you'd much rather go to work to get away from the family, and of course, you could sit down and watch your income reducing box eating your doughnuts and drinking your beer.

What a wonderful life that would be!

Play is all about rejuvenation, and it is also a great way to give the brain a break. When you go out and play, you are switching off from your daily activity consciousness, and for a while, you are in the moment.

Many people engage in daily meditation, and I applaud anybody who does this. If you have never tried meditation, go, and try it now. It is relaxing, and it is a form of recreation and one that can certainly free up your mind even for just a handful of moments. When you engage in a fun activity, it is much the same as meditation because you leave your external stresses behind and move into that fun environment.

It is, therefore, not only a source of relaxation but a way to stimulate the brain as well.

If you have a partner, awesome friends, or some co-workers, even your pets and children, you will feel so much better by participating in recreation with them.

Human beings like to be part of a tribe, and they want to associate with other human beings. Adult play is the real-time to forget about work and commitments and to be social but in a creative, fun, and unstructured way.

It is not about winning. It really is about participation.

There doesn't need to be a reason you engage in the activity other than enjoying yourself. Being with the people you want to be with you is not breaking any rules, and you should not be guilty if you are having fun and relaxing. Permit yourself to enjoy the playtime to enjoy having fun and understand that there needs to be no hidden agenda.This is helping you mentally.

There are so many benefits of fun, and whilst fun is crucial for a child's growth and development, it is beneficial for people of all ages. Fun can add joy to your life. It can release stress, supercharge your body, connect you with others around your environment; it can make you more productive and more pleasing to be associated with.

If you go out and have fun and enjoy some form of recreation, you will probably be less grumpy. You will be of a more positive disposition, and you have lots of things to talk about.

Who would have known it? Going and having fun engaging in recreation could make you a more interesting person.

So, we've ascertained that having fun relieves stress we've also mentioned that it improves your brain function. If you are having fun engaging in some form of recreation, it stimulates the mind. It boosts creativity while also enhancing relationships with your loved ones, family, and friends.

This is why many businesses take some of their employees out to do team bonding sessions. At that moment, when you're trying to create some form of log raft to go across a river, or the swing that you have to get across a ditch, you forget about the trivialities in the workplace.

It fosters more outstanding teamwork, a higher level of bonding where people from all sorts of personality traits can work together for a common fun goal.

In the wheel of life, we have a segment specifically for relationships. If you engage in recreation with your romantic partner or your children and dare, I say it, both, you will bring happiness to the family unit. What will also happen is during playtime, you will get to know each other even more, and you will trust each other even more.

Fun and recreation within the family unit build up resilience. It strengthens the relationships, and playtime can also heal any rifts within it.

Trust allows us to work together and open ourselves up more intimately; it will enable us to try new things. By making a conscious and regular effort to incorporate more playtime into the mundane of some of our lives, you can improve your relationships' quality.

It is not limited to your romantic partner, children, other members of your family, friends, or colleagues. You can have fun and recreate with anyone! When it comes to the work environment, those organisations that encourage players within their teams to have fun and spend some form of recreation create a formidable unit. They get to know each other and realise that they maybe aren't the personality that they see within the office environment. When you have fun with other members of your workplace, you start to grow a more remarkable likeness for them, and this then triggers creativity and innovation.

By encouraging employees to have fun and play with each other, you can create a more light-hearted work atmosphere. This light-hearted work atmosphere stimulates creativity and innovation.

The social interaction between employees improves the harmony within the workplace improves, and the productivity is affected too.

As we suggested with your health and fitness and within your business and career, it is essential to schedule some playtime with the people who matter the most.

Recreation could include a date night with your romantic partner. It could consist of a day or a weekend to a theme park with your children. It could involve going to the beach and having fun with you, your romantic partner, your children, and your dog.

Scheduling in recreation time with your family will help your family bond and stick together.

You could even place the schedule of your recreation time on your fridge, so everybody in the family can see it, and by planning weeks and months in advance, make the rule that these dates are not for negotiation.

Make those days extra special days in your memories and the memories of people that you are doing them with. Do not take your work with you. Leave it behind. Do not engage in some form of recreation and continuously refer to your smartphone.

If necessary, leave the smartphone at home.

**They say that laughter is the best medicine, and you know something it really can be.**

Going out on a family day trip and laughing and joking with each other, having some fun, stopping, and having lunch or an evening meal is all about bonding and making people feel secure.

The mother or father who is continuously at work and spends little or no time with their children is causing so much damage to their child or children's subconscious mind.

Their minds start to make up stories as to why the mum or the dad is working so much. And why whenever the mum and dad come back from working so much, they're always grumpy and telling them off and not having any time for them. You see their young minds repeated overtime, manifest the belief that they are not loved or not wanted.

Those above then create a negative vortex where they start to misbehave, they begin to misbehave not because they want to misbehave but because they are craving your attention. You see, children crave the attention of their parent by doing something wrong, because at least some attention is better than no attention.

How sad is that? Not only has it damaged their subconscious mind, but now they're doing something naughty so that they can feel something from you.

If, of course, you do not have children but are planning to have children, you can prevent all of this by being a more accommodating and understanding parent.

Here is quite an interesting paradigm story about a father and son. I have summarised it, but you will still get the point. The story is about a father who was getting to the twilight years of his life. His wife had recently passed away, and he decided to go into the attic to look for a particular photograph of him and his wife. As he went into the attic, he found box upon box of some of his children's comic books and diaries.

He never understood why his wife didn't just throw these things away as they were just taking up space.

Curious and lonely, he began to flick through some comics and found his sons diary. He read the journal and enjoyed listening to the stories within it. In his son's left-handed scrawl of writing, some of it was hard to read, but his son had kept a diary and dated each of the entries.

The old man went out of the attic downstairs, taking the diary along with him and then went to his drawing-room to find his journals. Side by side, he placed his son's journal with his journal and went through the date orders of times they had spent with each other.

One such entry Broke the old Man's heart.

His entry was simple: "Went fishing with Johnny. He didn't catch a thing".

Son's entry was equally simple: "I went fishing with dad. It was the best day of my life".

You may have experienced this with your parents, but it is vital to understand that you can't read your child's mind, and you may not understand the emotions that are going through that young person.

But do not assume for one moment that they do not want to be with you and they're not enjoying your company. If you can create a fun environment, your children will want to engage in many different recreations with you and your partner.

These will bring about lifelong memories for both you and for them.

By setting this precedent when they, in turn, have their own families, they will demonstrate the very same love and support that you did to them.

If you have hobbies such as golf or dancing, enjoy these hobbies as often as you can but make sure that you keep a balance between your family life.

If you like to golf and your partner loves to go dancing, there is no problem with you going your ways and enjoying your hobbies. When you return, you can talk about those hobbies, having enjoyed the fun and recreation benefits they bring.

Try to find some common hobbies that you can do together while also maintaining your independence.

Most of my life's best times have been when I've spent time playing my sports with my son, my wife, my mum, my dad, and my sister. We haven't done enough, and as time passes by, the opportunities to do so are reducing.

Those unforgettable trips with some of my friends consuming too much alcohol and some feeble golf along the way. And that is the balance we are talking about work hard, and play hard, and live your life on purpose.

I want you to imagine a world where the money is no object and time is yours. You no longer need to go to work for a living, even though I'm quite sure some of you will wish that you could work forever. Please take an out of body experience and think of all the things you would like to do.

Imagine that you are writing a movie or a book about your future life. You and your partner and your family are all primary characters within this movie.

Let your mind just drift away to all the things you could do with each other, remember you are writing the script, so neither your hormones nor your children's attitudes need to be in the movie.

If you could do those fun things, what would you do? If you could go on the most brilliant holidays, where would you go?

If you had the choice of where to send your children to school, where would that perfect school be? Where would you live?

Would it be a modern house and an old house, an apartment, a coastal development, or would it be in the middle of the countryside?

And what would you do daily if money and time were not an issue?

As I write this book and let my mind wander, I can create the most vivid movies for me, my wife and family.

Today there's a slightly different theme to what I may like to do. Remember earlier in this book; we have a property in Yorkshire, Spain, Florida, and New Zealand.

That's not a bad start. Canada is one of my second favourite countries. I just love the Canadian Rockies around Alberta and British Columbia.

So today, because money is no object and time is my friend, we've decided to start our skiing experience at the southernmost ski resort of the American Rockies. Then we're going to navigate North to the most northerly of the Canadian ski results.

As a family unit, we're just going to take our time, and when we get bored of a resort, we will move up to the next one and so on. We will ski hard and fast in the mornings when the snow is at its best, and then we will recover in some of the spa facilities during the late afternoon. I'm sure a cheeky aperitif might come into the equation from time to time.

In the evening, we will watch some movies, go tenpin bowling, play some games, or just relax and watch television.

We're going to eat fantastic breakfasts and lunches, and we're going to have some lovely evening meals prepared by us in these top-quality resort hotels. Every day we will do some form of activity, it may not be skiing, but it could be trekking through the mountains or enjoying some Husky rides. After we finished our rocky extravaganza, we will take a flight from Vancouver to Hawaii, where we will spend three weeks relaxing on the Big Island. Lost in Hawaii, we will spend lots of time snorkelling, jet-skiing, fooling around on the beach with a volleyball and just generally having a fantastic time.

After we have enjoyed our Hawaiian adventure will jump on a plane, and as it seems logical to do so, we'll go to Lake Taupo in New Zealand. New Zealand is such a therapeutic island, and yet whilst it is such a relaxing place, it is also the home of outdoor pursuits.

As a family, some of us will do the wildly outrageous and thrilling outdoor pursuits such as white-water rafting, bungee jumping or going on one of their range of crazily fast speed boats up the river.

We will continue to enjoy all the culinary delights, including my favourite wines from the Marlborough region.

We'll just enjoy the beautiful scenery of Lake Tekapo, watching the beautiful stars in that area where there's little artificial light. Having enjoyed our time in New Zealand, we could pop on a flight and head towards Spain. Some of the family may head back to the UK, but we will head to Spain.

In Spain, we go golf crazy, and we spend so many beautiful mornings playing on some of the best golf courses, walking off the 18th hole into the 19th and enjoying a nice-chilled beer.

On our return to the UK, we will have circumnavigated the world. And that ticks off yet another goal of mine.

Just one of my stories, a ramble of how I would love to have such a brilliant time. Interestingly you don't need to leave your house for the serotonin to start kicking in.

Just by spending time in the silence of your room and allowing you to think of all the things that you would love to do when you put yourself in the picture, that happy hormone comes out to play. When you embellish on the story, you could introduce yourself and your partner enjoying some memorable moment. Maybe, snorkelling in the Hawaiian reefs, enjoying that beautiful underwater world when you are next to each other, just occasionally holding hands.

Or if you are like our family having a fantastic golfing duel between your dad and your son. Having this three-generation rivalry is such fun, and whilst we're all competitive in the moment, the excellent banter that unravels during four hours of a golf match is just entertaining by itself.

Whether we are skiing or golfing or playing pool, we like to be competitive, and we want to have fun.

A family that plays together will stay together irrespective if they go through their teens into their early 20s and 30s. Once you have created that bond with your family, that bond can never be broken. You get the opportunity to design your life, so ensure that you develop your life on purpose and ensure that it is filled with an abundance of fun.

## Personal Growth

Reading or listening to a personal development book and not acting on the new learning is like reading a Stephen King novel and putting it back on the bookshelf.

The difference is the horrors he shares are just fiction and stay in the book. If you have a habit of just reading or listening and not acting on the new information, your life won't improve.

Your horrors and demons will follow you everywhere!

A key spoke within the wheel of life is the belief that human beings develop and grow through the drive for continuous and never-ending improvement.

In every aspect of our lives, if we can strive to do just a little bit better every time, we grow as people.

How often during this book did we refer to the jam in our doughnuts or the phrase you don't know what you don't know?

As we develop from young people into young adults and then started to mature, we became more aware that there was a world of personal development. I certainly recall no time during my school days as a young man in the army, or as I approached my 30s in the police service, any mention of personal development.

It could have been that my reticular wasn't open to hearing these words, and maybe, just maybe, I wasn't even open to personal development then anyway.

Many people fall into the world of personal development because they either want to avoid pain or make it again. There is a certain amount of dissatisfaction within their life, but they have taken steps to see if there is a way that they can achieve their ultimate goals.

The very fact that you are reading this book, a personal development book, and are nearing the end of it implies that you are already open to the thought process you'd like to improve your life. You should be congratulated for that, and may we urge you never to lose the thirst to learn.

Suppose you were to listen to 15 minutes of personal development audio or read 15 pages of a personal development book every day. In that case, you will have digested some excellent material for a year.

Investing just 15 spondoolies or thereabouts per month, buying personal development, would serve you well over the forthcoming years.

Remember, reading one book will not change your life; it will take time to grow personally. Just as it will take time for you to achieve your fitness and weight goals or your financial goals, growing personally will take time. There is no instant gratification for you here. But when you engage in personal development and understand that you and your life are moving forward in a positive direction, it does serve as an excellent source of motivation. The compound effect of getting lots of small wins in your life causes the release of our favourite happy hormone, serotonin.

The more we feel this way, the more we thirst for such positive internal feedback.

One key thing to understand in our world is that some people believe that they are entitled to a better life, and other people go out and create that life. The latter are the ones that are motivated and move towards a goal in a purposeful direction, engaging in goal-directed activity.

These people are also likely to absorb personal development material like drinking water. Never mind listening to personal development for 15 minutes a day. If they have any sounds in the car or first thing in the morning or late at night, you can be assured they will be listening to something that serves their mindset.

**Earners are learners. Leaders are readers.**

Many anecdotes would demonstrate the importance of personal development; I believe the best stories come from successful people. Speak to any successful person worldwide, and they will have spent time learning throughout their life.

Sir Richard Branson, Charles Wigoder, Jeff Bozos, Elon Musk and John and Jane Smith, down the road from you that live in a colossal mansion driving nice cars and always going on Holidays.

It isn't just the mega-successful people who have always embraced the need to learn daily. Many people from all walks of life are improving their lives every day. And so, could you.

Throughout my 20 years of business, I have come across so many people who talk about professional development. Still, their results over such a period demonstrate that they are not walking the walk.

When you go through living your life on purpose and set your goals when you engage in regular personal development, you are selecting books and audios specific to your goals, not somebody else's dreams.

Some people want to earn masses amount of money, and some people like to generate massive amounts of free time on the other end of the spectrum. Others want to spend their lives giving, and they see the attainment of money as a way of facilitating those goals.

In life, therefore, if you see somebody that is living a modest life and not the life that you are aspiring to, it does not mean they are not successful. Indeed, they could have reached their goals and could be internally very satisfied with where they live, the car they drive, and the lifestyle they have generated.

If we look at Maslow's and his hierarchal needs, each of us has the same initial needs, and all of us also want to achieve some form of self-actualisation.

Maslow's theory is that we all have basic food and water needs. It also includes rest and generating some warmth for those cold days and nights. Such a basic need also provides shelter, somewhere to live.

If we are talking about gratitude in your life, understand that there are people worldwide who struggle for even this basic need, they struggle to find food, water, warmth, and rest.

Many of us have been to poverty areas; I mean real poverty. During my time In the British Army during active service, we flew into Incirlik airport, in southern Turkey for the first Iraqi conflict. Our journey took us along what are described as roads, but not as we know them in modern western societies. As we passed through Towns and Villages through southern Turkey and into northern Iraq, you could see genuine poverty.

People living huddle together in mud huts in 1990/ 91 is quite incredible, and even as we passed through 2021, there are people around the world living in similar conditions. No running water, no electricity, and none of the luxury are that you take for granted.

When you drive along these roads in southern Turkey and northern Iraq, children are alongside the roadways begging for any scraps or morsels of food.

I was also fortunate to climb Kilimanjaro, and as we passed through Tanzania and saw some of the ways the Africans live. It Was genuinely impressive. There were similar mud houses, but some had electricity, and some had running water. What amazed me most is that literally, everybody had a mobile phone device to their ear.

They had prioritised a mobile phone in their life, how very bizarre!

Though, whilst climbing Kilimanjaro, you had a mobile phone signal to the very top. You certainly do not get full mobile phone reception everywhere in the United Kingdom, far from it.

You are already in a great place, a phenomenal platform to develop your life into the one you so desire. The next level up from the basic needs or physiological needs is safety.

Once we have satisfied our physiological and basic needs, we can focus on our safety needs. The idea from Maslow's teaching is that you move further up the triangle and achieve self-actualisation. The further you progress up the hierarchy of needs, the more complicated life becomes. On the second level, our safety level, we introduce security and safety needs, and these become our primary objective.

Human beings naturally like to have order within their lives, and they want to control their environments.

The basic security and safety needs include our financial security, being healthy, and just safeguarding our families from injury, accidents, and illnesses.

It is at this tier on the hierarchal needs where people will find a job or work to generate the income, required to satisfy these security needs.

Many people want to earn just enough money to put food on the table, have a roof over their heads, and their family surrounding them.

The next two stages of the hierarchal tier system are physiological needs. The first is the need to have friendships, be part of community groups, and belong to something. At this level, we start to form intimate relationships.

Human beings are not meant to be lone wolfs. Having this sense of belonging, being part of groups or family circles are intrinsic to our development and growth. Being part of a group with a circle of friendships also reduces the risk of depression and loneliness.

Having accomplished levels one, two and three, many human beings can be internally satisfied with their progress in life. They are not necessarily drawn to the 4th level, self-esteem needs.

This level of esteem needs is quite basic when you first understand it, but this is a level that can destroy and cause people more hardship is necessary.

It starts where the human being strives to gain respect, appreciation, and recognition from other people. It is where people feel that they have a need to accomplish something to have their efforts recognised by somebody they deemed to be in an important position in life.

Some people seem to think that they can achieve this level in the hierarchal needs by having "things" that give an exterior illusion of personal worth.

At this stage, some people spend more on material things than they can afford to keep up with the Joneses or look good in society.

If only they knew those good people in this world like others irrespective of the type of car they drive, their house or the apparent status within societies.

People who succeed at this level are the people who feel Naturally valued by others because they contribute to society and either their local community or to the larger community of the world.

Moving away from materialistic things, self-esteem can be improved by taking part in fun and recreation, those hobbies that we mentioned previously and testing their abilities in the field of sport.

Then Maslow highlights that the higher tier of his needs structure is self-actualisation.

The summary of this is where someone achieves their full potential in life. If you don't have any dreams, goals, or aspirations and don't know where you are going, you could quickly achieve self-actualisation. Some people don't even think about their imprint or their impact on the world. There is nothing wrong with this because they choose to live their lives. But for you living your life on purpose, this deep understanding of who you are and where you want to go may take years to reveal itself.

Do you want to be remembered for being a good person who donated not only money but time to your local community? Do you want to be remembered as somebody who left a fantastic legacy for your family and friends?

Do you want to be remembered as somebody who was continuously growing personally and that you made massive advances from the early years of your life?

In our wonderful world, as we grow through time as human beings, we can move through Maslow's hierarchy tier system, and as we move through the tier system and as we move through tiers within each tier, as people, we change.

Maslow used a basic series of hierarchal needs. The fact of the matter is that each need can be broken down into several smaller sections.

Self-esteem, for example, can be improved by gradually improving oneself.

Suppose like many people in the world, you are caught within the debt trap. You own a lovely house, a nice car, and you go on plenty of excursions and holidays. Extrinsically, you have met your esteem target because people are looking at you, and they are applauding you for your success in life.

Internally you know the truth. That you do not own your house or your car, and the holidays are typically bought on a credit card.

As you follow the finance section tips of this book, you change your relationship with money. When you no longer have a debt associated with a motor vehicle, and you own it, intrinsically, you have moved up another smaller level within the self-esteem tier.

You eliminate your debt, and you have now moved up another level within that tier. Without a mortgage, you own your house outright. Further up you go.

What is happening here is that because your net worth is increasing all the time, the internal value system that you have is, in reality, kicking into action. When you own what you want to own in life and live a life of abundance, you start to realise that you become the key person of influence and people then start looking to you for guidance. You move from an apprentice in life to a master in life.

As your net worth continues to grow, you are now in a beautiful place. Suppose you have spent time understanding the wheel of life, ensuring that you pay particular attention to all segments in the said wheel. In that case, you should have an excellent relationship with an intimate partner. If you have children, you should be getting along with them fantastic. You will have a great circle of friends and have an abundance of hobbies engaging with lots of fun and recreation.

You no longer need to force your personality on anybody because you become the person you always wanted to become. You have achieved self-actualisation; you have arrived.

As a young person going through college, my qualification was in business strategy. Whilst doing this degree, somebody once told me about a book called barbarians led by Bill Gates.

They told me that Bill Gates was a ruthless operator and acquired new businesses and software programmes by muscling in and threatening the people that were his competitors.

I never read the book; it just wasn't my style to listen to or read unless the facts were facts.

I always found that anybody that was further up the food chain in human society would always attract people that would want to bring them back down a notch.

When you investigate Bill Gates more from an exciting point of view, you can see that he and his company did engage in an aggressive growth strategy.

If you investigate Jeff Bezos of Amazon and look at how he built his business, you could also assume that he engaged in an aggressive growth strategy.

I don't think their early lives have defined either of these people. Maybe, just maybe, they stepped into a grey area, and they achieved some of their successes by stealing ground in a fair but assertive manner. If you speak to any person involved in a sport, they will take fair use of any rules of the game.

We all know too well about the Bill and Melinda Gates Foundation's generosity and how much money Jeff Bezos invests in charity and other initiatives to help and save our planet.

Elon Musk is another philanthropist. If you study in-depth Elon Musk, he is not motivated by money.

There are so many wonderful people in our world donating so much back to the planet, yet lesser people like to sniper them.

As you grow through your life and develop personally, understand the further up the apparent food chain you be you go, the more likely someone will start to take pot-shots to try and bring you down a step or two. Through the laws of association, where you are only associating with other people of the same mindset and philosophy, you will grow with these people in your mastermind groups. It is not up to you to worry about what people think about you, and with a growth mindset, you can reciprocate any negativity fired at you by replying with kindness and not anger.

The reality is if somebody is taking pot-shots at you, they probably want to be you, and the most remarkable thing you could do is to give them some knowledge and some wise words to help them get where they want to get to. Now that would be a phenomenal test of your self-actualisation.

This chapter is all about personal development. I suspect you will never stop developing if you are relatively new to this arena; in this section of the chapter, I'd like to run through some of my top titles that have enormously improved my life.

I would recommend that you take the time to buy these books or audios and many others that the authors have written.

**Napoleon Hill's Think and Grow Rich**

There is a common saying that successful people leave clues. Napoleon Hill spent 25 years of his life interviewing some of the most successful people of his time. Over 500 successful people were interviewed, and the overriding beliefs and philosophes were distilled into this book. That in itself is sufficient reason to give this book some serious consideration.

This could be one of the most challenging reads of any book when you go through it the first time. When I speak to people around the world who have also known about Think and Grow Rich, you would be surprised by how many people failed to finish the book. Quite ironic that one of the main chapters in the book is persistence! Therefore, we like to study, "Think and Grow Rich" in mastermind groups. In these groups that I mentioned last for 26 weeks, we meet every two weeks reading one chapter of the book.

Within the mastermind group, it is fascinating how different people interpret each chapter. Through a discussion, however, a greater understanding of the book is revealed, but more importantly, strategies how we can implement it into our lives are revealed.

With that said, if you have read or attempted to read, Think and Grow Rich, give it another go and then read again and then read again. If you can participate in a mastermind group with this book as the centrepiece of your discussions, it will be a great way to start. There are so many other titles that can be subsequent titles used within your mastermind sessions.

Throughout the many mastermind sessions that we hold, one clear message always seems to reveal itself, and that message is that in the modern interpretation of Think and Grow Rich, money is not the road to riches. Instead, it is an understanding that through goalsetting, where someone identifies what they need in life that they will need an equivalent amount of money to fund the said acquisition.

As Zig Ziglar states, “Money isn't that important; it ranks right up there with oxygen”.

For some people, the discussion about money seems vulgar, and it seems to be something that they want to avoid talking about.

Interestingly, if you speak to anybody who has participated in a mastermind group and then moved on to achieve high levels of success in their lives, they do concede that their understanding of vulgar money alters.

When they didn't have much money, it was easier to relegate money to something horrible. When they earned money, they promoted money as something worth aiming for because you can do wonderful things.

Wouldn't it be a great world to trade things in life based on our self-esteem?

Let us now summarise just some of the critical chapters within Think and Grow Rich that are important if you are going to live your life on purpose.

The first chapter in Think and Grow Rich is desire. Called the starting point of all achievement, the first step to riches.

In this book, we discussed that if you have a little why or a little desire that this small why would generate little power to achieve your why. If you have no real desire, it is probably easy to achieve it, so no real power is generated for its acquisition.

If you start to understand that thinking big is a good thing and that just because you don't hit your target straight away does not mean you haven't succeeded in it, then you will start to fuel your mind with some exciting things.

The whole point of desire is that if you have something that becomes not just a desire but a burning desire in your life, you will do what it takes to achieve it.

Whoever you are right now, whatever your life circle circumstances, does not define your future. The big problem with desire is that people have had the wrong jam injected into their doughnut, and they have lost the ability to dream big. Through time and societies conditioning, they feel as though they have achieved their lot, and at best, they may be able to achieve just a little more.

That couldn't be farther from the truth, and the reason they are not growing is that they haven't attached any value to their lives and their desires are too low. There is no energy being created; there is no structure to their lives, and they're not living their lives on purpose.

Seriously, if you are sitting reading or listening to this audio, you have thousands of spondoolies of debt. Yet, you want to own your own home, own your car, live an extraordinary life, understand this; you can achieve it.

**"If you say you can, you can, and if you say you can't, you are right" Henry Ford.**

Through the continuous and never-ending improvement and the ideology that you are moving forward every day of your life, even if it is unnoticeable, you are moving towards your objective. If you genuinely desire an improvement in your life, you can get it.

Do not listen to the dream stealers, do not listen to that horrible mind monster on your shoulder, as you associate with other people, and just like a rising tide lifts or boats, you shall be lifted to where you want to get to.

Hill, tells some wonderful stories throughout "Think and Grow Rich" to demonstrate some of the philosophies he learned. This is why I urge you to buy the book.

In the desire chapter, he gives you a formula or a method as he defines it, on how your desire for rich's or those material things can be transmuted into reality.

This chapter reiterates the importance of making sure that whatever you desire is always at the forefront of your mind and that this burning desire becomes all-consuming. He discusses the need to convince yourself that you already have it. Even though our modern interpretation of the nasty thing called money, Napoleon Hill states, only those who become money conscious ever accumulate great riches.

When we discussed the finances section, we do become money conscious. We implement a plan to do just that for those who want to eradicate debt. For those people who want to assume more wealth, we implement a plan to do that. We become conscious that that is our goal.

The more conscious you become of your desire, and the more time you invest in this desire achievement, the more momentum you create. Napoleon Hill also states that you don't get anything unless you are prepared to pay the price, and you are ready to invest the time and the labour needed to do what it is you want to do.

The second chapter is faith, the visualisation and belief in attaining desire. The second step to riches.

It's pretty much what it says in the last sentence; it's how you make sure you translate your desire into reality. First, you visualise what you want, and then you must believe that you can achieve it.

This paragraph can be blended with another section called autosuggestion. Napoleon Hill talks about the vibration of thought; if we get up each morning and go through our purposeful morning routine each morning, we will be running through our afformations and reminding ourselves what we want when we read our goals.

We must do this not just in the morning and not just last thing at night before we go to bed but all through the day, and what we want to do is to fake it until we make it and ensure that our subconscious mind accepts what we want to be our reality. Whatever it is you want to achieve, you must put yourself in the picture as though you have already achieved it and attach emotion to this. How will you feel when you have earned it?

You need to be already in possession of what you desire in your mind long before you achieve it. You need to have faith and belief that doing the right things repeatedly every day will lead you to achieve your burning desire.

A hit and hope Harry approach to life is not likely to lead to riches.

Most people are defeated by themselves before they start on any quest for improvement or riches because they don't believe that they can do it.

You need to have faith that you can achieve whatever you want to achieve. Through the power of autosuggestion, or by transfusing the jam in your doughnut, you need to understand that not only can you achieve these things but that you already have done so.

> *If you think you are beaten, you are*
>
> *If you think you dare not, you don't*
>
> *If you like to win, but you think you can't,*
>
> *It is almost certain you won't*
>
> *If you think you'll lose, you're lost*
>
> *Four out of the world we find*
>
> *Success begins with a fellows will*
>
> *It's all in the state of mind*
>
> *If you think you are outclassed, you are*
>
> *You've got to think high to rise; you've got to be sure of yourself before*

*You can ever win a prize.*

*Life battles don't always go*

*To the stronger or faster man,*

*But soon or late the man who wins*

*Is the man who thinks he can!*

That has to be one of the most powerful and understandable poems I've ever heard; it is just fantastic and summarises so many reasons why so many people fail. Make this your mantra.

Napoleon Hill also discusses the need for specialised knowledge. Whatever your chosen profession is or wherever you'd like that profession to take you. You need to know about that profession.

It is not just enough to scratch the surface, but enough that will give you a competitive edge in this world.

You will also need imagination, and a lack of creativity is a contributor factor to why some people don't have a Big WHY power

Think and Grow Rich, then moves on to a chapter about organised planning. In this book living your life on purpose, we plan in every segment of the wheel. We know that in modern society, with some of the new things that we know that focusing on all aspects of our life will give us that balance that we crave.

So we need to plan, and we need to plan appropriately. Living your life on purpose should eliminate some of those dead periods within our day and instead allow those quiet times to become productive.

**“A voyage of 1000 miles begins with a single step; this step must be in the right direction”.**

You will not be zigzagging through organised planning, but instead, you will be moving straight line to your objective. If those objectives are small wins, you will go from dot to dot quickly.

By accumulating lots of little wins heading in the right direction, our serotonin, the happy hormone, will be continuously kicking in to help us. Our confidence will be growing because we are achieving more quickly.

None of this can happen by accident; we must make sure it happens on purpose through organised planning.

A further chapter is that of decision. Once you have set your goals and believe that you can achieve them and are now well organised, armed with your special knowledge, and you have decided that you're going to move forward to attain said goals, do not let anything distract you.

Many successful people in our wonderful world have been ridiculed for the attainment of their desires. These dream stealers are so devastating for so many people, but not you.

Decide to do what it is that you want to do and understand that you can do it.

Master your procrastination. Do not let anything get in the way. If you have something you need to do every day, it is imperative, not a choice, that you fulfil those high pay off activities first.

Persistence is the chapter that discusses that sustained effort is necessary to induce faith to believe that you can achieve your goal.

Persistence is not optional if you want to be successful in your life. Persistence is an absolute necessity. Time after time, you will feel down, you will feel beaten but understand that "winners never quit, and quitters never win".

If you get knocked down, you get back up again; if you get a rejection or you feel as though you are not moving closer to your next intended goal, take stock of where you are, take stock of what it is your desires are, and then implement strategies to get to that next stage in your goal path.

This is one reason we follow a 13-week massive action plan. We have broken down our goals into easily manageable achievements. We are not zigzagging; we are straight-line goal acquiring.

Your persistence will increase through marginal gains.

That is why in your goal setting phase, make sure some of your first and early wins are achievable.

You can start to stretch them out as you go along but make sure that you build your persistence muscle with regular exercise.

By maintaining your daily method of operation and focusing on the target activities and being persistent in them, you cannot fail.

**Napoleon Hill listed eight factors of persistence:**

1: Definiteness of purpose knowing what you want is the first and perhaps the most critical step towards developing persistence. A strong motive forces one to surmount many difficulties.

2: Desire, it is comparatively easy to acquire and to maintain persistence in pursuing the object of intense desire.

3: Faith and belief in one's ability to carry out a plan encourages one to follow the project through with persistence.

4: Definiteness of plans. Organise plans, even though they may be weak and entirely impractical, encourage persistence.

5: Accurate knowledge. Knowing that once plans are sound, based upon experience or observation, encourages persistence. Guessing, instead of knowing, destroy persistence.

6: Cooperation, Sympathy, understanding, and cooperative association with others tend to develop persistence. Cue, the mastermind group!

7: Will power. The habit of concentrating one's thoughts upon building the plans for the attainment of a definite purpose leads to persistence.

8: Habit. Persistence is the direct result of habit. The mind absorbs and becomes part of the daily experiences upon which it feeds. Fear, the worst of all enemies, can be effectively cured by forced repetition of acts of courage.

Think and Grow Rich continues to talk about the mastermind group's power.

We have already discussed this within the book, and then it moves on through to the chapter of the subconscious mind. We have certainly covered this off and living your life on purpose.

To summarise, go and buy the book Think and Grow Rich. If you feel like this is a heavy read, join a mastermind group. Here at living your life on purpose within our community, we can assign you to a forthcoming mastermind group with peers you do not know but who have the same attitude and mindset.

**The Compound Effect by Darren Hardy**

This is a cracking book to either read or listen to. Darren delivers this content in such a free-flowing and easy to digest manner. Having met him, you know only too well that this person practises what he preaches.

I would certainly recommend that you put this book towards the top of your list of things to buy.

The simple summary of this book is that we make simple choices every day. By implementing seemingly insignificant steps towards our attainment of those choices, we will achieve our desires through the mastery of the compounded effect.

We have discussed that if you were to eat one of those wonderful Five Guys burgers occasionally, it would not have a detrimental effect on your physiology. On the flip side, we know that the compounded effect of eating this for breakfast, lunch and evening meal will undoubtedly have a negative impact on our physiology if we were to repeat this poor eating habit over a long period.

The same principle applies to physical fitness; if we go for a one-kilometre walk each month, we will not get physically fit. If, however, we go for a one-kilometre walk every day for 14 days, then transition into a majority walk to a minority-run for another 14 days and then move to a majority run. Over weeks and months, we will ultimately become fitter physically.

If we were to focus on eliminating any debt that we had and therefore stop paying those excessive interest payments, the amount of time to reduce those payments would be significantly reduced through the compound effect's power. Once we had eliminated the debt and those horrific interest rates, we would have more disposable income than we can reinvest into assets rather than liabilities.

In the compound effect, Darren highlights the eighth wonder of the world. To demonstrate the power of the compound effect, he shows how if you doubled just one penny every day over 31 days, that penny would be worth over 10 million spondoolies.

Just try the exercise; it is quite mind-blowing.

Day one, you have a penny. On day two, you have two pennies. Remember, it's doubling every day.

On day three, you have 4 pennies; on day four, you have 8 pennies; on day five, you have 16 pennies; on day six, you have 32 pennies; after seven days, you have a whopping 64 pennies.

There's nothing exciting happening now, but as you move into day eight, 64 pennies doubles up to 128 pennies, which then doubles up on day 9 to 256 pennies, and by day 10, we have reached a massive 512 pennies.

There is now a level of excitement starting to brew.

On day 11, we now have 1024 pennies, moving up to 2048 pennies on day 12, and 4096 pennies on day 13. Our pennies have now doubled up to a. significant 8192 pennies after a fortnight.

Isn't that amazing? After just a fortnight, we have now moved from only one penny to 8192 pennies, and the power of the compound effect will continue to accelerate; we've come this far we may as well continue for another fortnight.

| | |
|---|---|
| day 15 | 16,384 |
| day 16 | 32,768 |
| day 17 | 65,536 |

| | |
|---|---|
| day 18 | 131,072 |
| day 19 | 262,144 |
| day 20 | 524,288 |
| day 21 | 1,048,576 |
| day 22 | 2,097,152 |
| day 23 | 4,194,304 |
| day 24 | 8,388,608 |
| day 25 | 16,777,216 |
| day 26 | 33,554,432 |
| day 27 | 67,108,864 |
| day 28 | 134,217,728 |
| day 29 | 268,435,456 |
| day 30 | 536,870,912 |
| day 31 | 1,073,741,824 |

With this straightforward scenario, Darren Hardy has highlighted the compound effect's awesome power. Throughout the book, he demonstrates how you can have the compound effect work for you in what we ultimately would call all the segments in our wheel of life.

In its very essence, the compound effect is all about causing the snowball effect of improvement everywhere that we focus upon. There are no quick wins, and there are no illusions about instant gratification. It is about creating good habits that serve you well, and through persistent regular activity, you can get to wherever you want to within time.

The principal rule in the compound effect is that it is a matter of choice for you, but you need to understand that the compound effect is either working for you or against you; it can't be neutral.

A lot of people do not comprehend the incredible power of the compound effect because they have never been conscious of it before in their lives.Through the constant application of processes repeated overtime where you manage your expectations and do not expect that instant result, you will hit something Darren Hardy calls big Mo!

Big Mo is momentum, and if you can get momentum in your life in every area of your life, you have cracked the principles of success.

Many people, which corroborates the chapter of persistence within Think and Grow Rich, don't understand that you need to apply consistent effort to attain your goals, dreams, and aspirations. It is why they fail to harness the benefit of the compound effect fully.

The penny analogy above is all about consistency in the penny's doubling. In 31 days of doubling that penny, the value is well over 10 million spondoolies.

The compound effect's excitement in the penny analogy doesn't kick in until day 14. And even on day 21, it is only starting to get slightly more exciting; in the last week, you begin to see and experience the most noticeable results.

If the compound effect of that penny doubling was not daily, we doubled it up monthly. The results would still be that after 31 months, that penny would be worth over 10 million spondoolies.

The problem is that for the first seven months or even 14 months, that isn't sufficient evidence to create excitement and activity to maintain the doubling of the penny, and most people will quit because they expected quicker results.

The secret in the sauce that Darren Hardy eludes is doing something every day and keeping on doing it over a more extended period. The theory of the compound effect, once you understand it, is merely common sense.

If you want something bad enough and have sufficient WHY power and you work on the plans and the systems to attain what you desire every day, you stand a greater chance of doing it.

The compound effect also majors on creating good habits and eliminating those bad habits; it centres upon the premises of choices that we make every day. The book also centres on the importance of having an attitude of gratitude. It highlights some simple ways to create triggers or memory joggers that will work for you whilst also identifying the things that don't serve you well.

As with so many professional development books or audios, Darren Hardy reminds us about the laws of association. If you haven't realised the importance of the rules of association by now, you need to give yourself a significant wake-up pill. Find a success buddy that mirrors you and what you want to achieve. Participating in a mastermind group is an excellent another way to do this.

Do not listen to the GUPTRs or the IBEs!

These people are poor influences on you, oh and don't forget about that horrible mind monster stop feeding that thing!

Stop giving the mind monster too much airtime. You can be whoever, and whatever you want to be, you can have whatever you want if you are willing to pay the price and understand that your adoption of the compound effect and its principles will get you to wherever you want.

The compound effect comes as a must buy-in in my mind; I love listening to the audio because I like stories, but equally, I have both the audio and the book. Another book on the same theme as the compound effect is a cracking book by Jeff Olsen called the "Slight edge". This book is all about turning simple disciplines into a massive success.

Whilst this book echoes what Think and Grow Rich covers, sometimes it is just good to get a similar message from an alternative source.

If you look at the slight edge paths diagram below, you will see a corroborating factor to Darren Hardy's "Compound Effect" and Jeff Olsen's "Slight Edge".

I would recommend that you buy the "Slight Edge" because there are specific influences within it covered by Jeff Olsen that will resonate with your subconscious mind and cause you to implement some of these things in your strategy.

Here are some key points of the slight edge.

People everywhere are clamouring for the formula, the secret ingredient, the path to improve their lives. The secret ingredient is your philosophy: what you know, how you hold it and how it affects what you do. Once you change the way you think, you can take steps to lead you to the how-tos.

The things you do every day, the things that look like they don't matter, do matter they not only make a difference; they make all the difference.

Suppose you learn to understand and apply the slight edge. In that case, your life will become filled with hundreds of thousands of small, seemingly insignificant actions, all of them easy to do, none of them mysterious, complicated, or difficult. These are the actions that will create your success.

That's what successful people do: simple things that are easy to do. Here's the problem: every action that is easy to do, is also easy not to do. If you don't do them, you won't suffer, or fail or blow it, today. But that simple error in judgement, compounded over time, will ruin your chances for success.

The most potent force for change is time. Position your daily actions, so time is working for you instead of against you. Because time will either promote you or expose you. What keeps you on the path is your slight edge philosophy, which includes your understanding of the secret of time. Knowing that I will get the results I want if I stay on this path long enough.

Everyone wants to go directly from plant to harvest in today's world. The step we keep overlooking is the step of cultivating. Unlike planting and harvesting, that takes place only through the patient dimension of time. The right choices you make today, compounded over time, will take you higher up the success curve.

People always look for the cure, the breakthrough, the magic pill, the scientific quantum leap, or the miracle, yet the solution already exists.

It always did. Is it magic? Yes, the same magic caused the problem: the power of daily actions compounded over time. The magic of the slight edge.

Over the years, I have identified seven principles to apply right now into life every day.

1: Show up consistently with the right attitude.
2: Over a long period of time.
3: Have faith.
4: A burning desire.
5: Be willing to pay the price.
6: Have slight edge integrity.
7: Discipline to do those things even when no one is looking.

The truth is everything is curved. There is no true straight line; everything is changing, including your life. You are on a journey, your life path. That path is a curve you are either curving upward or downward.

Wherever you may be in your life, understanding the slight edge gives you the tools to start fresh right now! And place yourself firmly on the upper curve.

Mastery is not some vaulted, lofty place that only the elite few ever land. The pursuit of any aim, goal, or dream, personal, professional, spiritual, in any area is a slight edge journey of continuous improvement, learning and refinement. But mastery is not an exalted state that lies at the end of the path; it is a state of mind that lies at the very beginning. Mastery is the act of setting your foot on the path.

And the final point to make within our highlighting of the slight edge is the following several faces.

Once you recognise it in your life, you can harness the slight edge in their pursuit of your dreams.

Momentum: steady wins the race. Once you're in motion, it's easy to keep on keeping on. Once you stop, it's hard to change from stop to go.

Completion: every incomplete thing in your life or work exerts a draining force on you, sucking the energy of accomplishment and success out of you. Take on those incompletions in your life just as you took on learning to walk.

Habit: your habits are what will propel you up the success curve or down the failure curve.

Reflection: being productive and being busy is not necessarily the same thing. Doing things won't create your success, doing the right things will. Were those actions productive? Did you take a step forward?

Celebration: carry on and keep your slight edge activities, your right choices, and incremental successes, right in the open where you can see them and celebrate them. Acknowledge those steps, no matter how small or insignificant they may seem at the time. Wow, oh wow, in the compound effect by Darren Hardy and the slight edge by Jeff Olsen, there are so many amazing lessons.

They are the same, but they are different, and I would recommend that you put down the slight edge as one of the need to listen to or reads in your library.

These two books deliver a clear and concise message that repeated activity over a period of time, will generate the results that you want or don't want if you are letting yourself drift. Other books are more practical, and I love how you can dovetail the 1st three books into the next books I would like to draw to your attention.

Being organised is a crucial principle for you to live your life on purpose and get those goals, dreams, and aspirations.

Procrastination is one of the biggest killers that stop people from achieving what they want to achieve.

The next book I would love to introduce to you is just one of the many books written by a personal development guru called Brian Tracy. Eat that Frog is a pure masterpiece.

**Brian Tracy's "Eat that Frog".**

Each day when you wake up in the morning, or even the day before, you are coached by Brian Tracy to write a list of all the things that you need to do. It would then be best if you prioritised the things you need to do into some form of order.

The primary and overriding premise of "Eat that Frog" is that you should always do the biggest, ugliest task first.

If it means eating a frog first thing in the morning to get that horrible task done and dusted, then that is what you should do. Nothing should be done until you've eaten your frog, and then after you've eaten your frog, everything for the rest of your day will become easier.

In the book, Brian identifies the need to develop habits. Have you noticed a theme appearing right now?

Every single book has a section about habits. Therefore, if every single book we have discussed so far has a section about habits, it is a key feature of success or failure.

One of the big habits that Brian Tracy so eloquently demonstrates is that one habit we need to eliminate is the habit of procrastination. Through his teaching and theories and diligent practice, you can reduce procrastination. Remember to consciously create better routines and have triggers to activate those better habits allow the subconscious mind to do them automatically and without thinking about them.

"Eat that Frog" demonstrates that if you can make a habit of the critical things, this has two payoffs. The first is immediate satisfaction, and the second is long term success.

When you complete those challenging tasks first, it then sets up a positive feedback loop. We know that the happy hormone serotonin comes into our bodies when we feel like we have succeeded. The more we can get these endorphin- induced feelings into our body, the more self-confident and capable we become. Brian alludes to the fact that subconsciously the more times that you complete such tasks, the more you become addicted to the success, and then this loop forms the increased repetition of the endorphin release.

One of the keys to long-term success and living a happy life is when you have a series of successful habits. Those habits will become easier to do as time passes by, which means you slip seamlessly into doing the important things rather than dodge them.

One of the principal features of eating that frog is the importance of preparing correctly.

Brian identifies several steps for setting and achieving goals:

1: Determine what you want to accomplish, then write down those goals.

2: Define your goal: be clear about what you're aiming for and in what order. This echoes our live your life on purpose strategy of chunking down small goals and setting them into an order.

3: Write your goal down. Writing down a plan makes it real. A goal or objective that isn't put into writing is rarely achieved.

4: Write down the steps you need to undertake to achieve that goal. Goal getting is far easier to accomplish when broken down into small manageable tasks.

5: Now turn the list into a plan: now is time to prioritise those tasks and then list those things in the order that they need to be done. Once you have that written goal, it has now formed a plan; when you have placed something in order, that needs to be completed. You will be far more productive than if you only ever had that plan in your mind.

6: Set a deadline for achieving the goal. We mentioned that goals need to have definite deadlines, and within those concrete deadlines, we need to put in specific responsibilities that need to be completed. You may also want to set the deadline and sub deadlines for smaller tasks that are leading towards the end game.

7: Act on your plan. It doesn't need to be perfect because it is far better to act on an average plan than to do nothing with a great plan. Do something every day to advance your project and schedule it in your diary.

When you create your plan, ensure that you keep focusing on the importance of that life-work balance. Write down a list of the things you need to do in all areas in the wheel of life. Balancing what you do daily and prioritising them will allow you to grow in an uninformed way.

You can't have satisfaction in your business and your relationships if you only focus on business. Equally, if you are only focusing on business and your fitness, the chances are your relationships could lose out. When you are planning, ensure you incorporate all segments of the wheel and allocate them and appropriate time.

When you read “Eat that Frog” by Brian Tracy, it will make sense, and you will start to prioritise your lists so that you sequentially work through them in a chronological order that moves you forward.

Brian shows that there are things that you think are important in your life that are easy to do, but that there would be no negative ramifications whatsoever if you never did them. These are the tasks that people do first because they are the easiest!

By formulating good habits and a daily written plan of what you want to accomplish, you will be moving forward when you prioritise those crucial functions in your life.

In his book, he superbly shows how you can transform something you fear, into something you enjoy. Indeed, he shows you how you can transform something that you fear, not only into something that you enjoy but into something you crave completing.

You will also be guided to identify your strengths and weaknesses and how you can transform those weaknesses into strengths.

There will be some tasks that you think you need to do, but frankly, they are not congruent with your skills or levels of interest, so it might be better to get somebody else to do them for you.

Freeing up your time and allowing somebody to do these tasks means that you can focus on the task that you enjoy doing. This will create better results.

When you have set some goals, identify the most significant limitation. Once you've determined that main thing that's holding you or your project or your company back, find a way to overcome it.

Removing this will massively speed up your progress toward your goal.

When you get rid of a limiting factor, this could be your most important task or frog to eat now.

If the limiting factor is you in a certain area of your life, you need to turn that weakness into a strength by improving your skillset. There is nothing that will stop you from skilling up other than yourself. So, with your growth mindset, invest time into your skills.

Don't plan occasionally; plan every single day. Buy yourself a "things to do" book" with a list and a box where you can take off your activities. According to Brian Tracy, it can save 10 minutes in implementation when you spend a minute planning.

**"Give me 5 hours to chop down a tree, and I will spend 4 hours sharpening the blade" Abraham Lincoln.**

Plan your day every day, and this will be one of the fundamental principles to avoid procrastination.

Eat that frog demonstrates that you can increase your productivity by 25% or two hours a day when you work from a list.

Pareto's principle is the well-known 80 /20 rule, and if you live by the 80/20 rule, you will understand that 20% of your efforts will produce 80% of your results. Focus on doing the few things that will make the most difference, or better yet, narrow it to one thing.

If you have ten things to do, doing the two most important ones will have a more significant impact than doing the other eight combined. Each of the ten tasks may take the same amount of time, but a certain one will generate more value. Perhaps as much as ten times more than all the others combined. The most valuable task you should complete first, or the frog you should eat first.

“Eat that Frog” is one of those books or audios that needs to be in the library of people who want to succeed. Once you have read or listened to this book, you will eliminate procrastination to a certain extent. There are occasions when you will not be able to eliminate procrastination; it is the way we are built, and yet Brian still has a cunning plan.

Accepting that we cannot eliminate procrastination, he suggests that we purposely procrastinate on those things that don't matter. So, we write them on our list, prioritise everything, and intentionally do not do the things that have been prioritised as least important.

Once you understand the power of some of Brian Tracey's material, you will then continue to invest in some of his other training and coaching programmes.

Another good book that I alluded to earlier in living your life on purpose is "The 5-second rule" by Mel Robbins. A fantastic read, not one I'm going to cover now, but it is another way to eliminate procrastination.

We have highlighted just a very small selection of personal development material that we would recommend you invest in and digest as we look to close off this chapter. I have some other personal favourites, one of without a doubt my favourite authors is Dr Tom Barrett.

His analogy of the Jelly doughnut, being ACE, speaking with Authority, Conviction and Enthusiasm and the brilliant way he demonstrates tips and tricks to be focused blow my mind away.

When you research Dr Tom and see his CV, you will know that he has advised, mentored, and been a public speaker in some of the world's most elevated environments. Being an adviser in the White House, I'm sure, is quite a good accolade; being hot property on the professional speaker circuit and speaking in front of 10s of thousands of people identifies Dr Tom's value.

The way he delivers his information is clear and precise; how I like it. Direct!

Dr Tom delves into psychology in a light-hearted way, and his humour feeds out through everything he does. Dr Tom unravels what could be complex discussion material into easy to understand and digestible strategies and techniques that, when implemented, cannot fail to work.

Two of my favourite books are" demystifying success cracking the code" and "easy street the facts about focus".

Once again, I would highly recommend that you add these to your development library.

Another good read or audio which takes no more than a few hours but can be highly impactful in your life is a book called "Go for No" by Richard Fenton and Andrea waltz.

I particularly like this one because it reminds me of the mind monster that sits on people's shoulders that stop them from achieving what they can achieve.

Far too many people have heard the word "no", so often that it paralyses them. The jam in their doughnut is no longer a runny jam. The term "no" has been received as a failure statement so often that the jam has been overlaid by more jam within the subconscious mind.

So much so it has turned into a thick and horrible black treacle. When you read "Go for No", it is like a treacle busting book.

The jam undoubtedly undergoes a transfusion within your subconscious mind when you read this fantastic little book. Instead of fearing the word no, you embrace it, and you aim for it; who cares if you get a no?

I want to highlight two other phenomenal books or audios: “Atomic Habits” by James Clear and the “Miracle Morning” by Hal Elrod. These two titles work synergistically, and it would not be an understatement if I were to say that if you employed some of their principles, scrub that, all their principles, that you would save so much time in your day, and you would feel so much better.

If you live your life on purpose, both titles are right up there at the top of the list of books and audios recommended to listen to or read.

Finally, in this chapter, invest some money in buying the video, the audio, or the book called £The Secret" by Rhonda Byrne.

This is nice and easy to absorb information. Discussing the laws of attraction and the power of gratitude in a heartfelt and meaningful way, Rhonda Byrne hits the nail on the subject matter.

When you absorb the material within the secret and apply that material into living your life on purpose and the wheel of life, you can combine all the theories to improve your life.

The Secret" is plentiful with knowledge and wisdom and contains some philosophies that I think the whole world would benefit from adopting.

With well over 100 books or audios in my library, distilling down to just a handful was tough to do indeed. This chapter's overriding message is that throughout the rest of your life, buy into this continuous, never-ending improvement mindset.

# Attitude

By now, you should have completed your wheel of life an allocated where you think you are with regards to attitude. It is improbable that you have completed this task properly because the interpretation of attitude can come in many forms.

In this chapter, we will discuss how others' attitudes can affect you and how your attitudes can affect others.

Many of us will have come across people who have an awesomely right attitude and, on the flip side, someone who has a bad attitude.

The likelihood is that if we have good attitudes, we will be automatically drawn to those who are equally good with attitude.

If we have a terrible attitude, we may resent those who have a good attitude and be drawn to those who have a bad attitude.

But what is an attitude, and can it be changed?

The actual definition and connotation of attitude have changed over recent years. The interpretation has changed, and therefore as learning individuals, we need to appreciate these different connotations.

The first definition of attitude includes “a feeling or an opinion about something or someone”.

The second definition of attitude includes the way people act or how we act in the presence of others. A sub definition of attitude is how people work when operating behind your back.

We can divide attitude into a good or a bad attitude in the simplest of terms.

In today's cynical society, somebody could say “that kids got attitude”, and instantly there is a negative connotation to that phrase. For example, the kid is deliberately going out of their way to go against society's grain and therefore have an attitude.

But that kid has a bad attitude for a reason, and one of the great things with attitudes is that no matter where you are in your life, you can alter yours.

You could have all the skills and talent in the world and with a lousy attitude go nowhere in life, you will reach some part of your life, some level of income in your life, but never able to break through to the next level. It certainly isn't because of your skills or your talents. Attitude can work for you in incredible ways. It can also be destructive to so many different people.

There are different personality traits in our world. Once you can identify the different personality traits of people you regularly encounter, you can mirror these people's attitudes and forgive them with the right attitude.

Let us now investigate the different personality traits so that we can respond to them in a different way when we come across these people. During later parts of this chapter, we're going to delve deeper into ways to improve your attitude but let us now see how we can respond better to other people for the time being.

Being aware of other people's personality traits and becoming a chameleon will give people a better impression of you.

We will divide the four personality traits into four different colour groups—red, yellow, green, and blue.

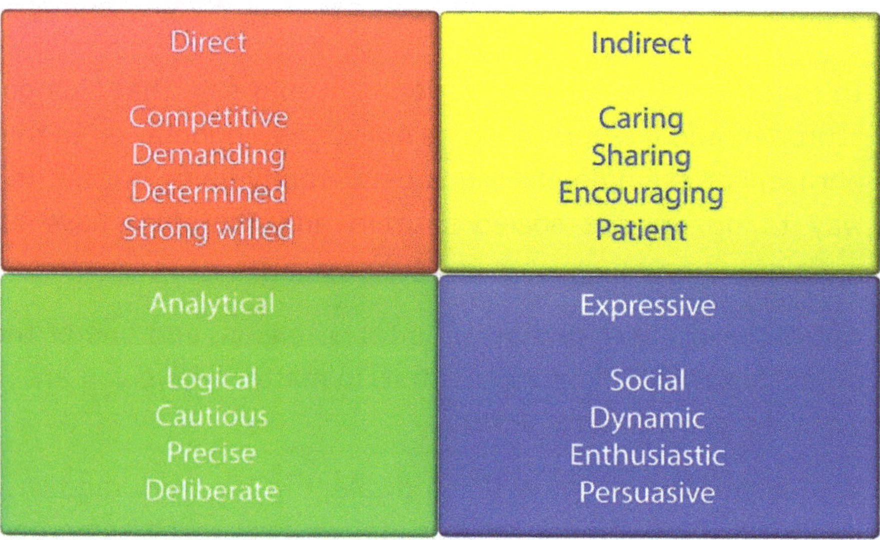


People have a dominant colour personality, but they can be a blend of all four colours. If you can master the skill of determining when you are speaking with someone what their dominant colour personality is, you can become the chameleon and change your dominant colour in that situation to reflect theirs.

This will create harmony in the way you are received and how you receive them.

Let us have a bit of fun because this should be fun, and whilst we go through this exercise, be mindful of where you think you are in terms of colour and your dominant colour. We will go through some of the personality traits, and whilst we are doing this, think, is this you? Do you know anybody like this?

**The Red Personality**

The red personality will be a direct communicator; they will be competitive, demanding, determined and strong-willed. They will be purposeful individuals who focus on results and generally like to take charge, no delete that they always try to take control, they like to make quick decisions, and they love challenges.

Reds are not good listeners, and they love recognition and competition. If you ever want to get a red personality on your side, give them lots of recognition and praise.

The Reds do like to speak their minds would be perceived as argumentative. Due to their low tolerance levels, they can seem to be impatient when they are dealing with somebody that is unprepared.

Their communication style would be that they tell people what should be done and control individuals.

It does not mean that they are bad by any stretch of the imagination; they are very confident people and know what they want.

When the red personality talks in their direct communication style, it is essential to understand that they mean no badness. It is the way they have been brought up to communicate. This communication style can immediately turn off some people with different personality traits.

If you are aware of it and interpret it as their personality trait, you can manage the way you receive that communication style. The red personality group is likely to be employed as

CEO, top-level manager, or run their own business. When you communicate with a red personality and become the chameleon, don't worry, you don't need to be abrupt, and you don't need to change your communication style, instead be more accommodating of theirs.

If the red personality expects decisions to be made quickly, allow them to make their decisions and not respond negatively to them. Instead, learn the skill of communicating back to them so that they can take from your interaction with them something that they can translate to being their idea!

Strengths: Planning and analysing.

Weaknesses: Perfectionists, critical, very opinionated.

Goals: Accuracy thoroughness and relentless.

Fear: Criticism.

Motivator: Progress and expect others to follow.

Irritation: Unpredictability, the slow decision of thought.

**The Yellow Personality**

The yellow personality is undoubtedly the most amiable of all personality traits. They are caring, and they love to share. They are encouraging and patient, they are relaxed, and they love to cooperate. In any form of discussion, they will always seek agreement, and they will always provide support to every single person within the team. These people like to communicate trust.

If you were to meet people like this to start with, they could be quite shy, but this does not mean they lack skill or talent. If you were to visit their home, this personality trait is likely to have a loving environment with lots of photographs of all their family scattered around every room. Chances are, if you have met many yellow personality traits, they will be the ones that like to bake and bring things to the office for other people's benefit.

Professionals with yellow personality traits seem to be attracted to the nursing profession, the teaching profession, counselling and caring. The yellow personality are the lovely people of the world.

The yellows need to be understood and appreciated, and sometimes they can come across as quite intense because of this need to be understood and appreciated. The yellow seek purpose in their lives, and that is why they love to work with people, especially children.

In a comical twist of fate, the yellow personalities usually are married to a red character. This is because the yellow personalities are the only personalities that would put up with the red abruptness.

The yellow personality politely always asks for help and guidance to commit to a decision. They will seek reassurance, and they will either show their emotion one way or another. If they are unsure, they may pretend to show emotion. When they pretend to show any emotion, for example, agree with a red personality, it is to keep the peace. As you can imagine, a yellow personality is a forgiving personality.

Strengths: They like to serve others and listen.

Weaknesses: Oversensitivity and indecision.

Goals: Acceptance instability.

Fear: Sudden change.

Motivator: Involvement they love to serve others.

Irritations: Instant insensitivity.

**The Green Personality**

The green personalities are typically the analytical people in the world. They are cautious, precise, and deliberate; they like to question and be satisfied with the facts. They are formal individuals, and they value logic. They commit slowly to something because they need to be sure of the data before proceeding.

Once a green personality has made their decision, and they mentally believe that decision to be correct they will be loyal people and act without reservation.

The green personality like to ask questions, and they also like control situations if they know they are right in their mind with their research. Greens are logical individuals; you could think about Spock from Star Trek!

You can always tell a green personality if you go to a party because they will be away from the main group; if you go to a seminar, they are sitting at the back. The green personalities are fantastic people, yet the problem is that so few green characters are recognised for their ability.

Because they are relatively introvert, unless someone takes the time to get to know these people, they will not break through that exterior protective shell.

Greens will typically resist confrontation at all costs, and they are generally quiet, but they do process things deeply. The greens are fantastic listeners, and whilst they do respect directness, they do recoil from perceived hostility and arguments.

A green personality type may be in accounting, engineering, technology, medicine, or some form of scientific work. Some of the most successful people in our world are green personalities. As young people, due to a certain amount of alienation from other peers in their schools, they withdrew to their world or associated with other green personalities.

Greens do like to work alone, and they can be perceived to be indecisive. Do not confuse indecision if they are still doing their research.

Fashionably certain sectors of the green personality can be referred to as geeks. Chances are you are employed by one!

Strengths: Planning, analysing and diplomatic.

Weaknesses: Perfectionists, critical.

Goals: Accuracy and thoroughness.

Fear: Criticism therefore can be quite stubborn.

Motivator: Progress.

Irritation: Unpredictability.

**The Blue Personality**

The best way to describe a blue personality is if you know Tigger from Winnie the Pooh. They are incredibly expressive; they are social and dynamic. They are enthusiastic and persuasive and can be highly motivational. They inspire and involve others, and they create excitement.

The Blues love adventure, and they seek to be popular. Of the four personality traits, the Blues will be the trendy people at a party, and they love to talk and tell stories.

If they are involved in a sales environment, which they are good at, their weakness is that they do not follow up appropriately. So, if you are working with a blue salesperson, develop a system to follow up on their activity.

The Blues believe they are multitaskers, but they are like a Tasmanian devil; they whizz around everywhere and create mayhem.

Sometimes the Blues can lack commitment, and they always need an out or an escape plan, a chance to run away.

The Blues are spontaneous. They love to entertain groups, and they need to be entertained.

They don't pay much attention to detail, and if it is fun, you can guarantee they will be in it. They are so caring and want to be friends and be loved by everybody. They will tell you that you should come to the party!

Like the yellows, they show their feelings, and they are compassionate individuals. With that sensitivity, such is their level of excitement and enthusiasm that if their sensitivity is questioned, it won't last long.

Strengths: Persuasion, interaction with others.

Weaknesses: Disorganisation and careless.

Goals: Popularity, applause, and recognition.

Fear: Loss of social status.

Motivator: Recognition.

Irritations: Routine.

This was a summary of those personality traits. Imagine that everyone has a primary colour in this personality grid, and you are communicating with a lot of different people.

You could perceive a red personality as having a poor attitude, and you could be right! But some personality traits like the Reds are misunderstood.

If you communicate with a red personality and a yellow personality, becoming the chameleon will serve you well. You understand the reds personality traits, and you respond accordingly, at the end of every interaction with the red personality, they will start to believe you have a good attitude.

It does not mean you have to be submissive and agreeing but learn how to respond correctly with these people.

The Reds do not mind having a constructive argument or discussion. The worst thing that could happen is if you communicate powerplay to powerplay with a red. It will be a volatile experience.

Suppose you are communicating with a yellow personality. In that case, you may need to be a different personality yourself. If you can get them to warm to you, trust you, they will open up to you, and they will move and demonstrate their skill set to you. Your yellow personalities could be your best allies in life. Because they are loyal once they have warmed to you and they like you they will tell everybody how nice a person you are.

Equally, suppose you are a blue personality, and you are communicating with a green character. In that case, you need to understand that you will have to temper down this level of excitement and this giddiness.

For the Blues, the green personalities can be superb allies. Remember the weaknesses of the Blues, they are unorganised and lack routine. On the other hand, the greens love organisation and enjoy routine.

When a blue communicates with a green personality, they need to calm down and give the green personality person all the facts at hand and let that green personality trait go away and spend time with the data.

No amount of enthusiastic coercion will ever work on a green personality. Please give them the facts, let them go away, and digest them. When they return to a blue character, they will have spent a lot of time and due diligence on the information at hand. If you are blue, make sure you acknowledge their work.

Of course, the blue personality trait person does not like systematic fashion, so if they are a chameleon, they need to calm down and bite their lips. The green personality trait will deliver back some facts and information that the blue personality will likely have overlooked.

The Green personality is the Ying to the blue characters Yang.

The quick fix on how people view you and your attitude is how you respond to your environment and its people. Therefore, your job is to become a chameleon, study other people's personalities, and become harmonious with them. This will make you a professional communicator of people.

The upside of this is that people of all four personality traits will look at you, and they will all put you into the category of someone who has the right attitude and someone they enjoy being with.

So that was the quick fix; now, we must look at the deeper issues as to what controls and created someone's attitude.

**Your attitude will determine your altitude.**

Let us agree that you are a highly skilled individual and superb at what you do. You are motivated, and you want to move through different life levels, as discussed in the personal development chapter. You are ambitious, and you want to improve your life and make sure you ensure balance in your wheel of life.

It does not matter how good you are, how motivated you are, how ambitious you are or how good you think you are! If you want to have an extra person on your team, so there is you and another person on your team, you want that person to be your attitude.

Having a good attitude is like having someone else on your team. If you have good ability and have the right attitude, this will generate a brilliant result.

If you have excellent ability but a poor attitude, this will generate a poor result.

People with good attitudes will naturally attract people, and on the flip side, those with a bad attitude will repel people.

The compound effect can work on your health, your fitness on your business and career can also work to your advantage with your attitude.

If you have studied the personality traits and put yourself in one of the colour categories, do you have a base to work from?

Now that you understand what personality trait you are, it would be foolhardy to believe that others will respond to your personality trait and accommodate you. It would be foolhardy because people don't know about the different personality traits you have a head start!

Indicators of a poor attitude include but not limited to:

They are always right.
They fail to forgive people.
They have a large ego.
They always like to take the credit.

Whatever your attitude is, it is vital to appreciate that you are in a constant flux of transition.

You know the phrase good vibes or bad vibes. When you speak to somebody, you get a good vibe, how interesting that you receive a good vibe from somebody that is not verbal.

We know that as human beings, we are natural transmitters on the way we feel, and we are natural receivers of the way people are and the way we think.

If somebody transmits something to us, where we get a hint of a poor or bad attitude, we will pick up on that instantly. You already know this to be true because you experienced it in your life.

You may not have been consciously aware of personality traits before, but for sure, you will have met people that you immediately want to either resonate with or get the heck away from.

If this is the case for others that we encounter, then by definition, whenever we speak to people, we will transmit our attitudes to them, and they become the receivers.

But what are we subconsciously transmitting?

Most people in this world have never looked at themselves to decipher what internally is being transmitted externally. The crux of the matter is that your internal belief system drives your external attitude.

We are talking severe jammy doughnut stuff right now!

Not many people know this, but even whilst you are in the womb of your mother, your attitudes are being formed. Whilst you are inside the womb and are developing into this amazing human being, you can still receive the transmission of the external womb environment. If you were developing within your mum's womb, and your parents always argue, you will detect this. If your parents had terrible temperaments, this character trait could be born with you. If, on the other hand, you detected nothing but love and care between your parents, this same trait will be born with you.

Then as you grow into the wonderful human being you are now; you will move through different period of life where your attitudes and belief systems are formed.

We discussed this with the jam in the doughnut theory, but it goes one stage further with attitude.

During your early years and up to 8/10 years old, you start to grow into the environment that has been forced upon you.

Suppose you were brought up in a nurturing environment where you were always supported and encouraged to do whatever you wanted to do. In that case, this becomes the primary operating system of your attitude.

If you have been constantly chastised and put down and had your growth-restricted up until eight years of age, this will become your base operating system.

As you move from 8 years of age to 12 years of age, you will become conscious of your self-image and learn through a new experience. If you are fortunate to go to a good school and have good associations, you will have experienced good things. The flip side is that if you had terrible associations, the school environment was not right, and you experience bad things, this then starts to create an overlay on your belief systems.

Up to the age of 23, this phase is where your peers and society's pressures can define your attitude.

During this phase of your life, you may be subjected to the pressures of conforming to the need to have a specific physical appearance. Some call this fashion.

The earlier attitude and belief operating systems are now working for you or against you. In the early years of life, you can escape being identified as having a poor attitude under the guise you are growing up.

When you enter the work environment, a good attitude or the lousy attitude is exposed. Those with a good attitude seemed to progress through their careers or running their own business, and then they seem to get that slight edge advantage.

Those with high skill levels but with a poor attitude seem to reach their ceiling and never progressed further. These people move from job to job, believing that it is the hierarchy or their fellow peers that are at fault for why they are not being promoted.

The problem, however, was much closer to home.

There is some excellent news when it comes to attitude. If you have a good attitude, you can still create a great attitude, and if you currently have a poor attitude, you can always make this a great attitude.

It is a case of identifying your internal drivers and then creating habits that change the operating systems that have served you poorly. Through that jam transfusion instal a brand-new attitude operating system.

The bad news is that there is no quick fix, as people who know you and have associated with you for many years, have already received the attitude that you have been transmitting.

Shouting to the world on day one that you have changed your attitude will not work. It will take time, like forming a good habit for people around you to pick up on your change of attitude and this increased positivity.

Being congruent in this world is essential for people to appreciate that you have an excellent attitude.

The great news is you can work on your attitude, and the bad news is it will take some time, but first, we must look in the mirror ourselves, and we must be brutally honest with what we see.

There is no person in this beautiful world that we live in that is perfect. And there is no need to be perfect. You don't need to be right all the time, and nobody cares too much about your ego. In this world, where we accept that we don't always get everything right, we flip that and identify that people we associate with don't always get it right. Therefore, we need to learn the skill of forgiving.

There is no point in collecting negative baggage throughout your life. The past is in the past. You can learn from it, but you cannot change it.

Near to the beautiful City of York is a monastery called Ampleforth. Many years ago, Ampleforth was occupied by a sect of monks; this set of monks had strict rules. One such rule was that they were not allowed to talk to or touch a female.

One day, the master monk and an apprentice monk had to walk from Ampleforth to York to run an errand. Before the journey, the apprentice monk asked the master monk how they would get from Ampleforth to York without encountering a female person.

The master monk explained that they would take all the back pathways, and there is an unlikely chance that they would encounter anybody, let alone a female. As they walked around a forest, they were met by a river's torrent and a female panicking as she needed to cross the river. The two monks stopped in their tracks, aware that they could not break the monastery's rules.

The lady pleaded with the monks to help her cross the river because she had to get across it to attend to her new-born child. The apprentice monk recoiled and wanted to walk away. Without uttering a single word, the master monk walked up to the woman, picked her up, waded through the river, dropping her on the other side. He then continued to walk towards York, without uttering a single word.

The apprentice monk caught up with the master monk, and throughout the next three hours of this walk, was moaning and groaning about what had happened. Then eventually, the master monk stopped and turned towards the Apprentice monk.

"What is wrong with you"? he proclaimed.

"Master, I cannot believe that you picked up this woman and broke the vows that we set and follow at Ampleforth."

The master monk replied, "You are right, apprentice. I did pick up this woman to do a good act so that she could attend to her new-born child, and whilst I did pick up and carry this woman across the river, you have been carrying her for the last three hours. Drop it and let us move on".

Many people throughout life have collected so many pieces of luggage that they are carrying too much. This luggage weighs them down, and they have so many grievances inside their minds that they're transmitting this all the time.

Indeed, some of these angsts are so well ingrained, and they never leave the person; the anger, the frustration is contained within and always being expressed out with. You are not always right, and it is a weakness to think that you are. It is a strength when you understand that somebody else's opinion is valid to them, and whilst it is not correct to you, it does not mean you have to impose your will.

We have identified that attitude is what we are inwardly digesting and what we are expressing externally. Attitude determines our happiness and success.

We have already spoken about emotional contagion and the laws of association. Why is it that grumpy people hang around with other grumpy people?

It's because this is where they get an agreement with each other. Some people get so entrenched with matters of the world that they cannot even influence, yet they become horrible anger vessels.

In this cracking world that we have, rewards are abundant for everybody to achieve in this time of opportunity.

**With the right mindset and attitude, you can achieve anything you want.**

If it can happen to them, it can happen to you. There are so many stories of successful people going from a minus bank balance to a multi-million positive bank balance.

There are so many stories of somebody that has been unhealthy, obese, and physically unfit, moving in a positive direction and becoming physically fit and running a marathon.

There are amazing stories of people who started in an organisation making cups of tea or sweeping the floors and becoming that company's chief executive officer or some other similar senior position.

It does not matter who you are, where you're from, what your education is.  Develop an understanding that if you learn to develop a great attitude and live in this world of continuous and never-ending improvement, you can genuinely get to wherever you want.

Look in the mirror and look in the mirror and give yourself an attitude appraisal.

SWOT analysis is how businesses work out how they can improve their business prospects.

The business identifies that it has strengths, weaknesses, opportunities, and threats. This is where the term SWOT comes from. Look at yourself and identify your strengths and jot those strengths down into your Journal. Then jot down your weaknesses.

Do not be afraid to confront your weaknesses because we all have them. Yes, 100% of this population have weaknesses. The winners in our world are the ones who identify their shortcomings and better still seek to transfer those weaknesses into strengths.

That is the great thing about the SWOT analysis. Once you have identified your weaknesses, you can turn them into a strength, and that will take time.

Once you have identified your weakness, we employ the same strategies discussed in the habit section of the book. We work on ourselves all day, during the day, being consciously aware of what we want to improve. We develop personally, and we work with other people that we know, like and trust to help us grow.

When it comes to opportunities and threats within the SWOT analysis, you identify where you are now and within your goal setting where you'd like to be in, let us say 13 weeks. Whatever goal we've decided, we already have agreed that we will chunk that goal into smaller bitesize and achievable targets. Each day we will move in a straight line towards attaining that goal. The threat is what is going to stop us from achieving our goal.

Let us assume, we have identified that one of our weaknesses is that we are always right and need to answer quickly. We've got a bad habit of butting in and talking over other people.

We've identified this to be a lousy attitude trait. We know that the threat is that when we engage in regular conversation at home, at work and even socially, that we have this habit of jumping in and exerting our belief in such a way that others can define it as being oppressive.

Remember, we don't mean to be oppressive, and we don't mean to exert our thoughts on other people. It is the way our attitude operating system currently works. We are conscious that we want to stop acting in this way, but how do you turn this threat into an opportunity?

The first win is that you have identified that this is a weakness, and you want to turn this weakness into a strength. After all, being confident in your ability is a strength. It isn't received the way you want it to be.

The next time you are in a conversation with somebody, the conversation matter interests you highly.

Within a group session, there is a discussion, and even before the conversation has started, you are mindful and conscious that you are going to hold back. You are going to bite your lip effectively.

The discussion is continuing, and other members of this discussion group notice that you are not butting in as usual. There will be a moment of silence until eventually, someone turns to you, and they will utter these words "it is unlike you not to be taking part. Is everything okay, and what are your thoughts on this matter"?

Even at this stage, subconsciously, your mouth wants to engage in top gear and unleash what you think. But at this point, you have mastered the art of diplomacy.

Suppose you respond something like this. "There is nothing wrong with me. I am fine; I am enjoying this discussion, and whilst I do have some thoughts of my own, I am inwardly digesting what you are saying. If you want me to give you my side of things, I'd be happy to share it, but I'm happy to continue listening until then".

First, that will be a shock and awe strategy. You will instantly have stunned the people with who you regularly have discussions, because they are already expecting you to give your opinion whether they want it or not.

Inwardly you are bursting, and you want to say what you want to say, but you're also conscious of what you want to do with this bad habit. You want to turn this weakness of attitude into a strength, and so you are inwardly holding back.

What is likely to happen is that members of the discussion group will instantly respect you for that statement. They are going to automatically warm to the fact that they are detecting a different characteristic trait.

They will ask you for your opinion on the discussion.

It is now your turn to deliver your opinion, but in such a way that it promotes further discussion, not to close down the conversation.

"My take on this is that (explain your thoughts) ........ and I can see pros and cons from (one group member) ... who gave a good explanation of... and I also liked what you (another group member) said about... I wonder if we can merge all of our minds if we can't come up with some symbiotic decision".

The result of this type of diplomacy is that if what you have said is right and a good course of action because you have delivered it more appealingly, the group is likely to accept all or some of your suggestion. By using multiple minds, you are more than likely to develop a better alternative, which is the strength of any mastermind group.

The result in that discussion is not a significant win; however, after the meeting concludes and you all go your separate ways, you have put a hand grenade into somebody's mind, and it has exploded. If you do this correctly, they will walk away stunned by this new reflective and diplomatic person.

When they talk about you behind your back, they are no longer saying that person is such a know it all. Instead, they say, "Wow, did you notice the change in that person".

This change cannot happen overnight, and this change cannot be false. If you employ a conscious decision to change your bad attitude, it will become a natural internal operating system with time. Until your subconscious mind accepts this to be accurate, you will have to keep your new attitude on track consciously.

If you have a dim view of the world and all the opportunities within it, you will get a dim result. If you appreciate that there are many opportunities within this world and that you want to build relationships with other people, you will get more from this world.

**You will get out exactly what you put in.**

Many of us have been to the school of Hard Knocks, and we know that through life, we can keep heading against a brick wall, or we can change. Life is more enjoyable with the right attitude, and with a good attitude, this starts to breakdown some of those limiting self-beliefs.

The law of attraction works for good things and bad things. If you are engaging with your purposeful morning daily and are deliberately working on your goals, you will attract those good things into your life.

We have said this before "Soldiers die for it, and babies cry for it. It is called recognition".

One of the critical things you can do to turn a weakness into a strength is to show mutual respect for people you associate with. Acknowledge and recognise the things that they do well.

One nice comment a day to your loving partner, to any children you have, to any work colleagues or friends that you have one piece of recognition to them every day will work wonders for their mindset and self-belief.

In this world, we have all been dealt a deck of cards, and we can sit with our deck of cards, and we can have a pity party about where we were born, the parents that we have, the school that we went to or the job we have. Yes, we can have a pity party, and frankly, nobody other than your other grumpy friends are going to listen.

On the other hand, we can agree that we have been dealt a deck of cards that might not be favourable, but like playing a game of cards, you can change them, and the changing of those cards can determine your winning formula.

We want to be aware of other people's attitudes, and we want to question whether they have a good or a bad attitude and we also need to look at these people and wonder if any of their bad attitudes reside within us.

If they do, we have identified them, and we can move them from a weakness to a strength.

Many times, you see that somebody partners up with another person in our world. During the relationship's courting phase, both people were of a cheerful disposition.

Through the school of hard knocks and overtime, if there are occurrences where one of that positive partnership starts to become negative, there is a high chance that unless this is addressed quickly, the other person will be dragged into a negative mindset and attitude.

Therefore, we recommend participating in living your life on purpose that you do this with your loving partner and, where possible other members of your household. It is like forming your very own mini mastermind group.

Remember, the best bit about most facets of life is there is no accountability, and the worst thing about most aspects of life is that there is no accountability.

If you buddy up with somebody else, it encourages a support system and accountability.

Earlier in the book, we introduced a vital exercise surrounding your purposeful morning and the introduction of some daily afformations. It is essential to positively paraphrase your language and the words that you openly speak and yourself talk.

Your attitude will determine your altitude—some of the first words in this chapter.

Eliminating some words from your vocabulary can help, especially when replacing those words with more positive ones. Light-hearted self-talk can be heard when watching Star Wars whilst Luke Skywalker is learning the ways of the force.

Yoda is getting Luke to do something in the swamplands, and Luke replies with the words “I'm trying”!

“Do or do not. There is no such thing as try,” replied Yoda.

It is light-hearted, yet there is a message that our daily self-talk determines whether we move forward to do a task or do not do a task. Our daily self-talk can grow our mindset or keep us exactly where we are.

Our modern world is moving at a rapid rate of technological growth. Some people instantly switch off the use of information technology because they believe that they do not understand it and will not understand it. They have effectively shut down immediately through the power of self-talk something that can enhance their life quite considerably.

Many people do not like new technology, and there is nothing wrong with that, but it can help us quite significantly. It can allow us to free up time and do the tasks we don't want to do.

Some self-talk words could include “I can't”. In the immortal words of Henry Ford

**“If you say you can, you can, and if you say you can't, you are right.”**

If you regularly say those words, “I can't”, be conscious during your day how often you say it, and when you say it, then change from “I can't” to “How can I do that?”

“I can't afford to go to Universal Studios with my family” can be changed to “How can I afford to go to Universal Studios with my family?”.

We have gone at great length through this book living your life on purpose to demonstrate ways in which you can do whatever you want.

We've covered ways in which you can change your financial fortunes so that you can make decisions positively and without worrying about the ramifications of a few thousand spondoolies on a holiday.

Other self-talk examples would be "I can't become a senior manager in my workplace" to "how do I become a senior manager in my workplace?"

By eliminating this negative self-talk and by positively paraphrasing your language into more positive self-talk, you will then work out ways to find solutions to whatever it is you want.

Anyone can develop a positive attitude, but first, we have already covered that you need to evaluate your attitude.

These attitudes that require attention could include your feelings towards yourself and towards other people, your current behaviours, how you think and where you see yourself in the future.

When we went through the personal development section of this book, Napoleon Hill reminds us that desire is the starting point of all riches, and faith is how we will achieve what it is we want to achieve.

Our attitude to our self-belief and the way we self-encourage is essential. If we have faith that we can achieve wins in those small, seemingly insignificant goal-directed activities, we will always move towards our goal and the closer we get to our goals, the better our attitude's will become.

We believe that it is essential to write down your statement of purpose. What do you want? Who do you want to become? Then chunk those goals down. They do say that a goal shared is a goal declared.

When you are within your mastermind group annual operating within a safe environment, you will be able to speak freely about your attitude and what you are doing to address the weaknesses and converting them into strengths.

Take action on your activity goals daily and harness the compound effect, knowing that you will be improving your attitude over time. Live one day at a time and do not expect seismic results overnight by changing your thought patterns and changing the way you feel and the way you think will improve your attitude.

It is your thoughts and not your environment that is determining your attitude and your happiness. By developing those good habits, you can control your habits, and therefore you can improve your attitude.

Like the formation of a good habit, remember you must be conscious daily of improving what you are looking to improve and understand that between days 21 and 28 is where other people are likely to see a change in your attitude.

Between days 21 and 28, if you have been focused daily on changing those weaknesses into strengths, then and only then will the operating system or, as we like to call it, the jam in your doughnut be transfused.

So, we must understand there are going to be the early days 1 to 7 where you are going to have to knuckle down and work hard on the things that you wish to improve.

Then through the middle phase of this period, from 7 until days 21, we will still be conscious, but at this point, we are now forming a daily operation method that should start to become more of a habit. It is during this middle phase, though, where danger is lurking. The danger is the danger of complacency; you still have to work hard every single day, every single time you open your mouth or think what you think until your subconscious mind accepts your new operating system to be true.

In the months ahead, having consciously been aware of the things that need to be altered then your natural operating system, your natural internal guidance system will be externally projecting a better attitude set.

With that in mind and with a positive paraphrasing statement to end this chapter, let the force be with you.

# Conclusion

Your tomorrow starts today.

If you want to win in this game of life, you need to get organised, and you need to know where you are going.

I cannot emphasise how important it is to incorporate systems and processes into your daily routine.

This is not exciting but getting organised will free up time for you to participate in more of the things you love.

Creating your purposeful morning and initiating a daily method of operation is imperative for your success.

This book or audio is just the tip of the iceberg when it comes to personal development. When you visit www.lylop.com, you will have the opportunity to associate with so many likeminded people.

Within our community, there are lots of mentors and coaches who can offer guidance and support to help you achieve your chosen goals.

This book is drawing to its end, but your participation within the LYLOP community is only just beginning. Every day you will be able to visit the community platform. You will help others within it just as much as others can help you.

Within the community platform, you will find an abundance of empowering, educational, and entertaining information. You will gain access to others' words and wisdom around the world.

Think of the community platform like your very own personal development smorgasbord. You will be able to self-select the information that you desire.

Each of the main chapters has been subdivided into a forum and support section within the community.

Don't forget success buddies are waiting for you if you need one. You will improve your life beyond recognition when you find that accountability partner.

If you like the idea of participating in a mastermind group, enrol and enjoy the journey.

There are so many overriding principles that have been repeated throughout living your life on purpose. They say that repetition is the number one rule of all learning!

This learning repetition is vital for you and everybody else who wishes to develop personally. Keep engaged and keep your mind active.

Each of us has different life circumstances, and the amount of time and effort that we can dedicate to each segment of the back and front wheels of life differ. Understand, though, but if you are not moving forward in your life, you will be moving backwards. So, keep involved and keep engaged and never give up!

When you participate in the wheel of life, and focus on every segment within both wheels, embrace this new philosophy 100%. Now that you understand that there will be no quick wins and that your success in life will be a direct result of repeated activity over a long time, you cannot fail.

If you only embrace this philosophy with a 30% attitude, you will likely get out what you put in.

Your job now is to go to the living your life on purpose Journal and complete the first tasks contained therein. Each month after that, redo those tasks and keep doing them every month. This will allow you to chart your continued growth.

Please make this an enjoyable journey too. You may have detected by now that I did not enjoy going to school. I only do things that I enjoy doing. The tasks that we have created within the Journal are simple to do, and they are simple not to do.

I will promise that if you go through each of the Journal's sectors and complete the tasks, you will see a noticeable difference in your motivation.

**Learn to master the mundane!**

Living your life on purpose is all about creating happiness. We want to help as many people as possible to have a more fun and fulfilling life. When you participate in the living your life on purpose philosophy, it should come as no detriment to other segments within the wheel.

If you wish to improve your friends and family relationships, this philosophy does not permit you to stop focusing on your income-generating tasks. On the flip side, if you wish to generate more income, you must not do so to the detriment of your relationships.

In the health and fitness section, understand that you can become fitter and healthier in a short time. Indeed. The moment you decide to become fitter and healthier is the moment that that happy hormone, serotonin, will fuel your body.

Making the decision alone will not get you fit and healthy. Instead, you will need to understand that it will take somewhere between 21 and 28 days of participating in the routines we recommend for you to see any noticeable difference. In the finance section, you need to appreciate that because you only get paid monthly and not daily, the noticeable differences could occur between 6 and 12 months. Do not get demotivated if you do not see instant wins. Remember the compound effect of the penny doubling up!

It was not until the last week of the exercise that the massive effects were noticed.

Hence, we highly recommend that you write down in the Journal what your current financial predicament is and then continue to replicate this recording every month. You will see that your financial circumstances are improving each month. The problem is the improvement during months 1 to 6 could be minimal.

With these minimal gains, you could be tempted to go back to the old ways of spending. We urge you not to embrace that quitting mentality. Like the compound effect works in the penny scenario, it will work for you to improve your financial circumstances. Just be patient!

Once you commit and understand that there are absolutely no quick wins, then, and only then, will you become a master within the living your life on purpose philosophy.

Within the book, we mentioned that there were four different levels of competency:

1: Unconsciously incompetent.
2: Consciously incompetent.
3: Consciously competent.
4: Unconsciously competent.

Through participation within this programme, you will move through each competency level.

The speed at which you pass from level 1 to level 4 will be entirely dependent on the amount of activity you employ within each of the wheel's different segments.

The more activity you do, the quicker you will pick up the skills, and therefore the quicker you will move through the levels of competency.

As with Maslow and his hierarchal needs, you want to become better in each of the disciplines as time passes by.

Creating new habits that serve you well will take time, and once you have made them, the old habits that weren't serving you well will be like the weight of your balloon being severed.

As you become better equipped and informed in each of the disciplines that you partake, you will move from comfort zone to comfort zone, improving all the time.

Each time one of those weights is severed, you are essentially improving your mindset, competencies, and belief system.

Be persistent and remain focused on why you want to improve your life. Understand that you have so many people around you and supporting you on this journey. It may be hard at times, and you may even cry on the odd occasion. It is OK to cry and is also OK momentarily to think about quitting.

But if you enter the valley of despair, you better have a strategy to get you out of there as quickly as possible.

This could be the role of your success buddy, reading your goals, reading your affirmations, or going for a nice walk and listening to some motivational music.

Do not have a pity party, because honestly, nobody really cares. The reason why they don't care is that they don't live with your consequences.

Ouch, that must hurt!

It is so true, though. You can bitch and you can moan, about anything you want. About how inadequate your life is and how you are getting the school of Hard Knocks. The people you communicate with maybe listening, and they may be nodding their head sympathetically. They may even cuddle you.

When they return home or hang up the phone, you are still alone with your same pitiful life circumstances.

There is only one person in your life that can make a change in it. Go and look in the mirror to find out exactly who that person is just in case you are not catching my drift.

**If it is to be, it is up to me.**

In conclusion, it is you that must decide to make the change, and be disciplined, but you are not alone. Far from it, and just like a rising tide lifts all boats, I want to reaffirm that we are with you, side by side.

Your LYLOP community awaits you, and we await you with open arms.

# References

During LYLOP we make reference to some outstanding authors and their works.

Below is a list of "must" read books.

Think and Grow Rich by Napoleon Hill

The Compound Effect by Darren Hardy

Eat the Frog by Brian Tracey

Atomic Habits by James Clear

The Slight Edge by Jeff Olsen

Demystifying Success by Dr Tom Barrett

Miracle Morning by Hal Elrod

Dare to Dream and Work to Win by Dr Tom Barrett

The Secret by Rhonda Byrne

The Five Second Rule by Mel Robins

Go for No by Andrea Waltz and Richard Fenton

If you wish to find them easier visit www.lylop.com

www.ingramcontent.com/pod-product-compliance
Ingram Content Group UK Ltd.
Pitfield, Milton Keynes, MK11 3LW, UK
UKHW021837270726
14058UKWH00002B/208